LET THE RIVER FLOW

I found Roger's book profoundly helpful yet easy to read and comprehend. As a theologian who is also a pastor, Roger helps those who might shy away from experience for fear of deception, and brings them into a safe place. Biblically, so as to have not only his theology, he also shares his life changing personal encounter with the living God. While 'in the river' himself, he 'blows' the arguments of critics and sceptics 'out of the water'.

JOHN ARNOTT, Senior Pastor, Toronto Airport
Christian Fellowship, Canada

Let the River Flow is an important book to read. Calm waters present little by way of navigational difficulty. The 'white waters' of revival, however, require knowledgable, experienced and humble guides. In this current outpouring of God's Spirit, Roger serves as a gifted river pilot.

GUY CHEVREAU, Teacher at the Toronto Airport Christian Fellowship,
Canada, and author of *Catch The Fire* and *Pray With Fire*

Roger Helland's excellent work is invaluable ... It informs those who desire factual knowledge by helping to overcome unsubstantiated allegations and objections, and it offers the wisdom of a pastor who has had extensive experience with the renewal ... [it] is a balanced and inviting book on the present renewal that deserves to be read by all Christians.

MARGARET M. POLOMA PH.D.,
Sociologist, the University of Akron, USA.

... a wonderfully helpful guide for those presently challenged with reconciling evangelical conviction and mission with new-found experience. On every page Roger's love for God's word, God's Church and the moving of his Spirit shines through.

GARY BEST, National Director, Association
of Vineyard Churches, Canada

... it is the most comprehensive, honest to the Biblical text, and theologically responsible insider response to modern renewal phenomena that I have seen ... One could only wish that all those who have written on this topic had gone to the lengths that Roger Helland has to be biblically honest and historically and theologically reflective ... this work should be required reading for students of this renewal.

PETER H. DAVIDS PH.D., Resident Academic,
Schoss Mittersill Study Centre, Austria

Roger Helland is a thinking person committed to thorough scholarship in the Word and history. This book is not only a biblically and historically based explanation of what is presently happening in the renewal, it is an exciting view of one who is pastoring and overseeing, and creates a hunger for God.

DEAN SHERMAN, International Dean of the College of
Christian Ministries, *Youth With A Mission*, USA

Roger Helland's book is a clear voice pointing the way out of a time of confusion. It is interesting, helpful and biblical.

RANDY CLARK, Senior Pastor, St Louis Vineyard
Christian Fellowship, USA

It has been my privilege to work on a pastoral team with Roger for over ten years. He has not just taught on renewal, he has experienced it, pastored it and matured it. This book reflects the distilling of a decade of pastoring in the midst of a move of the Holy Spirit ... As you read it, I am sure the lights will go on and it will bless you.

WESLEY CAMPBELL, Senior Pastor, New Life Vineyard
Fellowship, Kelowna, British Columbia, Canada

Roger Helland's insights on the latest powerful move of the Holy Spirit are lucidly portrayed against the background of revival history, and are refreshingly expressed in this helpful and exciting teaching manual.

BISHOP DAVID PYTCHES

Roger Helland

LET THE RIVER FLOW

Welcoming Renewal into your Church

Marshall Pickering

An Imprint of HarperCollinsPublishers

Marshall Pickering is an Imprint of
HarperCollins*Religious*
Part of HarperCollins*Publishers*
77–85 Fulham Palace Road, London W6 8JB

First published in Great Britain
in 1996 by Marshall Pickering
1 3 5 7 9 10 8 6 4 2

A catalogue record for this work is
available from the British Library

0 551 030666

Printed and bound in Great Britain by
Caledonian International Book Manufacturing Ltd, Glasgow

Dedicated to my wife Gail, the crown of my life
(Proverbs 31),
to my daughter Melissa, the love of my life,
to my first son Joel, the delight of my life,
to my second son Micah, the joy of my life,
to my Lord Jesus, who is my Life.

CONTENTS

ACKNOWLEDGMENTS

In many ways this book has been in the making since late 1987 and early 1988 when 'the Spirit came in power' to our church. One evening at the home of one of our elders, Terry Lamb, a prophetic person who was visiting us, simply declared from the Lord, 'Roger, you are going to write a book.' My reply: 'I don't have time and I don't have anything to say.' That was eight years ago. Much water has flowed in the river since. This work originally began in the summer of 1994 as a smaller duo project with Wesley Campbell, Senior Pastor of New Life Vineyard Fellowship. As I began to compile the data, it gradually consumed my efforts and grew into a full-scale solo project. Wes and I then agreed that he should write his own book while I waited and continued to develop the present work for the future.

Winston Churchill said, 'Writing a book is an adventure. To begin with it is a toy and an amusement ... Then it becomes a master and then it becomes a tyrant.' Writing a book is a bittersweet experience of labour and love which involves the help of many people to whom I owe debts of gratitude.

I wish to thank Dr John White, who paved the way and helped my understanding of the ways of the Spirit with his seminal work *When the Spirit Comes With Power*. Dr

Peter Davids offered valuable theological, exegetical and practical insights and corrections. He read the full manuscript three times and made scrupulous comments and suggestions which I believe improved this work considerably. Thanks also to Dr Guy Chevreau who read the full manuscript twice and offered important counsel on many details and to Len Hjalmarson, a friend, who worked through an early draft.

I am grateful for the now deceased Pastor George Mallone of Grace Vineyard in Texas. Several years ago at a simple lunch meeting he aroused my vision for getting my ideas into print.

Special indebtedness goes to Wesley Campbell, whom I've worked with on our pastoral team for ten years. His keen theological insights and passion for renewal influences my thinking and inspires me to 'never be lacking in zeal, but to keep [my] spiritual fervour, serving the Lord' (Rom. 12:11). As well, I will always owe gratitude to John Wimber, who is a true leader in renewal and church ministry, both in practice and in print.

I so appreciate the editors and staff at HarperCollins who made haste to accept my manuscript and get it into print this year, and Simon Fox, my copy editor, who did much to make my awkward paragraphs understandable. I would particularly like to thank Philippa Linton and Vicky Marquina of the editorial team for their patience and help.

Finally, *most* appreciation goes to my wife Gail, and my children, Melissa, Joel and Micah, who loyally supported me in this project from start to finish. They patiently allowed me to sit in front of my computer for many hours and at times sacrificed their need for my presence. Gail also challenged me to keep in touch with the needs of people who aren't always affected by the more demonstrative

ACKNOWLEDGMENTS

aspects of the renewal. My gratitude also goes to the pastors, staff and incredible people of New Life Vineyard Fellowship who have all done their best to let the river flow. They are a living laboratory of inspired people who always want 'More, Lord, more!'

Roger Helland
Kelowna, British Columbia, May 1996

FOREWORD

Roger Helland, who wrote *Let the River Flow*, is convinced that a river of divine waters is currently flowing from God's throne. I share this view. His statement is prophetic.

Roger begins his book by asserting that many pastors he meets say, 'I am dry. My church is stale. I'm ready to quit...' He is convinced that such pastors must start wading. They may not get to the middle of the river immediately, but all of us are invited to seek God's face. He longs for our fellowship. However, once you begin to swim, you must lose your fascination with the novelty of the experience, and like the early church, go out into the highways and byways. There are many degrees of empowering, and *you must use what you have before asking for more.*

The church's activity must not be confined to preaching. Preaching, it is true, lies at the core of what we must do, but the world must see reality in us. To have been touched by the love of God means you start loving others in practical ways. This is one of Roger's central appeals in 'letting the River flow'. Many Christians these days have begun to clothe and feed the poor. But may heaven defend us from getting into the welfare mess! Feeding and clothing is stage 1. Stage 2 is to develop new forms of business, in which profits are never an end in themselves, but provide a basis to expand and give work to more people. I predict that this will be the wave of the future entrepreneurial endeavour. It has to be. And the church will be its source.

Roger Helland loves Scripture but sees that our Western approach to it has become increasingly anti-supernatural and anti-subjective. Yet the Bible itself never ceases to deal with supernatural events, winding up in John's Revelation in a gala of supernaturalism. Roger quotes Guy Chevreau, author of *Catch The Fire*, who rightly asserts that the apostle Paul's 'understanding and experience of the Spirit of the risen Christ was always experiential. It was not primarily theological. The thinking about it came after, secondarily. First and foremost it was experiential.' Paul had to be overwhelmed first. Later, he asked, 'What *was* that?' Then God began instructing his servant in Arabia (Gal. 1:17).

Roger has an early and hard look at Scripture, experience and cessationism. He discusses manifestations, describes them carefully and in light of Scripture. But his book goes further. Written with pastors and leaders in mind, it helps them decide for themselves what is of God and what is not in this renewal. It shows them the importance of taking to the unsaved whatever God does for us. It is exciting to experience tongues of flame, but there are people outside who need to hear about God. The early church knew this and recognized the importance of bringing men and women to repentance and faith in Christ. What took place in an upper chamber thrust the early disciples into the middle of crowded places. In Roger's words, 'what comes down must go in (the church) and out (to the world).' The Holy Spirit filled them with power to be witnesses.

But power is dangerous. There are two dangers: one danger is that of having it; the other is that of not having it. Shakespeare understood that danger:

There is a tide in the affairs of men.
Which, taken at the flood, leads on to fortune;
Omitted, all the voyage of their life
Is bound in shallows and in miseries.
(*Julius Caesar*, IV, iii, 217)

God invites us to swim. This is the day of the greatest flowing River the world has ever seen. It is a River that empowers. We must wade in it ever more deeply, until we find ourselves borne wherever the Spirit would carry us. We are neither to die of thirst, nor to perish in 'shallows and miseries'. I heartily recommend Roger Helland's book as a valuable contribution to the literature, and as an aid in helping church leaders and people to cope with a River that could drown the unwary, sweeping them into by-waters.

John White
Psychiatrist, Author and Speaker

THE RIVER IS HERE

The man brought me back to the entrance of the temple, and I saw water coming out from under the threshold of the temple toward the east (for the temple faced east). The water was coming down from under the south side of the temple, south of the altar. He then brought me out through the north gate and led me around the outside to the outer gate facing east, and the water was flowing from the south side. As the man went eastward with a measuring line in his hand, he measured off a thousand cubits and then led me through water that was ankle-deep. He measured off another thousand cubits and led me through water that was knee-deep. He measured off another thousand and led me through water that was up to the waist. He measured off another thousand, but now it was a river that I could not cross, because the water had risen and was deep enough to swim in – a river that no one could cross. He asked me, 'Son of man, do you see this?' Then he led me back to the bank of the river. When I arrived there, I saw a great number of trees on each side of the river. He said to me, 'This water flows toward the eastern region and goes down into the Arabah, where itenters the Sea. When it empties into the Sea, the water there becomes fresh. Swarms of living creatures will live wherever the river flows. There will be large numbers of fish, because this water flows there and makes the salt water fresh; so where the river flows everything will live. Fishermen will stand along the shore; from En Gedi to En Eglaim there will be places for spreading nets. The fish will be of many kinds – like the fish of the Great Sea. But the swamps and marshes will not become fresh; they will be left for salt. Fruit trees of all kinds will grow on both banks of the river. Their leaves will not wither, nor will their fruit fail. Every month they will bear, because the water from the sanctuary flows to them. Their fruit will serve for food and their leaves for healing. (Ezek. 47:1–12)

Then the angel showed me the river of the water of life, as clear as crystal, flowing from the throne of God and of the Lamb down the middle of the great street of the city. On each side of the river stood the tree of life, bearing twelve crops of fruit, yielding its fruit every month. And the leaves of the tree are for the healing of the nations. No longer will there be any curse. The throne of God and of the Lamb will be in the city, and his servants will serve him. (Rev. 22:1–3)

Everyone loves to see a great river. I've seen many – the Thames, the Mississippi, the Colorado, the Danube, the Seine and the Volga. Great rivers provide beauty and bounty to their regions. But greater still, 'there is a river whose streams make glad the city of God, the holy place where the Most High dwells' (Ps. 46:4). A biblical symbol for life-giving blessings that come from God's presence is the river or streams of God. Ezekiel was a prophet, not an architect – one whose department is not the hands but the heart.[1] His visionary report in chapters 40–48 does not refer to a literal temple but to the conditions of the Messianic age. It lay in the future but grew out of the present. It is a comprehensive view of God's purposes in restoration. As John B. Taylor comments, 'The vision of the temple represented all that God stood for, all that He required and all that He could do for His people in the age that was about to dawn.'[2] Ezekiel writes God's Word about an idealized future for God's people, who went into Babylonian exile in the sixth century BC. It's also God's Word for his people today.

Ezekiel speaks of renewal and revival. Where God restores his people, worship is central, his presence is with his people, and the blessings of his presence bring life and refreshing to barren places. Ezekiel sees a River that swells as it makes its way to the desert ('the Arabah') and the Dead Sea ('the Sea') to the south. It brings life, freshness, fruit and healing. This vision is a timeless message to last-days people who 'live between the times' of the already and the not yet, in the age of Messiah, the New Covenant and the Spirit. It is a foretaste of the age to come. With the coming of Jesus a new age has dawned. God's Kingdom is partial, but will also come some day in fulness. Ezekiel's vision is a word for each generation since Christ came to earth as the Messiah until he returns to earth as the King. Ezekiel's River is timeless, not timely.[3]

Jesus said, 'I have come that they may have life, and that they may have it more abundantly' (John 10:10, NKJV). He also said, 'Whoever believes in me, as the Scripture has said, streams of living water will flow from within him.' John comments, 'By this he meant the Spirit, whom those who believed in him were later to receive. Up to that time the Spirit had not been given, since Jesus had not yet been glorified' (John 7:38–39). In Revelation 22:1–3, John applies Ezekiel's imagery to the realm of eternal life. A realm of abundance and magnificent perfection. The purpose of Revelation was to encourage persecuted Christians with the hope of Christ's victory over the world, the flesh, the devil and evil government and religion. Heaven is the finale of all God's purposes described in chapters 21–22. Renewal and revival bring heaven to earth. Eugene Peterson writes:

> Heaven is not what we wait for until the rapture or where we go when we die, but what *is*, barely out of the range of our senses, but brought to our senses by St. John's visions ... The vision of heaven is an affirmation of correspondence: that which we have begun to experience corresponds to what we will completely experience ... St. Teresa says ... 'The pay begins in this life' ... Just as the actions of earth flow into heaven, so the actions of heaven descend to earth ... Heaven is not fantasy. We have access to heaven now.[4]

What Ezekiel describes of the Messianic age and John describes of heaven, is taking place spiritually today. For Ezekiel the imagery is progressive. For John the imagery is final. But today, for you and me, the River is progressive as it rises, expands and yields life, fruit and healing. Heaven is coming down and glory is filling many souls. The blessings of God's presence are reaching deluge proportions globally. For almost three years a major headwater for this

River – at least in the Western world – has been in Toronto, Canada. The so-called 'Toronto Blessing' is a River of God whose increasing velocity and size can't be stopped. It rages on as the downpouring rains from heaven make it flow.

The local Indian word *Toronto* means 'meeting place'. By 20 January 1996, the Toronto Airport Christian Fellowship had completed their second year of nightly meetings. They report:

> The total attendance at the Toronto Airport Christian Fellowship since the meetings began on January 20, 1994 was estimated at 726,300 people, including approximately 25,000 Christian leaders from virtually every country and denomination. The statistics are based on an average of 800 per day in 1994 and 1500 per day in 1995. This includes an estimated 9,000 first-time commitments to Christ and prodigals who returned to God.[5]

The *Toronto Life* magazine billed the Airport Vineyard meetings as the number-one tourist attraction of 1994. Some hotels, airlines and restaurants give discounts to attendees. Falling, shaking, laughing, roaring, crying, prophesying, healing, tongues, demonic deliverance, visions, 'drunkenness in the Spirit' and intimate encounters with God are commonplace. Participants have even had these experiences before and after the meetings in taxis, in the lobbies of hotels, in restaurants, or simply while waiting in lines outside to get in. Hundreds of backsliders are returning to God and others are coming to salvation.

People from all over North America and as far away as Britain, Chile, Argentina, Switzerland, France, Germany, Scandinavia, South Africa, Nigeria, Kenya, Japan, New

Zealand and Australia have come to receive the outpouring. Terry Virgo, leader of the New Frontiers network, felt that God told him, 'I have attended a lot of your meetings, now I am inviting you to attend some of mine.' Leaders are affected and then return to pass on the fire to their locations. Similar renewal experiences have even appeared in conservative churches in Communist China. Dennis Balcombe of Revival Christian Church in Hong Kong, gives Sister Ding Xianggao's testimony about a ministry trip she and a group of Henan preachers took in 1994. When in Zhibo District, they came across some very conservative nominal believers. She reports:

> They were all very conservative, old-fashioned and backward ... and the leaders were opposed to everything relating to the Holy Spirit ... After preaching, we invited the Holy Spirit to come. Many fell on the floor speaking in tongues and some also laughed for hours. Others began to clap their hands, shout and dance. The Lord did it, not us. Those who were the most opposed to these 'manifestations' also received the blessing.[6]

Dennis Balcombe also sent a video to me. It shows the work of the Spirit upon thousands of Chinese. It shows believers in house churches and in open meetings crying out to God with tears and travail, dancing and worship. It also shows them falling, shaking, becoming drunk in the Spirit, laughing and prophesying. The primary fruit of this gifting is evangelism and revival. Multitudes of Chinese are converting to Christ. Very few, if any of them have been to Toronto or have been taught about the 'Toronto Blessing'. God is releasing blessing around the world.

In March 1996 Randy Clark, Senior Pastor of the St Louis Vineyard, took a team of 21 people to lead a renewal conference in Moscow. About 1,000 pastors and leaders from numerous denominations – some travelling by train for up to 30 hours – assembled to worship God, to be equipped and to 'Catch the Fire'. Several team members reported that it was the most significant move of God they had ever seen. His presence during the worship was overwhelming, and his power during the ministry times was impossible to describe with words. Here is an Internet report on the Moscow conference by one of the team members:

Day three of 'Catch the Fire' Russia was the final day of the conference and it was the day that all heaven broke loose … Even as the teaching time began it became clear that several in the audience were being touched by the Lord. Here and there people were shaking. Some were in a deep state of worship with hands raised and eyes closed, their heads tilted back while they quietly gave praise to God. As the meeting continued the shaking intensified, praises increased in volume and the manifestations began spreading to several parts of the room …

By the evening service there were about eleven hundred people crowded into the hall, filling all the chairs and most of the aisles. The worship was indescribable. Almost heavenly. Nearly every hand was raised in adoration to the Father. During the song 'Alleluia, Glory', written by one of the team members, the entire throng was jumping up and down in unison for several minutes. Most of the American team, who were not in the band, just stood in the front corner of the stage looking out into the congregation with absolute awe and amazement ...

The afternoon session saw a continuation of the Lord's healing hand that had been present all week. Two people were healed of severe curvature of the spine before our very eyes. With one young man we actually heard his vertebrae popping as he received prayer. The evening meeting was punctuated with an array of prophetic words, mostly centred around God calling Russia to send missionaries to the nations of the world. At the end of the meeting an invitation was given for those who believed God was calling them to missions. Some 300 Russians came forward to receive prayer from those who were already missionaries. It was an amazing sight to witness the fervent desire of this formerly persecuted people to reach this world for Christ.[7]

Today's renewal is transdenominational. God meets expectant people, regardless of their denomination or location. Catholics, Baptists, Presbyterians, Reformed, Pentecostals, Anglicans, United Church, Mennonites and Nazarenes have been touched. There are other significant 'watering holes' such as Sunderland Christian Centre, Sunderland, England; Holy Trinity Brompton, London; Brownsville Assembly of God Chruch, Pensacola, Florida; Tabernacle Church, Melbourne, Florida; Mott Auditorium, Pasadena, California; and various centres in Argentina. The powerful presence of God, often producing extraordinary effects, continues to increase.

The following account is typical. A Christian man named Jon at Grace Christian Fellowship, who attended a conference at Sunderland Christian Centre, England, in

September 1995, posted this report on 'New-Wine' through the Internet (25 September 1995):

About 700 people had been turned away. The leaders closed the evening down and then encouraged everyone to spend a little time with each other in prayer. Out of nowhere the fire fell. The manifest presence of God came on the meeting! The air was thick, all my friends were crawling about on the floor. People were roaring, shouting, crying, travailing all in the same moment. About 600 people were on the floor or swaying, bending, etc.

Five lads came in the church wondering what all the sudden commotion was about (this was *loud*!). Three of them gave their lives to the Lord, the Spirit of God came on them, I saw one of them fall, the other began shaking, the other peeped at the other two wondering what on earth was going on. Some taxi drivers came in to see what the buzz was and were promptly placed on the register for the next Alpha course! Landlords and hotel owners telephoned to find out why people were staggering around their hotels. They too were placed on the Alpha register.

Friday morning the first session was to be at 11:00 a.m. By 9.30 the church was full. When I arrived at 9:00 a.m., outside the church was a queue, bodies were on the pathways by the cars, on the grass, everywhere groaning, roaring, twitching. Some people were obviously carriers of the Holy Spirit, walking past people and totally oblivious to the fact that the people they passed fell to the floor. Friday night the Lord moved through the room quickly. Everywhere you went groups of people were going through the usual manifestations, but it seemed a lot more intense. All the chairs had been moved and about 850 people had crammed into the downstairs room that seats 600.

People were prophesying everywhere, most spoke of a wind blowing across the nations, one spoke of a volcano of grace and mercy erupting and covering the earth, someone else was prophesying continuously about the Day of the Lord and an imminent return. Throughout this I could hear a heavy rumble, like thunder. Then two drunkards staggered over to us (drunk in the Spirit). The one called John fell over. I picked him up and carried him around the auditorium. As we passed people, I placed his hands on their heads. As soon as he touched them they fell. Some of these people were looking away from him with their backs towards us. They still fell. Paula and two friends prayed for a young girl. After a few moments our friend prayed that God would heal her. The girl felt God touch her stomach. She had had a stomach tumour that stuck out under her skin. It had entirely gone. With many tears the girl went up to testify. During the meeting the conference prayed for the Holy Spirit to visit the Catholic churches. Somebody who is paid to pray for the Catholic church (a practising Catholic) gave his heart to the Lord and was very powerfully touched by God. A Catholic priest came to the platform and lay on the carpet for a long time under the presence of God!

This is not about manifestations but about the magnitude of the effects of God's presence. However, the manifestations draw the attention of even the secular press. The

BBC and CBC, *The Sunday Telegraph*, *The Daily Mail*, *The Times*, *The Independent*, *The Globe and Mail*, *The Toronto Star*, *The Vancouver Sun*, and *Time Magazine* have reported on this 'revival' or 'curious spiritual wind'. At a high point, on 10 May 1995, Guy and Janis Chevreau and Daina Doucet from the Airport Vineyard, Ken Gott from Sunderland Christian Centre, Mike Thompson of Tabernacle Church and a team of others appeared on the Phil Donahue show in New York City. This programme aired on 19 September 1995. An estimated 13 million viewers watch this American talk show daily. The world is aware of the renewal. Multitudes are reading and watching and coming.

On 13 March 1995, *MacLean's Magazine* – the Canadian counterpart to *Time Magazine* – published a favourable article entitled 'Going to the Mat for God: Tales of Ecstasy Draw Hundreds to a Toronto church.' The journalist opens the article with the following song lyrics: 'The river of God fills our mouths with laughter, and we rejoice, for the river is here.'

Indeed, the River is here. It will qualify as a most remarkable move of God in this century! Perhaps, in proportion, it will exceed the Pentecostal revival of the early 1900s. The world has entered a new era.

As I write about the current renewal, I am aware that people define this term differently, such as new structures for body life, new church management and ministry models, church vitality, retooling the mission and strategies of evangelism and church growth, gift-based ministry, charismatic experience, etc. I long to see all these types of renewal, but I do not use the term in these ways.

To renew means to 'make new again, to replenish, to revive'. Biblical renewal is God's presence and power, through his Word and his Spirit, bringing new life and replenishing spiritual fruit and power to his people. In times of extraordinary renewal (and revival), God pours out his Spirit through a heightened visitation of his manifest presence with dramatic results. This is what is occuring today around the world and what I mean by the current renewal. It is not confined to Toronto, Sunderland or Pensacola, as there are different streams and expressions coming from the River flowing from God's throne. This is a time of God's visitation.

In Greek there are two terms for 'time'. The first is *chronos* – that is, chronological time: minutes, hours, days. Another is *kairos* – that is, a season or era of time. Many believe that this is a *kairos* time of God. It is a special era where the manifest presence of God intensifies.

Answers are needed for relevant questions. Teaching is needed for understanding and correct practice. The Bible states: 'Always be prepared to give an answer to everyone who asks you to give the reason for the hope that you have. But do this with gentleness and respect' (1 Pet. 3:15). A 'reasonable defence' is an *apologetic*. We can safely defend what God is doing so that it will benefit others. We must understand principles and practices that will release rather than restrict what God is doing. This is the purpose of this book.

THE PURPOSE OF THIS BOOK

1) *To give church leaders and people a reasonable defence for the current renewal.* Many Christians have belief systems that have been tainted with a cessationist, anti-supernatural bias. Many desire to enter into what is happening but need an intellectual and experiential balance in order for them to welcome this. I want to help them think through the biblical, theological, historical and practical issues.

2) *To help leaders and people overcome obstacles and objections to release and not inhibit the waters of renewal.* Leaders and people also come across situations and people that they do not know how to handle. My purpose is to impart principles and practices that will help people overcome obstacles and objections, either in their thinking or in the thinking or writing of others. I address 'open' critics who are looking for a biblical defence. I do not address 'closed' critics who want to debate.

3) *To give insights on how to receive the renewal in the church and direct it outside the church.* I want to encourage people to go for it – to be involved, to wrestle with the issues, to spread this renewal so that the River has a widespread welcome *in* our needy churches and *out* to a needy world. My goal for my readers is that the first nine chapters will help them work through the problems, the phenomena and the practices, so that there will be a practical response, described in the last three chapters.

PART ONE

PERCEIVING
THE RIVER

CHAPTER ONE

FORGETTING THE FORMER THINGS

Forget the former things; do not dwell on the past. See, I am doing a new thing! Now it springs up; do you not perceive it? I am making a way in the desert and streams in the wasteland. The wild animals honour me, the jackals and the owls, because I provide water in the desert and streams in the wasteland, to give drink to my people, my chosen, the people I formed for myself that they may proclaim my praise. (Isa. 43:18–21)

Have you seen the six-hour Beatles anthology which was first aired on British television in 1995? I watched it with great interest, because I was a teenager in their heyday. This documentary covered the rise and fall of the greatest pop group of all time. There was ecstasy in their story. With their youth and their originality, these four young men moved the Western world into a musical and cultural revolution. Their song-writing and concerts were unsurpassed. But there was also agony in their story. At the height of their success they met Bob Dylan, who introduced them to drugs. Then they encountered Mahareshi Mahesh Yogi, who introduced them to Eastern mysticism. They left any path that might have brought them to the celestial city, where only Jesus Christ is King. Thus began the

3

downfall of the Beatles, as they searched for meaning in the dark. Their low point came in 1969, when they recorded their final album, *Abbey Road*. In 1970 the four Liverpool musicians went their separate ways. As a group they still had glory, but as individuals they ceased to shine.

By contrast, 1969 was the high point of my life, because that was when I came to know Christ. A high-school friend who was a 'Jesus freak' shared the gospel with me one evening. This was the ray of light in my darkness. Jesus brought meaning and deliverance into my life then, and he is still doing it today in new ways. I have experienced healing, mingled with pain, agony and ecstasy. The Beatles sang 'All you need is love', and 'There will be an answer, let it be, let it be'. But 'Beatle mania' is no more and John Lennon is dead. It makes me sad to think about the decline of such a talented group of musicians who were so important to me when I was young, but I don't dwell on the past, because God is doing a new thing in my life today.

In some ways the Beatles remind me of the experience of the church in recent decades. Many Christians are broken people who have been struggling to keep their moral and spiritual compasses pointing north. They have experienced pain and disappointment mingled with victory and success. Like the Beatles, the church had a glorious and spectacular beginning in the time of the apostles. When it is united and pure it is still glorious today, but when it is divided and contaminated, it has no glory. It ought to be able to move the world into a cultural revolution, and at times it has done that. Jesus Christ is the King of the Celestial City. But some Christians have left the path to that city as they look for meaning in the wrong places in the dark. The church in recent times has had some victories and some defeats; she has had the successful missions of Billy Graham and the moral scandal surrounding Jimmy Swaggart.

The church has been through a long season of spiritual drought. Some pastors I meet today say to me, 'I'm dry and burned out. My church is stale. I'm ready to quit. I need a fresh touch of the Holy Spirit.' And yet others are content with the past – they relish the good old days of the Azusa Street Pentecostal Revival of the early 1900s, or the Healing Movement of the 1940s and 1950s, or the Charismatic Renewal of the 1960s and 1970s, or the Third Wave Renewal of the 1980s. Some would say, 'Let it be! Let it be!'

GOD IS DOING A NEW THING

And yet today the world-wide church is living in times of historic significance. Certainly there were successes and failures in the past, but God is in the present. Right now he is the I AM of new things. In some ways the current renewal is similar to things which he has done before, but in its great breadth and momentum it is most extraordinary. It is not like Azusa Street, or the Charismatic Renewal or the Third Wave or the early days of the Vineyard Movement. This renewal is built on those earlier renewals, but it is different. It is crossing all denominational and theological boundaries and traversing the globe with a tidal wave of God's power. It is not a new revelation, but a new understanding of old truths. It is a new outpouring of the Holy Spirit according to ways in which God has worked in the past.

In early 1995 I spoke at a renewal conference at Edmonton in Alberta, Canada. About 1,500 people had gathered from over 60 churches and 20 denominations, including Roman Catholics, Greek Orthodox Christians, Lutherans, Baptists, United Church members and Plymouth Brethren. To many of them, God was doing a new thing. Mike Bickle and the Metro Vineyard in Kansas City have spent years praying for an outpouring of the Spirit. Leonard Ravenhill has preached and prayed about revival for decades, and now we are 'surprised by joy' as we realize that God is doing a new thing in the earth! Do we not perceive it? He is providing water in the desert and making streams in the wastelands to give much-needed drink to his people – finally!

In the passage from Isaiah quoted earlier, the prophet, writing in the eighth century BC, told a future generation of Israelites in the Babylonian exile which was yet to come that they should forget the Exodus from Egypt. Even though it was glorious and historic in its day, it belonged to a former generation and it was designed to meet their needs. There was going to be a new exodus from a new captivity for a future generation. The prophets always saw a continuity between history and prophecy. Isaiah's prophetic focus changed from God's past acts of redemption to the present ones which he was about to accomplish. It takes spiritual eyesight, by faith, to perceive the new things of God.

AN EXTRAORDINARY RENEWAL

Today we stand in continuity with past generations as the Word of God and the purposes of God continue to address and unfold for contemporary generations. In some ways 'there is nothing new under the sun'. Renewals and revivals have come and gone. Manifestations and bizarre phenomena have caused controversy before – people love or hate revivals. God builds his Kingdom layer by layer, with each generation building on the previous one. In this generation we can trace a direct renewal lineage back to the Pentecostal movement of 1906–1909. We can trace that movement's lineage back to the Holiness and Methodist movements of the 18th and 19th centuries. We can trace the roots of the Methodist movement back to the Pietism of the 17th century. And yet there is a sense in which the present renewal *is* something new – although it bears certain similarities to previous renewals and revivals, there has never been anything quite like it before.

God is pouring out the new wine of the Spirit, which requires new wineskins or church structures. We tend to get used to things as they are, and then there is the danger that we will reject God's new visitations. These words of Jesus are a warning for all generations:

> As he approached Jerusalem and saw the city, he wept over it and said, 'If you, even you, had only known on this day what would bring you peace – but now it is hidden from your eyes. The days will come upon you when your enemies will build an embankment against you and encircle you and hem you in on every side. They will dash you to the ground, you and the children within your walls. They will not leave one stone on another, because *you did not recognize the time of God's coming to you.*' (Luke 19:41–44)

The King James Version translates the last phrase as 'thou knewest not the time of thy visitation'. When Jesus came into the world, many people did not recognize him for who he really was. He said, 'If you have seen me, you have seen the Father' (John 14:9). In Luke 19 Jesus was prophesying the destruction of Jerusalem in AD 70 by the Roman general Titus. God finally judged Israel because they had rejected his visitation – they had refused to acknowledge Jesus as the long-awaited Messiah. Jesus was the ultimate new thing that sprung up like a spring in the desert. He was the River of Life. He wept over Jerusalem because the people could not or would not perceive God's visitation. As Joseph Roux says, 'God often visits us, but most of the time we are not home.'[1] Luke tells us that when some of John the Baptist's followers came to Jesus, they said, 'John the Baptist has sent us to You, saying, "Are You the Coming One, or do we look for another?"' (Luke 7:20, NKJV). Jesus replied by listing his messianic works: healing, miracles and preaching to the poor (verses 21–22). He concluded by saying, 'And blessed is he who is not offended because of Me' (verse 23). Will his mighty works today offend us? Will we recognize God's visitation today?

God is always at work in the world, always present. This is his *omnipresence* (see Ps. 139:8). Periodically, God makes a special visit to the world in which he becomes 'closer' and 'more present' than he usually is. This is his *manifest presence* (see Ps. 51:11). Because he always takes the initiative, God will do new things to meet the needs of the present. Throughout biblical and church history we read accounts of times when God came with his manifest presence in renewal and revival to revitalize people's hard and dry hearts. Often the human reaction to God's manifest presence has been physical and emotional manifestations.

God came with his manifest presence to our church in Kelowna, British Columbia, Canada. Here is my account of what happened.

OUR STORY

In 1986 I was part of the founding team when Wes Campbell and David Ruis planted what was then called the New Life Fellowship Baptist Church in Kelowna. In 1985–86 some of our leaders went to their first John Wimber conferences and saw supernatural gifts and manifestations of the Spirit for the first time. This made us hungry for renewal. In late 1987 and early 1988 we invited some well-known church leaders to come to us and lead some small conferences on Kingdom ministry and the Holy Spirit. Through the influence of people like George Mallone, Bob Birch and John Wimber, God introduced our church to renewal. During this time God invaded our leadership team.

On 9 December 1987 the eight couples who made up our pastors' and elders' team gathered for a Christmas party at an elder's home. At about 10.00 p.m. I strongly felt that we should spend some time in prayer, but my suggestion went unheeded. I again suggested that we should pray, and so we did. Within minutes, the presence of God came like an atom bomb into the living room. David Ruis began to shake. One of the elders was thrown onto the couch, and then he came springing out to the centre of the room, shaking and speaking in tongues. Next, Stacey Campbell flew off the couch into the centre of the room, where she began to shake, bounce and prophesy. Then these three together began to shake violently, jump up and down, twirl around, do chopping motions and prophesy to the group and to each individual there. The rest of us spent about four hours listening to this and watching it, all the while worshipping God, repenting, rejoicing and wondering what it was all about. We finally staggered home at about 2.30 a.m. We had not sought this or asked for it. We tried to keep what had happened to ourselves and not to tell anyone. We certainly didn't want this to spread!

A month later at a prayer meeting involving the same people, God visited us again. After this, in practically every staff meeting and elders' meeting these phenomena would be there – you could count on it. You could sense it beginning to rise in people, and then we would suddenly have these intense times of manifestations and prophecy that would last for hours. We began to tape-record the prophecies. We were seeing repeated manifestations, such as people blowing their breath over others and making chopping and waving motions over them. Then we started to invite other members of the church to these meetings, and they too would be hit by the same phenomena. It spread in the church like wildfire. We knew that we could not contain it any longer, and we knew we had to go public at last.

In February 1988 we felt that God wanted a church-wide time of repentance. After taking one Sunday morning to explain what had been happening, we called the whole church to a 'repentance weekend'. During that weekend the Lord moved upon people with prophecy, shouting and shaking. They did all these things in public, in full view of everyone else. Several people fell under the power of the Spirit. Everyone eventually went to the carpet on their faces in repentance, weeping and wailing. We were respectable Baptists and Brethren! Many people were frightened by what was happening and left the church. After this weekend the manifestations of the Spirit began to sweep our church like a flood. We began to hold prayer meetings throughout the week in the evenings, and we held special ministry nights at the weekends. Every time we worshipped and prayed, powerful displays of God's presence would occur.

This all grew in intensity throughout 1988 and 1989, but it gradually began to decline as fear, controversy, misunderstanding, internal church problems and lack of effective administration began to quench the Spirit. And yet we still grew as a church and continued to see the gifts and manifestations of the Holy Spirit as a regular occurrence in our church services and in our home-group meetings. Between 1990 and 1994 we still saw manifestations of the Spirit, but they certainly waned. Our 'great visitation' became a story of 'the way we were'.

From 1988 to 1990 we experienced healings, prophecies, words of knowledge, physical manifestations, deliverance and repentance. The church grew to about 1,000 adults and children. Our leadership felt increasingly drawn to the values and relationships among the Vineyard association of churches. We finally became an official Vineyard church 'by adoption' in the Spring of 1991. But God had first visited us when we were still a Fellowship Baptist Church. He revisited us in an even more spectacular way in March 1994 during the dedication weekend for our new church building. The children were especially touched by God. Our three-day celebration looked like a disaster area in the evenings! God came to us even more dramatically than he had done in 1987–88.

This intense activity of the Spirit occurred again during our 21-day time of prayer and fasting three months later in June 1994. We saw literally hundreds of people – the elderly, the young, children, conservatives and charismatics – dramatically impacted by God. Most of the meetings looked like a battle zone!

Some pastors from other churches in the city also attended some of these meetings. A conservative Mennonite pastor with a hunger for renewal came to one of them. He went up on the 30-foot prayer scaffolding which we had erected outside the church on our parking lot on the main highway. Here people were praying for the city below them in shifts around the clock for 21 days. Also on the scaffold at that time were Wes Campbell and Marc Dupont from the Airport Vineyard Church in Toronto. While they were up there Marc gave a prophetic word to this visiting Mennonite pastor (a word which was later confirmed by at least three other people, who independently gave him similar words). The pastor reported to me afterwards that when he heard the word, he shook violently and had an out-of-body experience in which he was in the sky far above Kelowna. He saw revival fires burning all over the city. He also saw the churches filling up with people. He felt the presence of God in such a powerful way that for two weeks afterwards he was constantly on the verge of tears and scarcely able to speak. He received a new boldness for preaching and evangelism. His story is just one out of hundreds of similar stories that could be told about the things which God has done at our church over the past eight years.

However, our church is not built on mere phenomena. Hundreds of people in the church have had their lives dramatically changed by God as they have experienced renewal – with or without manifestations. What matters is the long-term fruit of the renewal – lives which have been changed by God. The phenomena of renewal came to us early on in our church history. We have learned a great deal first-hand. So we are primarily after the fruit, not the fun!

MY STORY

When people ask me, 'What was your background?' my reply is 'Pagan.' I grew up in Southern California as an immoral hippie, drug dealer and rock music junkie. My lifestyle was not unlike that described in 1 Corinthians 6:9–10. I became a Christian during the Jesus Movement in late 1969. I served in the US Army in Vietnam and Germany and eventually grew into a Bible-believing, God-serving Christian. My later roots as a Christian were with the Baptist General Conference. However, all through those early years I lived a double life, until one of my Army buddies in Germany said to me, 'Roger, get your story straight! You have a beer in one hand and a Bible in the other!' And so I began to take being a disciple of Jesus Christ more seriously. Four years later I moved to Canada to study at a Bible college near Vancouver. Having received God's call to serve him in the ministry, I went to Dallas Theological Seminary for further study. I spent four years there studying theology, Greek and Hebrew, church history, preaching, how to interpret the Bible, missions and evangelism. As my theological thinking developed, I was influenced by a Dispensationalist-Cessationist point of view, believing that the gifts of the Spirit were for the apostolic age but not for today.

Dallas Theological Seminary is not known as a place where church renewal is taught, but while I was there I attended an excellent course on this subject with Dr Gene Getz. He focused his renewal teaching on three vital experiences: Vital Learning experiences (the Bible); Vital Relational experiences (fellowship and worship); and Vital Witnessing experiences (evangelism). He derived these principles from Acts 2:42–47. This list of three experiences is biblical, but it is also incomplete. I later saw that there was one more vital experience that was needed in church renewal – the power of the Holy Spirit. Acts 2:43 says that 'everyone was filled with awe, and many wonders and miraculous signs were done by the apostles.' Of course, Dr Getz taught that only the apostles performed signs and wonders. He actually believed that no spiritual gifts are operative in the church today. He felt that all of Acts 2:42–47 was for today, except for verse 43. This is what I call selective hermeneutics!

Having studied in that environment, I emerged as a respectable conservative theologian. However, over a period of about ten years, God changed my thinking so radically that it can only be described as a paradigm shift. I began to see and experience God moving in ways that were new to me – in fact, I did not really believe that God *did* work in such ways! And yet as I saw supernatural gifts and phenomena, I knew that I was seeing God at work.

In 1988 our church sponsored a renewal conference. One of the people who were leading it gave me the first word of knowledge I had ever received. It depicted me as a young boy, running round the bases after scoring a home run in baseball. This was symbolic of the joy that God was releasing in me. The supernatural thing about this word was that I actually did hit a home run while playing baseball as a young boy. In fact, that day I hit two home runs and was on top of the world. The person who prayed for me saw this in his mind's eye. This conference was the beginning of a decade of on-the-job training in the school of the Spirit. Over the next few years I received other words from God and gave many words of knowledge and prophecies to other people. I also saw thousands of cases of phenomena.

During our church dedication weekend in March 1994, a couple prayed for me. As they prayed I could feel the presence of the Holy Spirit. I had felt his presence many times before and I had been 'slain in the Spirit' before. I stiffened my knees, but I couldn't resist. I fell on my side on the floor. After about ten minutes I decided to get up. One problem: I couldn't. I could only lift my head. I started to laugh, and I also felt tremendous waves of love and prophetic revelation and a desire to pray for people. A couple of men helped me up and put my arms around their necks as they supported me. I could not speak clearly. My speech was slurred, my eyelids were heavy, and I could not stand or sit without falling over. In a nutshell, *I was drunk in the Spirit*. This had never happened to me before. I had never seen this before. I had only heard about it. I wanted to minister to people and to worship the Lord. I felt tremendous freedom and joy and a spiritual euphoria which I can't describe. My mind was clear and my spirit was alive. I was then inspired to begin writing this book.

Since 1988 I had seen thousands of people have 'peak experiences' with God, and I had had some of my own. But all the while, I had never shaken, bounced, roared or manifested, and I did not care to or seek to. I always felt content to observe others. But then, when I was at the Sunday evening meeting at the Toronto Airport Church on 21 January 1996, I had a major 'peak' experience. The worship had ended, and Paul Cain was about to speak. There was nothing to suggest that anything dramatic was about to happen to me. Then suddenly, like a bolt of lightning, I was struck down by God's Spirit, and I was lying on my back across several chairs in the second row. I began to shake violently and uncontrollably. I ended up on the floor as my body twitched, heaved and shook like bacon in a frying pan.

Several months later I learned that Jim Goll and Randy Clark had simultaneously reached out their hands towards me from where they were sitting. At that moment 'heaven came down and glory filled my soul!'

Waves of the Holy Spirit's power were causing my whole body to go into the most wild contortions and reactions imaginable. I felt a surge of holy energy and revelation gush from my inner being. People who were near me fell back or began to shake as the Spirit's power spilled over into them too. I felt as if I were the Incredible Hulk bursting with God's power, or Popeye after eating his can of spinach, ready to go and fight Brutus! This lasted for three and a half hours non-stop. I left the meeting that night soaking wet with perspiration. Wes Campbell told our church the following Sunday that what he had seen happen to me was the largest impact of God's Spirit he had ever seen happen to one person on one occasion. The day I had left Kelowna for Toronto, our Church Secretary Darlene had been praying for me. She said the Lord gave her one word for me: 'awakening'. I think my peak experience was similar to the one which Saul had: 'The Spirit of the LORD will come upon you in power, and you will prophesy with them; you will be changed into a different person' (1 Sam. 10:6). I certainly had an awakening!

WHAT'S THE POINT?

Conservative evangelicals reading this book may be thinking, 'Oh come on! That isn't orderly and godly! God doesn't do things like that!' You may think it is unbiblical for God to invade a Christmas party or to overcome a pastor so that he can't walk and shakes uncontrollably for three and a half hours. But I know that God did it for me. I was

16

there! I'm not crazy, I'm not a fanatic. My life is going through a process of incredible change – not because of mere phenomena but because of an encounter with God himself. When I had that experience, I was not being psychologically manipulated by the people leading the meeting. I know the Bible. I am a graduate of Dallas Theological Seminary. But God took my life and reordered it. The fruit of that experience was that I felt humbled and literally shaken to the core of my being. I experienced the fear of God. I was full of prophetic revelation that blessed people. I wanted to give away to others whatever God was doing in me. I laughed, I cried, I worshipped.

We Christians all say we believe that God can do whatever he wants. This is our 'theoretical theology'. But then, when he does things that we don't like or understand, we say that God wouldn't do that. What we really believe is that God only does certain things which fit in with our way of thinking. This is our 'operative theology'.[2] But what God does in renewal and revival may not always accord with our own preconceived notions. So we need his help to welcome and understand his work.

WHAT IS THIS NEW RIVER OF GOD?

This new River is an *extraordinary* time in which God is visiting individuals and groups in such a way that his presence and its effects are intensified. This does not mean that unless someone experiences a manifestation, God's manifest presence has not reached them. The effects can be quiet, personal and undramatic. Although a visitation does not equal phenomena, phenomena often accompany extraordinary visitations of God. God is always present and imminent in his church and his world. We can see from Scripture and from contemporary experience that there are exceptional times when God comes closer, moves in *kairos* action, and leaves very dramatic effects and results.

God prepares his people for his plans. He discloses them through prophecy. Isaiah 42:9 proclaims, 'See, the former things have taken place, and new things I declare; before they spring into being I announce them to you.' Amos 3:7–8 declares, 'Surely the sovereign LORD does nothing without revealing his plan to his servants the prophets. The lion has roared, who will not fear? The sovereign LORD has spoken, who can but prophesy?'

In the past 20 years or so, scores of people have prayed for and prophesied that renewal and revival would come to Canada and elsewhere. Here are some of those prophecies.

Dr David (Paul) Yonggi Cho

David Yonggi Cho, Senior Pastor of the world's largest church, Yoido Full Gospel Church in Seoul, Korea, delivered the following prophecy in October 1975 while speaking at Evangel Tabernacle in Kelowna, BC:

> When I came to Canada, the Holy Spirit spoke in my heart, 'Son, you have come to the place which I chose. This country is the country I chose to fill the gap.'

In 1984, while Dr Cho was speaking at a church growth seminar in Sackville, Nova Scotia, he related his earlier prophecy, and added the following:

> Five years ago I visited Canada and travelled from Montreal to Vancouver by car. I was preaching from town to town, and while I was speaking, I felt somewhat depressed. The Canadian church seemed so

small. But wherever I went, the Holy Spirit spoke in my heart that God was going to raise up tremendous churches in Canada and that Canada would be used as a missionary sending country ... If ever God would use any country, he should use America instead of Canada because America is a ... country with greater resources and more population. But again and again God spoke to my heart that he was going to use Canada, so finally *in Toronto*, with great inner faith, I prophesied as the Holy Spirit anointed me ... I really believe that God is going to bless Canada and the Canadian church is going to rise up once again and go to the four corners of the world and bring the gospel of Jesus Christ ...

Further to that, in 1991, David Yonggi Cho also prophesied a revival that would come to Pensacola, Florida. On Father's Day, 18 June 1995, revival began and continues to this day there through the renewal meetings at the Brownsville Assembly of God Church. By May 1996, 500,000 people had come to the meetings with 18,000 decisions for Christ. It is now known as the 'Pensacola Outpouring'. Cho recounts his prophecy in the foreword of the book written by Senior Pastor, John Kilpatrick. In it, Cho says:

When I was ministering in Seattle, Washington, in 1991, I became deeply concerned about the spiritual decline in America. I began to pray even more earnestly for revival in these United States. As I prayed, I felt the Lord prompt me to get a map of America and to point my finger on the map. I found myself pointing to the city of Pensacola in the Florida panhandle. Then I sensed the Lord say, 'I am going to send revival to the seaside city of Pensacola, and it will spread like a fire until all of America has been consumed by it.' That revival fire has now come to Pensacola's Brownsville Assembly of God church.[3]

Larry Randolph

Larry Randolph is a prophetic pastor who originally came from Arkansas and now works in California. One evening in 1986, the Lord visited him. As he lay on his bed, the Lord began to 'rain' on him. He could smell, feel and hear rain. He jumped up, opened his window, but saw nothing outside except clear sky. Thinking that this was strange, he returned to bed. Later the same things happened again. This time, like the young Samuel, he said, 'God, what's happening? It's not raining outside. Speak to me.' Then he felt the Lord speak to him in an audible way. The Lord said:

As it was in the days of Noah, so shall it be in the coming of the Son of Man. I'm going to bring an un-precedented outpouring of my Spirit upon the church and the world. Just as Noah received a rain that was unprecedented in his generation, I'm bringing a rain of my Spirit unprecedented upon this generation.

Larry asked the Lord, 'How long?' The Lord said, 'Seven years.' He said this would begin in the autumn of 1993 in seed form, and it would develop into a great revival. Larry preached this message all over the world, and he even pro-duced a three-tape series on Noah. Seven years later, on 1 January 1993, he said, 'Okay, Lord, it's coming – this is the year. Give me a sign.' That day, Larry received a phone call from Elder Artish Cash of Crenshaw Christian Fellowship in Los Angeles. He wanted to interview Larry on his radio programme on station KTYM. While he was on the air, the following prophetic words came out of Larry's inner being: 'The Lord is bringing an unprecedented revival. The fall of 1993 is the beginning. A sign will be that the nation is going to have one of the wettest years ever in the last hundred years. It's going to rain in the Midwest, it's going to rain in California. It's going to rain, rain, rain.'[4] By February 1993, mudslides were devastating homes in California. That summer torrents of rain pounded the Midwest. It was the most rain the country had seen in a century!

In 1984 the Lord said to Bob Jones in Kansas City, 'Keep your eyes open for the "great flood". Here is going to be a sign to you. Rain, rain rain! Rain is coming! The waters are going to flood and when the Mississippi River changes its direction, that is when it will signal the beginning of the time of the visitation.' In mid 1993 the Missouri River overflowed its banks and went into the Mississippi River. So powerful was the flooding that the Mississippi also overflowed its banks as it changed its direction – just as Bob had prophesied in 1984. This flood was regarded as one of the worst in US history. In June 1995, over the phone, Bob Jones told me that he feels that the Mississippi will change its direction again.

Terry Lamb

Terry Lamb is a man with a prophetic gift who comes from Ontario. He spent several years on the staff of Burnaby Christian Fellowship in British Columbia. In 1990 he and his family moved to Kelowna and joined our church. He has a ministry as an itinerant preacher and he also ministers in very accurate prophecy. In April 1992, while Terry and I were going for a walk together, he told me about a vision which he had had that sunny morning. He had seen snowflakes falling outside his living-room window (it doesn't snow in Kelowna in April). He also saw an arrow shoot from heaven into the bullseye of a target which had a maple leaf in the middle (the maple leaf is on the Canadian flag). He asked the Lord what it meant. He felt the Lord say in his spirit, 'I am bringing renewal to Canada.' A few nights later, he had a dream in which he saw a key being thrown out of heaven and landing beside his bed. He saw written on it the words, 'renewal and revival'. In the dream he saw himself pick up the key. As he did so, it turned into the Canadian maple leaf. He felt the Lord say, 'Through Canada renewal and revival will touch every nation of the world.'

Paul Cain

Paul Cain is a well-known prophet. Three weeks before the first Toronto Airport Vineyard meeting in January 1994, when he was at the New Year's Eve service at the Anaheim Vineyard, he prophesied that 'There is coming a fresh release and visitation of the Spirit to John and Carol … This move of the Spirit will bless the whole Vineyard.' Later that evening, Paul talked to John and Carol Wimber and said that the Lord had told him, 'John and Carol, *not Wimber.*' The only other John and Carol in the Vineyard movement whom John Wimber knew of were John and Carol Arnott. The rest is church history!

Marc Dupont

Marc Dupont is a staff member at the Toronto Airport Church. He has delivered some very significant prophecies in recent years. In May 1992 at Toronto he had a vision of vast quantities of water falling over and on to a very large rock.[5] God said through Marc,

> Toronto shall be a place where much living water shall be flowing, even though at the present time both the church and the city are like big rocks – cold and hard against God's love and his Spirit. The waterfall shall be so powerful that it will break the big rocks up into small stones that can be used in building the Kingdom ...

> There will be a radical move in late '93 and through-out '94 of many ordinary Christians beginning to form, on their own, prayer groups of intercession for the city, the nation, and the peoples ...

> Like Jerusalem, Toronto will be a centre from which many are sent out to the nations, on all continents. It is of God that there are so many internationals in this area. The Lord is going to be sending out many people, filled with his Spirit with strong gifting, vision, and love to the nations on all continents.

In July 1993, while he was in Vancouver, Marc felt God saying that the moving of the Holy Spirit in Toronto was going to happen in the summer and autumn of 1993 and would accelerate in pace in 1994. These predictions are turning out to be very accurate.

IS THIS THAT?

Some people may seriously question whether *this* (i.e. the present renewal) is *that* (i.e. what the prophecies were predicting). For example, Dr James A. Beverley, theology professor at Ontario Theological Seminary, not only questions but undermines the prophecies of Marc Dupont, Paul Cain, Bob Jones and Stacey Campbell.[6] I will deal with the subject of prophecy in chapter 6, but for the time being I will try to respond to Dr Beverley's criticisms and suggest a few guiding principles.

First, if someone's experience with genuine prophecy is limited or non-existent, then that person is in a weak position to judge it, especially when they do so *alone*.

Secondly, prophecy must be weighed and waited on to see how it develops. Prophecy often comes in parts and develops progressively. Sometimes it is general, sometimes it is specific, or sometimes it is a combination of the two. Sometimes it comes in riddles, dreams, visions and symbols. For example, Marc Dupont's prophecies are partly general and partly specific, they are fairly symbolic and have not yet been completely fulfilled.

Thirdly, New Testament prophecy is not the same as Old Testament prophecy. New Testament prophecy is meant to strengthen, encourage and comfort (see 1 Cor. 14:3). It may have predictive elements and may actually be a 'word of knowledge', but it does not necessarily have to speak to the whole of the contemporary national scene with profound power and insight, as, for example, Isaiah and Amos did.

Fourthly, not all the predictive elements in a prophecy should be pressed to yield minute detail about future events, for 'we know in part and we prophesy in part' (1 Cor. 13:9).

We must also agree on the terms we use. For example, some people call what is happening now renewal while others call it revival.

Fifthly, prophecy must be judged in the context in which it was given, according to the character and track record of the prophet, and in submission to the Bible and the church leaders. It should also be submitted in advance and it should be weighed by more than one person (1 Cor. 14:26–32). Re-read the above prophecies for yourself. I think that cumulatively they are very compelling!

God is today releasing a new River of his Spirit. He sovereignly chose Canada to play a central role in a great move of the Spirit which would affect the whole planet. He calls us to forget the former things and not to dwell on the past. We will have water in our deserts and streams in our wastelands. This new River is rushing with the vitality and power of the Niagara River in Ontario. According to Isaiah's promise, if we will perceive what God is doing, we will drink and we will worship. The Lord says that he will 'give drink to my people, my chosen, the people I formed for myself that they may proclaim my praise' (Isa. 43:21). Let the River flow!

CHAPTER TWO

SCRIPTURE AND EXPERIENCE

'Is this renewal *biblical*?' This is the most common and important question which people are asking. The root problem in this question is the manifestations and gifts of the Holy Spirit. Are *they* biblical? In other words, are they from God? We will answer that question in later chapters. We must first ask how we interpret Scripture to determine what is biblical, and how experience affects that process. This is the goal of *hermeneutics*.

Hermeneutics is the study of the principles for interpreting and applying Scripture. It is both a science and an art, and it involves both exegesis and exposition. Worldview, experience and theology affect our hermeneutics, which affects our application. Interpreting Scripture begins with *exegesis*.

EXEGESIS

Exegesis means to 'draw out' the meaning of the Bible. The task is to determine the meaning which the writers intended to communicate and which their readers were expected to understand. Exegesis is *not* studying the text to 'read in' *what it means to me*. That is application. Before we apply the text we must understand the text and then ask, 'How does this apply to me today?'

When we read passages in the Bible about miracles and unusual phenomena, we must first ask, 'What did the author mean and what would his original readers have understood him to mean?' Should the things we are reading about be a *normal* part of church life today? As we do exegesis, we must be aware that our worldview shapes our interpretation.

WORLDVIEWS

Our *worldview* is our assumptions, values and commitments (conscious and unconscious) about our perceptions of reality. It is the grid through which we process and explain reality as we perceive and experience it. We largely see what we are taught to see by our culture. A perception is a conclusion which we make about an experience after we reflect on it. It may or may not be in line with reality. We perceive selectively, we accept things that confirm what we have been taught, and we believe what we think is possible. What we think determines what we see; what we see often does not determine what we think.

If we saw someone shake during a prayer meeting, our learned perception would be that the person was having a convulsion, an epileptic seizure, an electrical shock, or a demonic manifestation. We are not taught and we do not easily believe that people can shake uncontrollably as a reaction to God's presence. We think and then we see. Therefore, our worldview can unconsciously screen God out of our perception. We can also tend to screen out bizarre or supernatural elements that we read in Scripture. Our worldview affects our perception of God in this present renewal, as we seek to 'biblically' explain the manifestations and gifts of the Spirit.

THE CHARISMATIC WORLDVIEW

Perhaps charismatic Christians can teach us a few things about exegesis and worldview. According to the Oxford researcher David Barrett, the largest Protestant group in Christendom world-wide is the one which includes the Pentecostals, the Charismatics and the Third-Wavers (the 'Third Wave' is a contemporary renewal movement of Evangelicals who are not necessarily Pentecostal or Charismatic). In 1990 these three groups numbered roughly 373 million, so they are about 23% of the world's Christians.[1]

C. Peter Wagner's latest statistics (adapted from David Barrett) show that in 1945 there were only 16 million Pentecostals. In 1975 there were 76 million of them (including the Charismatics). By 1985 there were 247 million Pentecostals/Charismatics. Barrett projects that by the year 2000 there will be 600 million Pentecostals/-Charismatics/Third-Wavers.

These Christians share a belief in and experience of God's supernatural power. This is consistent with a biblical worldview. Wagner, formerly a Dispensationalist missionary to Bolivia, was always encouraged by his mentor, Donald McGavran, to study growing churches to discover church growth principles. He came to realize that the fastest growing churches in Latin America were the Pentecostal ones.[2] They ministered in the power of the Holy Spirit, and the people of Latin America expect the miraculous. When we Westerners do exegesis, we have a tendency to screen out the miraculous, the bizarre and the supernatural. Therefore, we often don't experience it or believe in it either.

THE ENLIGHTENMENT WORLDVIEW

The philosophy of the 18th-century Enlightenment still strongly influences our Western cultures.[3] The goal of this philosophy was to counter superstition, the miraculous and 'divine revelation' with reason and science. Major philosophers and politicians like David Hume, Immanuel Kant, Benjamin Franklin and Thomas Jefferson championed this worldview. It is based on a desire to control, order and predict. One of its major concepts is that of cause and effect. It supremely values the senses or experience (empiricism) and the mind or reason (rationalism).

Enlightenment rationalism trusts the scientific method and sees no 'supernatural' intervention in a closed universe. It believes only in the visible world of the five senses. It is naturalistic and materialistic. Its assumption is that matter is more 'real' than spirit. On the Greek model, it divides reality into the natural and the supernatural, rather than seeing reality as one indivisible whole made up of the natural and the spiritual, as the Hebrews did. It is largely anti-supernatural and humanistic.

Enlightenment philosophy is also *deistic*. Deism reduces God to the First Cause. Like a great clock-maker, God made and wound up his world clock, leaving it to run on its own natural momentum without his further intervention. He is a First Cause, but he does not intervene by the supernatural or miracles after that. I believe that many Christians are theological theists but practising deists, due to their Cessationist and anti-supernatural beliefs. They believe that we cannot trust emotion, intuition, the invisible and the realm of the spirit. An Enlightenment worldview influences their hermeneutics.

29

To any Christian who is bound by the Enlightenment worldview but wants to get free from it and to experience God more fully, I would make the following recommendations:

1) Reject the Enlightenment, deistic, anti-supernatural bias. Do not read the Bible as a book of words but rather as a book in which God speaks. Read the Bible and expect to have biblical experience. Allow the Bible to reshape your worldview and experience. *Enter into* the text yourself.

2) Expose yourself to experiences where the Holy Spirit is moving (churches, conferences, prayer times, etc.), and read books and listen to tapes about renewal and revival.

3) Meet with people who have the same hunger for God. Pray, worship and minister to one another in small groups. Discuss and apply what the Bible says about the supernatural and the Spirit.

4) Make a 'paradigm shift': believe in order to see (see John 20:29–31). As Bernard of Clairvaux said, 'I believe in order to experience.' Matthew wrote about Jesus' hometown, 'He did not do many miracles there because of their lack of faith' (Matt. 13:58).

EXPERIENCE

Personal experience has a crucial place in biblical interpretation. Our experience influences our interpretation of Scripture and our perception of our world. According to Jesus, to *know* the Word of God (i.e. to hear it) is to *practise* it (i.e. to obey it). We learn truth by doing it. Ideally, we must *test* our experience by Scripture while we seek to *align* our experience with Scripture. Experience is crucial to Christian knowledge and fellowship.

The apostle John heard, saw and touched Jesus the Word (1 John 1:1–3). John's *experience* of Jesus Christ, through the five senses, is a valid means of knowledge and understanding. The fact is, salvation and sanctification are both experiences with God. *I would argue that the theology and doctrine expressed in the Bible are largely developed from the biblical authors' experiences with God.* This provides the basis for preaching the gospel message and enjoying its reality through Christian fellowship. Dr Ray Anderson expresses this idea, and links experience and theology by the term *praxis*. He writes:

> *Praxis* is quite different from the mere application of truth or theory. The word *practice* ordinarily refers to the methods and means by which we apply a skill or theory. This tends to separate truth from method or action so that one assumes that what is true can be deduced or discovered apart from the action or activity which applies to it in practice. *Praxis* is an action that includes ... the final meaning, and the character of truth. It is an action in which the truth is discovered through action, not merely applied or 'practiced.'[4]

Anderson asserts that through the action itself, the truth of the action is revealed. The purpose or meaning of something is discovered in its action, not in its theory or practice. For example, we learn the truth and goal of love by the action of loving. We do not really know its truth by theory but only by *practising* it. The goal and meaning of love is giving and nurturing for the benefit of the loved one. It is intimacy and relationship. Before I was married and had three children, I did not particularly enjoy or want children. But as my own children arrived on the scene, I began to *experience* for myself the parental love for my children that other parents had told me about. I had known parental love by theory and had even tried to *practise* loving *their* children! However, I did not really *know* parental love until I discovered it through the *action* of loving *my* children. Anderson writes:

> In *praxis* God's truth is revealed through the structures of reality by which God's actions and presence are disclosed to us through our own actions ... God acts through our human actions to reveal truth. The truth of God's Word, for example, is not something which can be extracted from the Bible by the mind so that one can possess this truth as a formula or doctrine without regard to its purpose of bringing us 'into the truth.'[5]

When Jesus healed on the Sabbath, he *demonstrated* the truth that God is interested in restoring human beings, not in keeping the law which was made for human beings (Mark 2:27). When Peter received a vision about how the gospel was for Jew and Gentile alike (Acts 10), he did not come to this theological conclusion by studying his Bible. Experience and theology meet.

A common accusation made against the current renewal is that it is based too much on experience. However, if people did not *experience* getting blessed, filled and healed, they would not go to renewal meetings![6] They would not get excited about the theory and theology of renewal, filling and healing. We learn best not by theory or theology but by experiencing the Holy Spirit who is the *praxis* of Jesus.

DOCTRINE FIRST OR EXPERIENCE FIRST?

Which comes first, the doctrine or the experience? Most Christians would probably say that doctrine comes first. But people do not base their doctrine on doctrine alone. They base their doctrine on experience. Even the biblical writers based their understanding of the Spirit on their experiences of him. First they experienced him, and then later they reflected theologically on those experiences. After his vision and his interaction with Cornelius, the apostle Peter had to change his theology to include Gentiles in the gospel (see Acts 10). When we first see him in the book of Acts, Paul was a persecutor of the Christians, but after meeting the risen Jesus on the Damascus road, he abandoned his Pharisaic theology of law and works and became a Christian himself. Truth was revealed as Peter and Paul experienced the *praxis* of the Spirit who inspired the Scripture and made it come alive in its effects. What we experience determines much of what we believe and therefore practise.

Ray Anderson states, 'The early Christians first experienced the presence and power of Christ in their lives and then produced theological reflection based on that experience.'[7] Dr Guy Chevreau agrees. He writes: 'For the Apostle Paul, his understanding and expectation of the Spirit of the Risen Christ was always *experiential*. It was not *primarily* theological, doctrinal or speculative. The thinking about it came after, secondarily. First and foremost, it was experiential.'[8] Chevreau also writes that 'We must understand that the manifest presence of God *is* highly subjective. It *is* experiential. It *is*, often, emotional. And, it *is* typically messy.'[9]

In January 1996, at a pastors' teaching session at the Toronto Airport Church, Guy stated that 'theology is biography'. He used the example of Paul, who did not wake up one morning and decide that being a Pharisee and persecuting Christians was tiring, and so he would try grace. No, he discovered grace when he experienced the risen Jesus. Guy also referred to Moses, who did not write the Law first and then have a burning-bush experience later. He concluded by saying, 'Theology without biography becomes dead orthodoxy.'

College students will go to one school and will believe what that school teaches. They may then go to another school that teaches the opposite and may come to believe that instead. Experience even shaped Martin Luther's theology. As a Catholic monk who despaired of trying to earn God's favour through discipline, piety and good works, he discovered the truths of justification by grace through faith alone in Romans and Galatians. Then he tried to reform Catholic theology – even though most of Paul's theology is centred on life in the Spirit and *not* on justification.[10] He adapted the text to 16th-century conditions as the Bible spoke to his personal situation.

John Calvin's experience also informed his theology. He reacted to the corrupt, self-appointed sovereignty of the papal system. He wrote his *Institutes of the Christian Religion* in order to assert the sovereign will of God in his appeal to King Francis I of France on behalf of persecuted evangelicals during the Reformation.

Perhaps Jonathan Edwards was influenced in his theology in favour of the miraculous and manifestations because of the experiences and healing that his wife had during the First Great Awakening. It is also possible that B. B. Warfield was influenced in his theology against the miraculous because of his wife's long-standing illnesses.

Those who have an experience that is closer to what we read in the Bible are better able to understand the authors. If I have been filled with the Spirit and have seen dramatic changes in my life as a Christian, I will better understand what Paul meant when he wrote, 'If you live by the Spirit you will not gratify the desires of the sinful nature' (Gal. 5:16).

Dr Roger Stronstad argues that Pentecostal interpreters of the New Testament are better able to understand what it says about the Holy Spirit because their theology is *experience-certified*.[11] He says their own personal experience of the Spirit 'results in an understanding, empathy, and sensitivity to the text, and priorities in relation to the text which other interpreters do not and cannot have.'[12] What this also means is that only a Christian interpreter is able to understand and produce 'enlightened' Christian theology based on first-hand knowledge. The non-Christian can't. Also, someone who has experienced renewal will be in a better place to understand similar biblical patterns like tongues, healing, prophecy, manifestations and so forth.

However, it is possible to go wrong with basing our theology on experience. For example, I believe the Montanists (an early prophetic movement), the Quakers and the early Pentecostals went wrong when they built their theology on their experience and did not ground their experience with biblical restraints and discernment. Their experience became normative. Charismatics can have this tendency too. But the issue is not, as Dr John MacArthur declares in his book *Charismatic Chaos*, that Charismatics rely on experience rather than letting biblical truth stand in final judgment on experience. The issue is, whose experience are we to trust? MacArthur's experience also influences his hermeneutics. Many Charismatics are also well-grounded in biblical truth.

THEOLOGY

Our exegesis, worldview and experience shape our interpretation of the Bible and the formulation of our theology. We must gauge the Bible with experience and we must gauge experience with the Bible. Our interpretation should work in a circular fashion, as illustrated below:

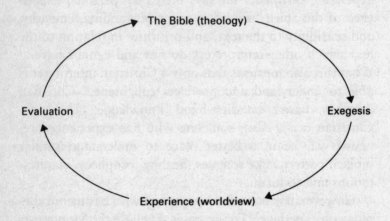

The Bible (theology)

Evaluation

Exegesis

Experience (worldview)

In the hermeneutical task there is a vital link between what you *understand* and what you *interpret*; what you *exegete* and what you *experience*; what you *perceive* and what you *practise*; what you *believe* and how you *behave*.

I have seen hundreds of sceptical, conservative Christians change their worldview and theology because of first-hand experiences with the supernatural. They are not unlike the man born blind whom Jesus healed on the Sabbath (see

John 9). Jesus put some mud made with his own saliva on the man's eyes and told him to go and wash in the Pool of Siloam. This offended the theology of the Pharisees. It did not look like God's actions, especially because Jesus did this on the Sabbath. But the man himself said, 'I once was blind but now I see', and he called Jesus a prophet. His experience influenced his theology. Our goal must be to balance reason with revelation, exegesis with experience.

NORMAL AND NORMATIVE

The *final authority* for faith and practice does not rest on theology, experience, tradition or reason but on Scripture alone. A difficulty lies in how we apply historical or cultural portions of Scripture. Application is how we personally appropriate Scripture. *But how do we distinguish between, on the one hand, that which is normative and is above culture or history and is therefore for today and, on the other hand, that which is not normative and is cultural or historical and is therefore not for today?* How are the books of the Bible the authoritative Word of God to us today?[13]

The author's *intended meaning* and how the readers would *understand* that meaning is what governs the *significance* of that meaning in application. Are miracles, prophecy and the gift of tongues *normal* for church life (i.e. they could or should happen) or *normative* for church life (i.e. they must happen)? We cannot suggest that didactic (i.e. epistle/teaching/instructing) books and passages carry more doctrinal weight than historical or narrative or poetic portions of Scripture. We must ask, 'How is this text the Word of God for us?' Which aspects of New Testament church life are descriptive (normal) and which are prescriptive (normative)?[14]

In order to form our theology from the Bible, we must understand the nature of historical narratives. Before it was written down, much of the Bible was passed on in the form of oral narrative – that is, story-telling. The stories were meant to be *heard* as the Word of God and applied in contemporary contexts. The Bible was not written and preserved in order to report what God *did* but rather to proclaim what God *does*. To determine what is normative and what is normal in Christianity, we must ask the following questions:

1) What does the biblical author *intend* to teach?
2) What is *incidental* in an account and what is of *primary significance* in it? Precedent must be related to *intent*. There may be patterns and practices that illustrate principles, but the author may not intend these as precedents.
3) What do the words and activities of the characters portray? Are they *interpreted* in the text or elsewhere in the Bible as normative?
4) Is the overall message and purpose conveying something which is an *expected* experience of believers (i.e. *normal* precedent, repeatable Christian experience)?
5) Is the overall message and purpose conveying something which is a *required* experience of believers (i.e. *normative* prescription, required Christian experience)?

The Bible as history and theology is biography which is meant to shape a community that enters commonly shared experiences across culture and time. We must therefore contemplate Scripture and not just interpret it. Eugene

Peterson calls us back to *contemplative exegesis*, in which we will be not merely *exegetes* who lead the meaning out of the text but also *guides* who lead others in the way of the text. He cites the example of Philip and the Ethiopian eunuch: 'So Philip ran to him, and heard him reading the prophet Isaiah, and said, "Do you *understand* what you are reading?" And he said, "How can I, unless someone *guides* me?"' (Acts 8:30–31, NKJ). Contemplative exegesis of historical narratives means that we, like Philip, who climbed into the chariot, seek to climb into the story and share the journey.[15]

SUMMARY

You might be thinking, 'He hasn't answered the question, "Is this renewal biblical?"' Well, it depends on your definition of 'biblical' and how you do hermeneutics. Our Enlightenment anti-supernatural worldview and our experience will affect what we read. If we read the Bible with a prior commitment to the supernatural occurring in our day, and if we progressively experience what we see in Scripture, then we are in a better place to verify what is of God. The Bible reveals that *supernatural Christianity is normal*. You might say, 'Well, I don't trust people's experiences, but I do trust the objective Word of God, and I still have a problem with the gifts and manifestations of the Holy Spirit. Are they biblical?' We will deal with these questions in the next three chapters.

CHAPTER THREE

SURPRISED BY THE GIFTS OF THE SPIRIT

A BIBLICAL BASIS FOR THE GIFTS OF THE SPIRIT TODAY

'Come, Holy Spirit!' and 'More!' are the most used words in today's renewal. Thousands have witnessed or experienced dramatic gifts of the Holy Spirit – especially 'the manifestation gifts' of 1 Corinthians 12:7–11.

People pray for renewal. But when it comes, some of them complain that it's 'not biblical'. Why? Because some people have theological problems with tongues, prophecy, healings, words of knowledge and demonstrations of power. Or, because some have had bad experiences or no experiences with the gifts of the Spirit, or have little or no theology for the gifts, they are surprised by them when they happen. Some of these people are *Cessationists*. I will now respond to Cessationist views so that these people will have a proper biblical worldview and theology which aligns with their new experience.

The Cessationist view

Cessationists believe that the so-called 'sign gifts' which are listed in 1 Corinthians 12:7–11 ceased after the early church, or when the canon of Scripture was complete. One system of biblical interpretation which works from a Cessationist viewpoint is *Dispensationalism*. The

Dispensationalist view is present, for example, at Dallas Theological Seminary, in the writings of Pastor John MacArthur, and in *The Scofield Reference Bible*. Reformed Theology (i.e. Calvinism) is Cessationist, but it comes to this view by a different theological route.

Former Dallas Seminary professor Dr Jack Deere states that over the years he has observed that the majority of what Christians believe is not derived from their own study of the Bible. What they believe comes from what authority figures and teachers have taught them. He writes:

If you were to lock a brand new Christian in a room with a Bible and tell him to study what the Scripture has to say about healing and miracles, he would never come out of the room a cessationist ... This is not a system of doctrine that I would have ever come up with on my own. I had to be *taught* that the gifts of the Spirit had passed away.[1]

Deere also says:

No one ever just picked up the Bible, started reading, and then came to the conclusion that God was not doing signs and wonders anymore and that the gifts of the Holy Spirit had passed away ... The doctrine of cessationism originated in *experience*. The failure to see miracles in one's own experience and to locate them in past history required an explanation.[2]

You cannot read the Cessationist position *out of the biblical text* through proper exegesis, but can *read it into the text* with an anti-supernatural, Dispensational, anti-charismatic *experience*.

There is not one explicit or implicit text in the entire Bible that affirms or declares that *any* spiritual gifts were confined to the early church or ceased at the completion of the canon (i.e. the 66 books of the Bible). Cessationists must resort to logical, theological and historical arguments to establish their position. They cannot prove it by Scripture alone. The following are the major Cessationist arguments, together with my responses to them:

Cessationist thesis 1

The commissions in Matthew 10 and Luke 10, which include preaching the gospel of the Kingdom and healing the sick, were given to the disciples and the 70, not to the whole church.

Response: In Matthew 28:18–20 Jesus tells the disciples to teach all the nations to *observe all that he had commanded*. He told his disciples to preach the gospel and heal the sick (Matt. 10).

The Gospel writers intended to write theological/historical manuals based on the written and oral accounts of the teaching and ministry of Jesus. The Gospels were written to address the contemporary needs and interests of the early church concerning discipleship, faith, evangelism, doctrine and church practice. We cannot selectively choose which Gospel accounts we will apply today. We cannot discard the miraculous accounts while retaining the non-miraculous ones. We are told to observe (i.e. obey) all that Jesus commanded in the Gospels. Paul and Barnabas took the teaching we read in Matthew 10:14 literally. In Acts 13:51 they were the only ones who shook the dust off their feet when the gospel was rejected in Pisidian Antioch. Is Paul then not a model for ministry today in obedience to Matthew 10:14?

Cessationist thesis 2

The 'sign gifts' and miracles were given to authenticate the apostles and to give them credibility as authors of 'new revelation' or Scripture (e.g. Acts 2:22, 43; Heb. 2:3–4; 5:12; 2 Cor. 12:12).

Response: Non-apostles such as the 72 (Luke 10), Stephen (Acts 6:8), Philip (Acts 8:6–7), Barnabas (Acts 4:3), Ananias (Acts 9:17; 22:12), Philip's daughters (Acts 21:9), the Galatians (Gal. 3:1–5) and the Corinthians (1 Cor. 12–14) moved in 'sign gifts' and performed miracles. Also, Mark 16:15–18 and John 14:10–12 are general promises of the miraculous for all non-apostles who will believe. Though one may dispute the original reading of Mark 16:9–20, the theological understanding of the church at this time must have endorsed miracles, signs and wonders in order for such a reading to appear in the manuscripts of later editions of Mark.

2 Corinthians 12:12 seems to say that signs and wonders authenticate the apostles. The New King James Bible captures the literal Greek text well: 'Truly the signs of an apostle were accomplished among you with all perseverance, in signs and wonders and mighty deeds.' Throughout 2 Corinthians, Paul seeks to prove that his apostolic ministry is authentic. The signs of his apostleship were performed (passive) in the manner of great perseverance, *by* signs, wonders, and miracles. As Victor Furnish comments, 'All three words stand in the dative case, expressing the means by which the apostolic signs had been exhibited in Corinth.'[3] These words in the dative case are not preceded by a preposition and are furthermore preceded by a verb in the passive voice. This would lead us to conclude, then, that these three words are datives of *means*

or *agency* – that is, they express how the apostolic signs were performed in all perseverance – by signs, wonders and miracles.

Furthermore, Romans 15:18–19, a parallel passage, is similar:

> I will not venture to speak of anything except what Christ has accomplished through me in leading the Gentiles to obey God by what I have said and done – *by the power of signs and miracles, through the power of the Spirit.* So from Jerusalem all the way around to Illyricum, I have fully proclaimed the gospel of Christ.

Therefore, a valid apostolic office should include signs, wonders and mighty works. It might also include suffering (2 Cor. 11:16–33), effectiveness in calling people to the obedience of faith by preaching and demonstrations of power (Rom. 1:5; 1 Cor. 2:5; 1 Thess. 1:5), and the call of God (1 Cor. 1:1). The Bible nowhere states that signs, wonders and miracles *were only given to authenticate the apostles*. However, a genuine apostle would perform these signs, wonders and miracles (e.g. Acts 2:43; 4:30; 14:8–10; 15:12; 16:16–18; 19:11–12; 20:7–12; 28:1–6, 7–9). Also, because a false apostle can do counterfeit miracles, the primary function of miracles cannot be the authentication of a true apostle.

Hebrews 2:3–4 states that: 'God also testified to it [i.e. the gospel message] by signs, wonders and various miracles, and gifts of the Holy Spirit distributed according to his will.' This passage indicates that signs, wonders and miracles were given to authenticate or testify to the gospel, not to testify to the apostles or their new revelation. The verb 'testified' in this verse is a *present* participle, indicating an *ongoing* reality of signs and wonders, miracles and gifts of the Holy Spirit. The testifying happened simultaneously with the confirming and continues as a perpetual reality in the Christian community.

The New Testament never speaks of so-called 'sign-gifts'. The terminology of 'distributed according to his will' is parallel to 1 Corinthians 12:11: 'All these [gifts of the Holy Spirit] are the work of one and the same Spirit, and he gives to each man, just as he determines.' Hebrews says that all the gifts of the Spirit, not only the so-called sign gifts, are distributed by his will as he determines. All of them authenticate the gospel. 1 Corinthians 1:7 also reinforces the *continuous* nature of all gifts: 'Therefore you do not lack any spiritual gift *as you eagerly wait* for our Lord Jesus Christ to be revealed.'

Again, the New Testament asserts that miracles, signs and wonders were given to confirm the message of the gospel: 'So Paul and Barnabas spent considerable time there, speaking boldly for the Lord, who confirmed the message of his grace by enabling them to do miraculous signs and wonders' (Acts 14:3). We need such confirmation as much today as they needed it then.

Cessationist thesis 3

Miracles were necessary for the gospel to gain a hearing in the first century. After the church became established and mature, confirmation by miracles was no longer needed.

Response: There is not one single scripture to defend this Cessationist argument. If the church needed miracles then, does it need them any less today? Is a 'mature' church one that can exist without miracles? Biblically, a mature church is one that has reached unity in the faith and in the knowledge of the Son of God, attaining to the whole measure of the fullness of Christ and building itself up in love as each part does its work (Eph. 4:13–16). Miracles or lack of miracles is not a measure of maturity. Are we to say that the post-apostolic church has displayed the maturity listed in Ephesians 4? Hardly. In Galatians 3:5 Paul asks, 'Does God give you his Spirit and work miracles among you because you observe the law, or because you believe what you heard?' The Greek for 'give you his Spirit and work miracles' is in the present tense. The implication is that the giving of his Spirit and miracles are ongoing, normal experiences that arise out of a proper belief system.

Furthermore, we read that prophecy, dreams and visions would attend the outpouring of the Holy Spirit in the 'last days' (compare Acts 2:17–21 with Heb. 1:2). The New Testament reveals that the 'last days' began at the Incarnation. We are in the last days until Christ returns (2 Pet. 3). Therefore, we can expect prophecy, dreams and visions to occur during the church age, from Pentecost to Christ's second coming.

Cessationist thesis 4

The Gospels and Acts were 'transitional' books in God's economy and therefore are not normative for today regarding miracles and sign gifts. Also, we cannot take doctrine from these narrative books but rather from the later epistles.

Response: Jack Deere comments: 'What this argument really means is that we may not use the Gospels and Acts to determine doctrine about supernatural events in the life of the church today ... You are free to copy the non-miraculous elements in the Gospels and Acts, but you are not free to copy the miraculous elements.'[4] This would be bogus hermeneutics. Much of the Bible is narrative. In the Ancient Near East, telling a story was a common way to communicate theology. Theologians have always used the narratives of the Gospels and Acts for doctrine (e.g. John 6:44; Acts 13:48; Matt. 28:18–20; Acts 4:12).

The Gospels and Acts together make up 59% of the New Testament. Are we prepared to read them only as interesting history that has no doctrinal and normative authority? Are we to suppose that the real-life model of a Spirit-empowered missionary church which is displayed in the book of Acts was only for a short transitional period? Scripture nowhere states that the Gospels and Acts are transitional books. These books were written long after the events they record. They were written to show later generations of readers what normal Christianity should be for them.

Cessationist thesis 5

With the completion of the canon of Scripture, the 'sign gifts' would cease – especially tongues, prophecy and miracles. According to 1 Corinthians 13:8–10, Paul anticipates that certain gifts of the Spirit will pass away – particularly tongues – as indicated by the middle voice of the verb '*they will cease* in and of themselves' (v. 8). The church no longer needed miraculous spiritual gifts when perfection came (some say this refers to the completed canon and others say it means the maturity of the church). The Bible alone is sufficient for doctrine, life and practice (see 2 Tim. 3:15–17).

Response: Paul is comparing that which is now *partial* to that which will be *perfect*. He is not comparing that which is temporary to that which is permanent. At the time of his writing, certainly neither Paul nor the Corinthians would have known about the idea of a 'closed New Testament canon'. The official closing of the 27-book New Testament canon did not occur until AD 393 and 397 at the Councils of Hippo and Carthage.

Contextually, Paul is referring to the *Second Coming* as that which is *perfect* (*teleios*) or has 'attained the end or purpose'. *Now* we are incomplete and childish, but *then* we will be complete and grown up; then we shall see face to face and know fully, even as we are known (1 Cor. 13:11–12). He also cannot be contrasting the immaturity and maturity of the church, because, as Dr Gordon Fee writes,

> the contrast has to do with the *gifts* being 'partial,' not the believers themselves ... Paul's point in context does not have to do with 'childishness' and 'growing up,' but with the difference between the present and the future. He is illustrating that there will come a time when the gifts will pass away ... at the Eschaton ... The gifts, are appropriate to the present life of the church.[5]

Only prophecy, tongues and knowledge would cease with the perfection. Certainly knowledge continues today. MacArthur, in *Charismatic Chaos*, places undue emphasis on the change of verbs and the middle voice with respect to tongues. Gordon Fee comments:

> Some (e.g. MacArthur; cf. Toussaint) have argued that the change of verbs (including the change of voice) with tongues (*pausontai*) has independent significance, as though this meant that tongues might cease before prophecy and knowledge. But that misses

Paul's concern rather widely. The change of verbs is purely rhetorical; to make it otherwise is to elevate to significance something in which Paul shows no interest at all. Just as one can scarcely distinguish between 'cease' and 'pass away' when used in the same context, neither can one distinguish between *katargeo* and *pauo* in this context (although the NIV's choice of 'be stilled' for tongues is felicitous). The middle voice came along with the change of verbs.[6]

Finally, the gifts of apostle, prophet, evangelist, pastor and teacher are still operative today. Ephesians 4:11–13 says:

It was he who gave some to be apostles, some to be prophets, some to be evangelists, and some to be pastors and teachers, to prepare God's people for works of service, so that the body of Christ may be built up *until* we all reach unity in the faith and in the knowledge of the Son of God and become mature, attaining to the whole measure of the fullness of Christ.

This passage states that apostles, prophets, evangelists, pastors and teachers will continue 'until' verse 13 is reached. Who today could say that Ephesians 4:13 has ever come to fulfilment in the church yet? Therefore the gifts of apostle and prophet must still be valid for today.

Cessationist thesis 6

Most miracles occurred in three main periods of biblical history: (1) in the time of Moses and Joshua; (2) during the ministries of Elijah and Elisha; and (3) in the time of Jesus Christ, the apostles and the early church. There were a few isolated incidents in other time periods, but these three are the main periods.

Response: While there is minor validity to this thesis, it does not argue for Cessationism. It's true that miraculous activity increases at special times. But that is my point – during a visitation of God, his presence and power are increased. However, God still performed miracles apart from these three main time periods.

Two citations are sufficient for the Old Testament era: '*You performed miraculous signs and wonders in Egypt and have continued them to this day, both in Israel and among all mankind*, and have gained the renown that is still yours' (Jer. 32:20); and 'Why have you rejected us forever, O God? Why does your anger smoulder against the sheep of your pasture? ... *We are given no miraculous signs*; no prophets are left, and none of us knows how long this will be' (Ps. 74:1, 9). Psalm 74:9 reveals that miracles were expected but were not taking place at the time of writing.

Two citations are sufficient for the New Testament era: 'Believe me when I say that I am in the Father and the Father is in me; or *at least believe on the evidence of the miracles themselves. I tell you the truth, anyone who has faith in me will do what I have been doing. He will do even greater things than these, because I am going to the Father. And I will do whatever you ask in my name*, so that the Son may bring glory to the Father. You may ask me for anything in my name, and I will do it' (John 14:11–14); and 'in the church *God has appointed* first of all apostles, second prophets, third teachers, then *workers of miracles, also those having gifts of healing*, those able to help others, those with gifts of administration, and those speaking in different kinds of tongues' (1 Cor. 12:28). Paul included what we view as non-miraculous gifts, such as teachers, helpers of others and administrators, in the divine appointments as much as apostles, prophets, miracle-workers, healers and tongues speakers. *All* these spiritual gifts are supernatural.

The whole Bible is full of miracles and supernatural activity. It is a model for what is 'naturally supernatural' for faith and practice. If the Scriptures are 'God-breathed and useful for teaching, rebuking, correcting and training in righteousness, so that the man of God may be thoroughly equipped for every good work' (2 Tim. 3:16–17), then we can safely desire and appropriate what they show to be normal. Throughout the Bible we can find visions, dreams, miracles, signs, wonders, healing, prophecy, 'power evangelism', exorcism, gifts of the Spirit and supernatural guidance. This is normal stuff.

Cessationist thesis 7

The testimony of church history shows that sign gifts ceased, and therefore what we see today is counterfeit or psychological. In addition, modern-day abuses only confirm that this theory is correct.

Response: Church history shows that miracles and gifts of the Spirit were cited and proclaimed during the period of the church Fathers, in the medieval era, during the Reformation and in the era of the modern church. However, there were times of less activity, due to a sterile institutionalizing of Christianity.

Until about AD 300, the practising of spiritual gifts was common. After that time, the church under Constantine (AD 313) became institutionalized with formalism, clergy domination, ecclesiastical hierarchy and political secularization. The church became office-based and clergy-based rather than spiritual gift-based and laity-based. But even before AD 200, a centralizing of ministry, with scribes and priests, discouraged 'body life' through spiritual gifts. Throughout church history, resistance to the Spirit has battered the belief in spiritual gifts. It began early on when Paul wrote these correctives: 'Do not quench the Spirit. Do not despise prophecies' (1 Thess. 5:19–20, NKJV). The natural response to the supernatural is rejection.[7]

Cessationism also fails to acknowledge contemporary reports of experiences of gifts and miracles around the world. The largest group in Protestant Christendom (Pentecostals, Charismatics and Third-Wave Evangelicals) are not Cessationists. The Oxford scholar David Barrett projects that by the year 2000 they will constitute 29% of all Christians worldwide.[8] Surely, they will not all be deceived!

I agree that there have been and will continue to be counterfeit gifts and miracles. However, if there are counterfeits there must be the genuine items as well. The devil seeks to copy the real and the valuable.

A HISTORICAL BASIS FOR THE GIFTS OF THE SPIRIT TODAY

When dealing with historical documents, the bias of the historian must be checked. Writers view the evidence through prior assumptions and interests. If someone wanted to prove that miracles largely ceased after the early church period, they could cite numerous documents that support that. One could cite an early writing of Augustine, *On the True Religion*, to present his view that 'these miracles were not allowed to last until our times lest the soul [of the believer] ever seek visible things and the human race grow cold because of familiarity with those things whose novelty enkindled it.' Furthermore, in another early work Augustine reasoned that Jesus performed miracles to give him public authority.

One could also cite Benjamin B. Warfield, who, after looking at the historical evidence himself, alleged in his classic work, *Counterfeit Miracles*, that miracles, healing, deliverance and the gifts of the Spirit ceased after the apostolic era. He went against the evidence by asserting that documents from the early church did not prove the existence of miracles in the first three centuries. Furthermore, he believed that the Catholic miracles of the Middle Ages had their roots in the pagan wonder-tales and were either myths or healings that resulted from the power of suggestion. This is a classic case of Western Enlightenment rationalism being read into the accounts.

The *selective* editing of historical evidence to support one's purpose and interests is widespread. It would be unfair to cite the early Augustine to show evidence that Cessationism was a widespread belief without also citing his later works. Before his death, in *The City of God* and *Retractions*, Augustine repudiated his earlier belief in Cessationism and affirmed the continued healing ministry in the church. He wrote: 'Even now ... many miracles are wrought, the same God who wrought those we read of still performing them, by whom He will and as He will ...'[9]

One's bias can get in the way of objective research. John MacArthur is a good example of one who argues a Cessationist position from a rationalist dispensational bias. In his book *Charismatic Chaos*,[10] he cites extreme cases of aberration in the Charismatic movement which are non-representative and novel. Charismatics themselves don't want to see what he reports. His study is not broad enough and it is unfair. He also does not seriously interact with either historical or exegetical studies that are non-Cessationist. Where he does, he selects very non-representative examples or evidence.[11] Another example of bias is B. B. Warfield, who appeals to Augustine for orthodox theology yet discounts his later favourable views on the miraculous. This is selective editing according to one's bias.

Space does not allow for documentation, but you can find other works that report on genuine experiences of spiritual gifts throughout church history.[12]

CONCLUSION

One reason why some Christians are surprised by the gifts of the Spirit today is that *they have not experienced good examples of them*. Their theology and tradition don't permit them. Jack Deere concludes:

No cessationist writer that I am aware of tries to make his case on Scripture alone. All of these writers appeal both to Scripture and to ... history to support their case. It often goes unnoticed that this appeal to history ... is actually an argument from *experience*, or better, an argument from *the lack of experience* ... It is common for Charismatics to be accused of building their theology on experience. However, all cessationists ultimately build their theology of the miraculous gifts on their lack of experience. Even the appeal to contemporary abuse is an argument based on *negative experience* with the gifts.[13]

PART TWO

THE PHENOMENA
OF THE RIVER

CHAPTER FOUR

THE MANIFESTATIONS AND PHENOMENA

The River of God produces much refreshing and power. But wherever his manifest presence is, there are often corresponding manifestations and phenomena. Wherever I go, I find that people in many other locations are also experiencing the same phenomena. In some cases people have not even heard of the 'Toronto Blessing' and still experience the power of the Spirit in all his fulness. For example, late in 1994 there was a move of God identical to that in Toronto at a church pastored by Clifford Kapofu in Gweru, Zimbabwe. No one had heard of the 'Toronto Blessing', and yet people experienced being slain in the Spirit, laughing and shaking. At the time Pastor Kapofu wrote to a friend near Toronto, asking, 'Is there anything like that happening where you are?'[1]

Another example is a young man named Noel Isaacs, a Bhoutanese church planter and evangelist who lives in Darjeeling near Tibet. When he went to Toronto in May 1995, what he saw was nothing new. He told me that in 1980 a mighty move of the Spirit had hit his church. People would fall (without 'catchers'), shake and prophesy, just like in Toronto. It was then that he was filled with the Spirit for the first time. God caused him to jump up and down about three feet high for three hours, while he spoke in tongues and prophesied. Because the local witch-doctors also did this, some people thought that it must be demonic. I asked Noel, 'How can a person know it was God?' He replied, 'If you seek signs, wonders and manifestations you might invite the devil in, and he can counterfeit it. If you seek God – and he is your sole focus – he will give you what you need and not give you the devil.'

As we saw in Chapter 1, God visited our congregation with his manifest presence in 1987–88 and 1994. It continues to happen unhindered in our church and around the world like a mighty tidal wave. So, what are these manifestations? What do they mean? What is their purpose? I do not claim to have absolute answers for each manifestation, nor can I 'prove' them all from Scripture. I affirm that most of them do not contradict Scripture – particularly when you see the lasting fruit in people's lives.

I do not give way to fanaticism or foolishness. I am known as the theological pastor on staff at New Life Vineyard. I went to Bible college and Dallas Seminary, taught at a Bible college for six years and became an elder at New Life at its inception in 1986. Our church started out as a Fellowship Baptist Church but eventually became a Vineyard Church. I joined the pastoral team full-time in 1991. I was in the thick of things 'when the Spirit came in power' in 1988 and in 1994. I declare the following:

1) I have never conjured this up, nor have I sought or prayed for manifestations for myself or for others.
2) I judge everything with close scrutiny by the Bible, personal testimonies, history, tape-recordings, transcriptions, personal observations and experiences, and historical research.
3) I measure it, I welcome correction and caution, and I want 'more'. I talk to renewal leaders.

4) I have observed thousands of hours of this and
   I have interviewed hundreds of people.
5) I have read dozens of books and articles and have
   investigated the Bible thoroughly.

THE CURRENT MANIFESTATIONS

I have witnessed the following manifestations in thousands of situations and locations over the last eight years. I have seen identical reactions to the Spirit, and I realize that not every manifestation has a 'meaning'. While the devil or the flesh can cause many manifestations, so can God. However, Christians don't usually interact with demons or allow their flesh to do bizarre things unless they are very immature. It is also difficult to produce this kind of behaviour through mental suggestion, imitation or practice, especially with young children and the elderly.

Also, I reject the allegation made by some that certain styles of meetings, with effects from music and crowd suggestion, can be a psychological cause for the manifestations. I've seen identical manifestations in large and small meetings, with and without fast or quiet music, with and without charismatic leaders and speakers, with and without direction, and in many nations in diverse settings. True, many behaviours are infectious and we are all sensitive to group conformity. But in any renewal meeting you might see incompatible yet simultaneous laughter, crying, shaking, falling, silence and loudness. Below are most of the current manifestations. I see them in three areas: physical, emotional and spiritual.[2]

Physical manifestations

- trembling and shaking
- bouncing and jumping, lifted up or moved around
- blowing
- heat or tingling in the body
- being pinned to the floor and not able to get up
- dancing in the Spirit
- being struck down
- twirling or running
- bent over forward or backward
- chopping and flailing
- eyelids fluttering
- convulsing and twitching

Emotional manifestations

- laughing
- crying and weeping
- groaning and travailing and 'giving birth'
- shouting, yelling and roaring
- floods of joy, euphoria, boldness, worship

Spiritual manifestations

- 'weighted down' by God
- overcome in the Spirit
- inability to talk
- 'drunk' in the Spirit
- trances and visions
- tongues
- journeys

GENERAL REASONS FOR THE MANIFESTATIONS

Manifestations can happen when a supernatural being comes into contact with a human being. Throughout Scripture, we read of people who react either to the presence and power of God or to that of demons and the devil. A 'power encounter' occurs. The way one might react to the spirit world is similar to how one might react to a bolt of electricity. A number of physical and emotional responses could happen: yelling, falling, shaking, hysteria, jumping and so forth. Dave Roberts states that there are two underlying schools of thought regarding manifestations: one says they are human reactions to a divine touch; the other says a person is overwhelmed by God and the manifestations may be involuntary.[3] While we cannot prove that God actually shakes someone or causes them to laugh, we can at least conclude that these are some of the reactions that people experience when God encounters them. Drawing on my own observation and research, the following are the best reasons I know of for the manifestations in the current renewal.

An enhanced state of awareness

Because of an increased presence and power of the Holy Spirit, many people are touched in such a way that their state of awareness is changed – where the temporal dimension fades and the spiritual dimension is enhanced. Medical perspectives reveal that there are parallels between what happens to people in altered states of consciousness and what generally happens to people who experience manifestations. There will be one or more of the following: an alteration in thinking or in perception of time, a loss of control, a change in emotional expression, dissociation between mind and body, perceptual changes, feelings of profound insight, a sense of the ineffable, feelings of rejuvenation, and hypersuggestibility. This is not to suggest that the renewal and its phenomena are nothing more than an enhanced state of awareness, but some aspects may apply. Do not deep spiritual experiences of prayer, visions, dreams and encounters with God bring us into another dimension? Surely it happened in Peter's trance on the roof (Acts 10); or in Isaiah's vision of God's glory (Isa. 6); or in Daniel's, Ezekiel's and John's revelatory experiences and Paul's experience of being caught up in the third heaven (2 Cor. 12).[4]

A *visible sign of 'anointing' or the presence of the Spirit (1 Cor. 12)*

A manifestation is sometimes a visible sign of anointing. When the Lord comes upon people, shaking is often the reaction. Sometimes it is a representation in the body of what is happening in the Spirit. Sometimes it's joy (laughter) or it's anointing (falling under the power of the Spirit or trembling slightly, etc.). At times people go into a series of motions that have recurring patterns. There are similar patterns of shaking, blowing over a person as if the Spirit was blowing, windmill motions, chopping, slapping or kicking motions and so forth. At times one can see what is happening spiritually by the physical reactions on people's bodies – whether the cause is from the Holy Spirit or a demon.

A *confirmation of direction in prayer prophecy or intercession*

As we pray for people, certain manifestations happen. Sometimes, as you 'chance' upon a certain topic or area of prayer, people might shake, cry out, weep, or prophesy simultaneously. It seems that the people praying are on track with the prayers or that they are 'praying according to the Spirit'. The manifestations, at times, are visible signs of confirmation. Once, at a conference, we were interceding with someone about a major spiritual warfare issue. Another person came up to us during the intercession and, without even knowing the subject of prayer, began to shake as he 'identified with our intercession'.

A natural visual aid of what God is doing in the supernatural

The visible speaks of the invisible. Our Western rationalist worldview does not easily perceive that the visible and invisible are part of the same reality. But body and mind, physical and spiritual affect each other. God works in the natural to illustrate the truths of his spiritual. In the Gospel of John, Jesus performed several major physical miracles to illustrate spiritual truths. He fed the 5,000 with bread to illustrate that he is the Bread of Life (John 6), and he healed a blind man to illustrate that he is the Light (John 9). I have seen thousands of hours of manifestations and the contexts in which they occur. Often, it appears that they are a physical illustration of what God is doing spiritually in the person's life. For example, a physical shaking may be a sign of God shaking and transforming the person's whole life.

People reacting to God's sovereign presence

Finally, in some cases one has to conclude that there is no specific reason for the manifestations: they are simply an expression of God's sovereignty. The Bible says: 'It is the glory of God to conceal a matter; to search out a matter is the glory of kings' (Prov. 25:2). Often manifestations are no more than a finite being reacting to the presence of an Infinite Being. Just as a tuning fork vibrates when in the presence of powerful sound waves, so some of God's people vibrate when in his presence.

ARE THE MANIFESTATIONS SECONDARY?

Some people want assurance that the manifestations are not the primary focus of the renewal. They want them to be secondary. This is valid. But it is not that easy to make manifestations secondary when they are so prominent and dramatic. God certainly gets people's attention. Frankly, I find many manifestations funny, awesome and inspiring visual aids. They have actually helped many people get in touch with a very present God! They are also God's advertising for the curious. If it were not for manifestations, thousands of people, unbelievers included, would not go to renewal meetings. They are a core element and not a peripheral element in the renewal, and yet they are not the renewal. They are attending circumstances. We cannot *make* manifestations less obvious. That would be like telling a seven-foot tall person to be less obvious!

We should not 'feature' manifestations or make them the central message and focus. But let's not do as James Beverley does[5] and prematurely criticize people like John Arnott, Randy Clark or Guy Chevreau. According to Beverley, they say the manifestations are secondary but still give them primary attention in their ministries and writing. It's not easy to tame people who shake, fall, laugh, or become drunk in the Spirit. The renewal is still new, and mature administration and focus will develop over time. Beverley is right to ask whether the manifestations are secondary. But perhaps we should be wary of undermining people. We must be careful not to quench the Spirit with our cautions and our ideas of 'order'. I feel that manifestations can actually build up the body of Christ, as we see spectacular reactions to God's presence.

CAN PEOPLE CONTROL THE MANIFESTATIONS?

To what extent do people have control over the manifestations? Can they stop them, release them, or curtail them? This is somewhat like asking, 'To what extent can people control their emotions?' Well, you can, but also you can't. John White has observed that powerful reactions to the Holy Spirit tend to produce newly learned patterns of behaviour with their own triggering mechanisms. New interconnections among nerves are started as we learn new patterns of behaviour. We become more accustomed to new impulses, to the point where we may find them progressively easy to control – in other words, we are more able to stop them, release them, or curtail them.[6] For example, the Bible shows that we can exercise control over prophecy and tongues (1 Cor. 12–14).

For those who manifest, the early stages are some of the most difficult times, where the manifestations feel so overwhelming or uncontrollable. It's like an electrical system that is designed for a certain voltage and becomes overloaded. As an electrical system responds to the voltage of electricity, so people respond to the voltage of the Holy Spirit. An upgrade in the wiring system is required to handle the increased voltage. In the same way, people's wiring systems get upgraded through experience and by learning to control, release, or curtail the manifestations. However, there are other times, when, like Ezekiel, the Spirit seizes people and causes physical phenomena to happen to them that they cannot control (Ezek. 2:2; 3:12, 14, 24). Jeremiah experienced physical and emotional reactions to God: 'Concerning the prophets: My heart is broken within me; all my bones tremble. I am like a drunken man, like a man overcome by wine, because of the LORD and his holy words' (Jer. 23:9).

WHAT IS THE FRUIT?

Some people suggest that these manifestations could come from 'focused attention' or hypnotic states. These manifestations could also come from psychosomatic disorders or demons. But what is the object of that focused attention? If our focus is on God, why would we expect the flesh or the devil to bring the results? We will later deal with how one can gauge whether something is from God or not. For now, let me say that the *context* of the manifestations is the key. The context has to do with what is taught and practised, the focus, the character of the people, and the spiritual fruit. Counterfeit or spurious experiences will always be with us, but so will the genuine. John White states:

> Surely it is fruit that matters. And specific fruits tend to be found in certain kinds of orchards ... In itself, a given manifestation is no sign that something of spiritual value has been accomplished ... How then is a manifestation to be judged? Partly by the orchard – the setting the manifestation occurs in, the kind of preaching the subject has listened to. And partly by the fruit – effects on the life, the ongoing testimony and the subsequent character of the person in whom the manifestation is observed.

We have the Holy Spirit, the Bible, the corporate wisdom of the church, the gifts of discernment, and the protection of God who gives good gifts and his Spirit to his church when we are truly open and obedient (Luke 11:1–13). Therefore, there is a great safety net to keep us from falling into hypnotic, demonized or psychosomatic deception! The phenomena produced by the River is not the River itself. They are effects. The goal of renewal is not to see how many manifestations people can experience. The goal is spiritual fruit. An example of this is David Mainse, Canada's leading Christian television talk-show host. In the spring of 1995 he openly endorsed the Toronto Blessing on the air during a week of programming dedicated to the renewal. He recounted, with tears, his own experience at a renewal service at Holy Trinity Church in Brompton, London in early 1995. God took him to the floor for 40 minutes (at first he had tried to resist by stationing himself against a large pillar at the rear of the church!). He experienced profound renewal and healing. Since his return from England, his colleagues have remarked on the changes which they have seen in him. Says Dr Chuck Borsellino, a clinical psychologist, 'I see in David a greater sense of peace, a greater sense of compassion, a greater freedom in worship and a greater sense of release to the Lord of this ministry.'[8]

Testimonies are good, but so is 'scientific' research. What follows are some results of a report issued by Dr Margaret Poloma.[9] She was a professor at the University of Akron specializing in the sociology of religion. She developed an extensive questionnaire which was completed by 866 people who went to the Toronto Airport Church meetings and conferences. She sought to answer the question, 'What are some of the effects of the Toronto Blessing?'

The average age of the respondents was 45 years, with an average of 15 years of formal schooling. 18% were pastors and another 30% were church leaders. 91% reported that 'I have come to know Jesus or the Father's love in new ways.' 81% reported an experience of 'a fresh sense of God's forgiveness'. 55% of the respondents indicated that they had been delivered from Satan's hold on their lives as a result of prayer at the Toronto Airport Church, while 78% had experienced 'an inner or emotional healing'. 83% of the respondents acknowledged that 'talking about Jesus to my family and friends is more important to me now than it has ever been before.' 88% claimed that they had more love for their spouses as a result of being blessed by God at the Toronto Airport Church. 71% asserted that 'my church has experienced positive benefits from my visit to the Toronto Airport Church', and 89% reported an affirmative response to the statement, 'I am more in love with Jesus now that I have ever been in my life.'

WHAT ABOUT 'HOLY LAUGHTER'?

Many people feel uncomfortable with showing emotion. To exercise 'self-control' is considered to be spiritual. We do need self-control, but this is about moral character and lifestyle, not emotion. Some Christians see weeping and repenting as more spiritual than laughing and rejoicing. But the Bible says that there is 'a time to weep and a time to laugh, a time to mourn and a time to dance' (Eccl. 3:4), and 'blessed are you who hunger now, for you will be satisfied. Blessed are you who weep now, for you will laugh' (Luke 6:21). Joy does not seem to be a common fruit of the Spirit in our churches. Why? Gordon Fee remarks, 'One wonders, does the general lack of joy that characterizes so much of contemporary North American Christianity suggest that the life of the Spirit has been generally down-played in the interest of a more cerebral or performance-oriented brand of faith?'[10] When the focus is on God, it is holy laughter. Joy and laughter are emotional blessings, not rational blessings from God's presence.

The Bible endorses both joy and laughter: 'He will yet fill your mouth with laughter and your lips with shouts of joy' (Job 8:21); 'Surely you have granted him eternal bless-ings and made him glad with the joy of your presence' (Ps. 21:6); 'When the LORD brought back the captives to Zion, we were like men who dreamed. Our mouths were filled with laughter, our tongues with songs of joy. Then it was said among the nations, "The LORD has done great things for them." The LORD has done great things for us, and we are filled with joy' (Ps. 126:1–3).

A common phenomenon in the Rodney Howard-Browne meetings and in renewal meetings in almost any location is 'holy laughter'. Why the laughter? Because people need it. They are so unhappy and discouraged. People can now get psychological help that is called 'laughter therapy'. Also, the Bible flatly declares that 'the joy of the LORD is your strength' (Neh. 8:10) and that joy is a fruit of the Spirit (Gal. 5:22).

Dr William Fry, professor emeritus in psychiatry at the Stanford University Medical School and founder of the Gelotology Institute, has done extensive research on the benefits of laughter and humour. (The word 'gelotology' is derived from the Greek word *gelos*, meaning 'laughter'; hence gelotology is 'the science of mirth'.) He has scientific laboratory evidence to demonstrate that laughter has pos-itive effects in the cardiovascular system, the respiratory system, the central nervous system, the immune system and the endocrine system. Laughter is also good physical and psychological exercise. Summarizing the positive effects of laughter, Dr Fry writes:

> Mirthful laughter has a scientifically demonstrable exercise impact on several body systems. Muscles are activated; heart rate is increased; respiration is amplified, with increase in oxygen exchange – similar to the effects of athletic exercise. Stress is antagonized by humor. Emotional tension, contributing to stress, is lowered through the effects of humor. Laughter is followed by a state of physical relaxation, diminishing physical tension.[11]

Oliver Cromwell, Lord Protector of Great Britain in the early 17th century, was a gregarious Christian who reorganized the Church of England, championed the rights of commoners, protected Quakers and Jews, and served as commander-in-chief of the army. After reorganizing the Parliamentary forces in the New Model Army, he won a key battle against the forces of King Charles I at Naseby in 1645. Immediately before this battle Cromwell experienced holy laughter and was drunk in the Spirit. The following quotation is from a book by Bishop George Lavington entitled *The Enthusiasm of Methodists and Papists Compared*:

> I don't remember any of these laughing fits among Papists. But they were very common among the French Prophets in their agitations. Mr Aubrey, in his Miscellanies (page 117), relates the same thing of Oliver Cromwell. 'Oliver, says he, had certainly this afflatus. One that was at the Battle of Dunbar told me

that Oliver was carried on with a divine impulse: he did laugh so excessively as if he had been drunk. The same fit of laughter seized him just before the battle of Naseby.'[12]

Holy laughter can promote good health and can give you the courage to face battles! In one of our meetings, another church joined us. The Spirit dramatically impacted a number of their youth who came. Many crashed to the floor, laughing for hours. One girl ended up laughing for 27 straight hours! Laughing is good spiritual and emotional medicine. On 'holy laughter', John Stackhouse, associate professor of modern Christianity at the University of Manitoba, comments: 'It seems to me that people are enthusiastic about Jesus, are happy to be a Christian, and there doesn't seem to be an oversupply of that in North American Christianity today. If you don't like the idea of holy laughter that breaks out in a church service, then what kind of laughter do you believe in?'[13]

IS THE RENEWAL
BIBLICAL?

People ask, 'Is the renewal biblical? Is it from God?' I think that this question is imprecise. What they are really asking is, 'Are the *manifestations* biblical? Are *they* from God?' It is *they* which cause the controversy. But what does 'biblical' mean? My dictionary defines the word in two ways: (1) of, in, or derived from the Bible; (2) in harmony with the Bible. If a person stresses the first use of 'biblical', it is not possible to show exact verses where many of the manifestations are 'in or derived from the Bible' (although there are manifestations in the Bible which have similarities to some of those which we are seeing today). But I would argue that the majority of today's manifestations are 'in harmony with the Bible'. It depends on how you interpret Scripture. I see lots of phenomena in Scripture, and yet I see few phenomena today that can be found there. However, they are not in contradiction to the overall gist of Scripture.

We all believe and do things that don't contradict Scripture and yet are not commanded in Scripture. The Bible does not command us to baptize by immersion or to rule by a congregational, Presbyterian or Episcopal form of church government. Yet, we could call any of these 'biblical' practices because they are in harmony with the Bible. Also, the Bible does not state that God is a Trinity. Yet, we believe this doctrine because the Bible reveals it. Billy Graham asks people to bow their heads and close their eyes while they repeat a sinner's prayer. Then he calls them to come forward to receive Christ. This is not taught in the Bible, but it doesn't contradict it either. Many things that we do can't be found in Scripture: using church buildings, closing our eyes during prayer, using little wafers and grape juice for communion, developing youth programmes and Sunday schools, standing to preach from a pulpit (Jewish rabbis sat down when they taught in the synagogue!), and using PA systems.

Are manifestations biblical? *Yes.* Can we give you a chapter and verse for all of them? *No.* But let me present evidence from the Bible and history to show that manifestations are in harmony with Scripture.

THE BIBLICAL BASIS OF THE PHENOMENA

Signs and wonders of the kingdom

As Israel awaited the promised Messianic King, the Old Testament era drew to a close. And then came the preaching of John the Baptist and the baptism of Jesus, which fulfilled the prophecies in Isaiah (Mark 1:2–11). The time of waiting had ended. The King had arrived. And 'After John was put in prison, Jesus went into Galilee, proclaiming the good news of God. "The time has come," he said. "The kingdom of God is near. Repent and believe the good news!"' (Mark 1:14–15). In the rest of Mark 1 the writer records several occasions when Jesus called people to follow him and confronted demons and healed people.

Mark's theological point is clear – the kingdom ministry of Jesus came suddenly, dramatically and confrontationally against sin, Satan and sickness. The Gospel writers show that Jesus was the promised Messianic King who had authority over sin, sickness, death, nature and Satan, and who summoned people to enter the kingdom through repentance and faith. Wherever Jesus went, he brought the kingdom to bear in the lives of people who were in bondage, sin and sickness. He preached and demonstrated the gospel of the kingdom. His ministry of freedom and joy is summarized in Luke 4:18–19.

In accordance with many Jewish theologies, Jesus thought in terms of two ages: this present age and the age to come (Mark 10:30). This age was controlled by Satan, sickness and oppression. God would cataclysmically terminate this age and create a new age where evil, sickness and injustice would end, and righteousness, peace and justice would begin. Jesus proclaimed that the kingdom was both present and future. He said that 'the kingdom is within you' (Luke 17:21), and when he cast out demons it demonstrated that the kingdom had come (Matt. 12:28). He also told his hearers that the kingdom would come in their generation (Matt. 10:23; Mark 9:1; Luke 22:32) and that the kingdom was near (Mark 1:15; Luke 10:9).

Yet Jesus also declared that the final coming of the kingdom was a future event (Matt. 24–25). How do we reconcile the present and future aspects of the kingdom? Dr Derek Morphew explains: 'The kingdom is "already" here but "not yet" here. Two ages coexist ... Everything that is still to happen at the second coming has already happened in Jesus Christ ... The end of the world has already taken place ... The "last days" came with Jesus and ever since we have been living in the last days.'[1]

To put it another way, Christ has ushered in the 'presence of the future' as the fulfilment of the gospel of the kingdom. The message and ministry of Jesus is eschatological (i.e. about the last days). For those who are in Christ, the transition from death to life has happened – they have eternal life but they will also inherit eternal life. The ministry of the Spirit which was prophesied in the Old Testament (Isa. 44; Jer. 33; Joel 2) and by Jesus and the apostles (Acts 1–2) means that the age of the Spirit began in the last days. The pouring out of the Spirit which is modelled in the book of Acts is a taste in this age of what believers experience from the age to come (see Heb. 6:4–5).

Renewal, revival and their manifestations are kingdom experiences and interventions of God in this age; they are signs of his present rule and foretastes of the age to come. They are appetizers. They are not the meal. We must 'taste and see that the Lord is good' (Ps. 63:5) and 'taste the heavenly gift and the powers of the coming age' (Heb. 6:4–5). Jesus sent his church both to preach the gospel of the kingdom (i.e. the Word) and to practise it (i.e. work) (Matt. 10:7–8; Luke 9:2; 10:9). God testified to the gospel by signs, wonders and various miracles, and gifts of the Holy Spirit distributed according to his will (Heb. 2:4). 'The Kingdom of God is about things going and coming,' says John Arnott. 'Sin, sickness, pain, and demons are going. Salvation, healing, joy and the Holy Spirit are coming.'

When people encounter the Holy Spirit, they experience the presence of the future. Miracles, signs, wonders, gifts and manifestations of the Spirit are merely 'signposts' of God's activity of the future age breaking into this age. They are effects of the kingdom pointing to something beyond themselves. It would be silly of us, while driving on a highway in Ontario, to stop our cars so that we could hug and kiss and give our attention to a road-sign that stated 'Toronto, 45 kms'. The sign is not the thing but is something that points beyond itself to that which it represents. Wesley Campbell declares, 'What do you do with signs? You read them!' The supernatural and miraculous are signs of God's rule.

However, Beverley asserts that 'the Toronto Blessing represents a *faulty understanding of signs and wonders*' because it is 'less than biblical in its views of miracles'.[2] He goes on to allege that manifestations are not proof of the outpouring of the Spirit. They are not inherently miraculous or supernatural, and can be imitated or explained psychologically.[3]

Beverley is right when he declares that manifestations are not proof of the supernatural outpouring of the Holy Spirit. The focus and the fruit in people's lives provides proof. When one is careful to observe manifestations and their circumstances, and when one interviews people who experience them, proof comes. I've seen 70-year-old grandmas and seven-year-old children under different circumstances experience identical manifestations. In the thousands of hours that I've been in this, I could not say that the manifestations lack the supernatural or that most of them could be induced psychologically or imitated. Beverley is not a psychologist. Some manifestations may be explained psychologically, but is that the best or only explanation?

What is a 'biblical' miracle? J. D. Spiceland writes:

It is important to bear in mind that the biblical concept of miracle is that of an event which runs counter to the observed processes of nature ... Biblical miracles have a clear objective: they are intended to bring the glory of God into bold relief ... The miracles are signs rather than merely wonderful works. They are,

however, signs only to those who have spiritual discernment to recognize them as such.[4]

Most of the manifestations that I have seen 'run counter
to the observed processes of nature', certainly 'bring the
glory of God into bold relief', are 'signs', and require 'spiritual discernment to recognize them as such'. A good actor
could not possibly imitate many of the manifestations because many are impossible to physically accomplish on
one's own. Some last for hours. Get an actor to shake for
two hours non-stop while he blows and chops the air! Or
get him to lie on the floor and tremble like bacon in a frying pan for an hour non-stop! There are 'intrinsically supernatural components' in much of what I've seen. But we
must 'perceive' it. There are things of the spirit that the
mind cannot understand. Paul deals with this issue in the
worship setting of tongues and prophecy in Corinth:

> So it is with you. Since you are eager to have spiritual
> gifts, try to excel in gifts that build up the church. For
> this reason anyone who speaks in a tongue should
> pray that he may interpret what he says. For if I pray
> in a tongue, *my spirit prays, but my mind is unfruit-
> ful. So what shall I do? I will pray with my spirit, but
> I will also pray with my mind; I will sing with my
> spirit, but I will also sing with my mind.*
> (1 Cor. 14:12–15)

The principle is that the Spirit does things which are unin-
telligible to the mind. If tongues or other non-rational
expressions of the Spirit occur, we ought to teach with
intelligible words so that we edify people. With the renewal the same applies. We should allow the non-rational

miracles and manifestations which the Spirit is doing to happen, but we should also give intelligible teaching that instructs. It takes eyes to see and ears to hear what the Spirit is doing and saying. Larry Lea warns, 'Those who pretend to pass judgment in spiritual matters must be prepared to show their credentials of personal spiritual experience. Unfortunately, many people condemning manifestations and experiences birthed by the Holy Spirit have had little personal experience with either.'[5] Even Machiavelli notes, 'Men in general judge more from appearances than from reality. All men have eyes, but few have the gift of penetration.'

When the natural and supernatural meet

When the natural and supernatural meet, sensational things can happen. In his song 'God is so good', Kevin Prosch sings 'the natural things speak of the invisible'. And so they do. What goes on in the natural reflects what God is doing in the supernatural. The Bible is replete with examples that show how the physical world can be affected by the invisible world of God, angels and demons. Physical manifestations are consistent with how people and places can be affected by the manifest presence of God.

The following passages represent a sampling of bizarre experiences that happened to people whom God encountered with his manifest presence. God has and does come upon people with such power that they sometimes change into a different person. In Judges 14 God empowers Samson to kill a lion with his bare hands:

> Samson went down to Timnah together with his father and mother. As they approached the vineyards of Timnah, suddenly a young lion came roaring toward

him. The Spirit of the LORD came upon him in power so that he tore the lion apart with his bare hands as he might have torn a young goat.

This is similar to David, who, after the Spirit came upon him in power (1 Sam. 16:13), killed a lion and a bear (1 Sam. 17:33–37). In Judges 15–16 God empowered Samson to defeat a thousand Philistines. After he had been tied up with ropes,

> The Spirit of the LORD came upon him in power. The ropes on his arms became like charred flax, and the bindings dropped from his hands. Finding a fresh jawbone of a donkey, he grabbed it and struck down a thousand men. Then Samson said, 'With a donkey's jawbone I have made donkeys of them. With a donkey's jawbone I have killed a thousand men.'
> (Judg. 15:14–16)

Later in the narrative, Delilah tricks Samson and he is captured by the Philistines. They cut his hair and gouged out his eyes. He was brought to the Temple of Dagon during a celebration to entertain the audience. Then God empowered him again:

> Then Samson prayed to the LORD, 'O Sovereign LORD, remember me. O God, please strengthen me just once more, and let me with one blow get revenge on the Philistines for my two eyes.' Then Samson reached toward the two central pillars on which the temple stood. Bracing himself against them, his right hand on the one and his left hand on the other, Samson said, 'Let me die with the Philistines!' Then

he pushed with all his might, and down came the temple on the rulers and all the people in it.
(Judg. 16:28–30)

A different experience is in 1 Samuel 10. Samuel prophesies to Saul that God's Spirit would come upon him to change him into a different person and cause him to prophesy:

'After that you will go to Gibeah of God, where there is a Philistine outpost. As you approach the town, you will meet a procession of prophets coming down from the high place with lyres, tambourines, flutes and harps being played before them, and they will be prophesying. The Spirit of the LORD will come upon you in power, and you will prophesy with them; and you will be changed into a different person. Once these signs are fulfilled, do whatever your hand finds to do, for God is with you. Go down ahead of me to Gilgal. I will surely come down to you to sacrifice burnt offerings and fellowship offerings, but you must wait seven days until I come to you and tell you what you are to do.' As Saul turned to leave Samuel, God changed Saul's heart, and all these signs were fulfilled that day. When they arrived at Gibeah, a procession of prophets met him; the Spirit of God came upon him in power, and he joined in their prophesying. When all those who had formerly known him saw him prophesying with the prophets, they asked each other, 'What is this that has happened to the son of Kish?' (1 Sam. 10:5–12)

Later, in 1 Samuel 19, a similar thing happens to Saul's men as they go after David in Naioth:

> Word came to Saul: 'David is in Naioth at Ramah'; so he sent men to capture him. But when they saw a group of prophets prophesying, with Samuel standing there as their leader, the Spirit of God came upon Saul's men and they also prophesied. Saul was told about it, and he sent more men, and they prophesied too. Saul sent men a third time, and they also prophesied. Finally, he himself left for Ramah and went to the great cistern at Secu. And he asked, 'Where are Samuel and David?' 'Over in Naioth at Ramah,' they said. So Saul went to Naioth at Ramah. But the Spirit of God came even upon him, and he walked along prophesying until he came to Naioth. He stripped off his robes and also prophesied in Samuel's presence. He lay that way all that day and night. This is why people say, 'Is Saul also among the prophets?'
> (1 Sam. 19:18–24)

This experience is sensational. Saul sends a battalion of tough soldiers to capture David. They were not worshipping God. They came to a group of prophets and the Spirit of God came upon them causing *them* to prophesy. Furthermore, after Saul was told about it he sent more men and they prophesied too. Saul sent men a third time. Again the same result. This is an example of an 'epicentre' or a concentrated area of God's power. When someone entered it, they were affected. To make matters worse, after Saul himself came, he removed his clothes and laid there all day and night. He also could not get up. Does this look like it is from God?

Ezekiel the prophet, had an incredible vision of God's glory as the heavens were opened. After seeing the vision of the living creatures and God's glory he fell prostrate, heard the audible voice of God, was filled by the Spirit, physically raised and transported, and felt completely overwhelmed (after all that, who wouldn't?):

> This was the appearance of the likeness of the glory of the Lord. When I saw it, I fell face down, and I heard the voice of one speaking. He said to me, 'Son of man, stand up on your feet and I will speak to you.' As he spoke, the Spirit came into me and raised me to my feet, and I heard him speaking to me ... Then the Spirit lifted me up, and I heard behind me a loud rushing sound ... The Spirit then lifted me up and took me away, and I went in bitterness and in the anger of my spirit with the strong hand of the Lord upon me. I came near the Kebar River. And there, where they were living, I sat among them for seven days – overwhelmed. (Ezek. 1:28b–2:1; 3:12, 14–15)

Daniel the seer had similar experiences as a result of a visitation from the angel Gabriel. He was terrified, fell into a trance-like sleep, could not move, received an overwhelming vision, was physically raised by the angel, resulting in a feeling of exhaustion from the experience:

> As he came near the place where I was standing, *I was terrified and fell prostrate*. 'Son of man,' he said to me, 'understand that the vision concerns the time of the end.' While he was speaking to me, *I was in a deep sleep, with my face to the ground. Then he touched me and raised me to my feet* ... I, Daniel was exhausted

82

and lay ill for several days. Then I got up and went about the king's business. I was appalled by the vision; it was beyond understanding.
(Dan. 8:17–18, 27)

Later, Daniel had an angelic vision that sapped his strength, rendered him helpless and speechless, and put him into a deep sleep. He was set trembling on his hands and knees and later recovered with strength from the angel's touch. Read the following accounts of phenomena:

I looked up and there before me was a man dressed in linen, with a belt of the finest gold around his waist. His body was like chrysolite, his face like lightning, his eyes like flaming torches, his arms and legs like the gleam of burnished bronze, and his voice like the sound of a multitude. I, Daniel, was the only one who saw the vision; the men with me did not see it, but such terror overwhelmed them that they fled and hid themselves. So I was left alone, gazing at this great vision; I had no strength left, my face turned deathly pale and I was helpless. Then I heard him speaking, and as I listened to him, I fell into a deep sleep, my face to the ground. A hand touched me and set me trembling on my hands and knees. (Dan. 10:5–10)

While he was saying this to me, I bowed with my face toward the ground and was speechless. Then one who looked like a man touched my lips, and I opened my mouth and began to speak. I said to the one standing before me, 'I am overcome with anguish because of the vision, my lord, and I am helpless. How can I, your servant, talk with you, my lord? My strength is gone and I can hardly breathe.' Again the one who looked like a man touched me and gave me strength. 'Do not be afraid, O man highly esteemed,' he said. 'Peace! Be strong now; be strong.' When he spoke to me, I was strengthened and said, 'Speak, my lord, since you have given me strength.' (Dan. 10:15–19)

There are also several New Testament examples of sensational experiences. The Book of Acts gives many. In Acts 2:1–4 we read:

When the day of Pentecost came, they were all together in one place. Suddenly a sound like the blowing of a violent wind came from heaven and filled the whole house where they were sitting. They saw what seemed to be tongues of fire that separated and came to rest on each of them. All of them were filled with the Holy Spirit and began to speak in other tongues as the Spirit enabled them.

We know that in Acts 2, these men prophesied, and the people said, 'These men have had too much wine to drink' (Acts 2:13–15). Peter said, 'We're not drunk, as you suppose.' Why would they assume drunkenness if not for unusual activity? This account is full of phenomena: a violent wind, tongues of fire settled on *each* one, *all* were filled with the Holy Spirit and spoke in tongues. This caused onlookers to wonder if they had had too much wine.

In Acts 7 Stephen had a vision of Jesus in heaven before he was stoned. In Acts 8 after Philip evangelized the Ethiopian eunuch the Spirit transported him from Gaza to Azotus, 20 miles to the north! In Acts 9 on his way to Damascus, Saul saw a great light, heard the audible voice of Jesus, fell to the ground, lost his eyesight, and got saved. In Acts 10 Cornelius had a vision where an angel spoke to him, and Peter fell into a trance and received a vision of a sheet containing four-footed animals and heard an audible voice. While thinking about the vision he heard the Spirit speak and give him information. He preached at the house of Cornelius, where the Spirit came on all who heard the message, and they spoke in tongues.

In Acts 12 Peter escaped from prison as an angel removed his chains and opened the iron gate leading to the city. In Acts 16 Paul had a vision of the man of Macedonia. Then while he and Silas were jailed in Philippi, a violent earthquake shook the jail, the door flew open, and their chains came loose. In Acts 19 Paul placed his hands on the Ephesian disciples to receive the Spirit, and they spoke in tongues and prophesied. You can continue through the book of Acts to see more 'sensational mystical experiences'.

Space limits me to these few biblical examples of phenomena and sensational experiences. As Wesley Campbell writes, 'There is still so much more that could be said about talking animals (Num. 22:28), walking on water or through walls (Matt. 14:29; John 20:19), riding with angels (2 Kings 2:11), bones that raise the dead (2 Kings 13:21), wrestling with theophanies (Gen. 32:28), and visiting the third heaven to receive visions of paradise (2 Cor. 12:2–3).'[6]

Shaking

As the Israelites came to Mount Sinai, it was ablaze with fire and smoke, accompanied by thunder and lightning. The people trembled as the whole mountain shook violently (Exod. 19:16–19). When Christ was crucified 'the earth shook and the rocks split' (Matt. 27:51). After their report and exhortation to the believers back home about their encounter with the Sanhedrin, Peter and John prayed, and 'after they prayed, the place where they were meeting was shaken. And they were all filled with the Holy Spirit and spoke the word of God boldly' (Acts 4:31). On this text I. Howard Marshall remarks that 'the effect of the prayer was remarkable. The room in which the disciples were gathered shook as if an earthquake was taking place. This was one of the signs which indicated a theophany in the Old Testament (Exod. 19:18; Isa. 6:4), and it would have been regarded as indicating a divine response to prayer.'[7]

In Daniel 10:7 the King James and New Revised Standard Versions mention the 'great quaking/trembling' that happened to the people who were with Daniel, and Jeremiah says that his 'heart is broken within me; all my bones tremble' (Jer. 23:9). But I do not believe these passages refer to manifestations of the Holy Spirit. They are emotional and physical expressions of the fear of God and the impact of his Word. Shaking is biblical, but I can't find any place in the Bible where people experienced a shaking manifestation identical to that in the present renewal. However, it is a biblical principle that God's presence causes shaking.

Slain in the Spirit

Many Christians equate biblical people falling under the power of God with being 'slain in the Spirit', but I'm not convinced that there is a clear example of this in Scripture. Yes, people fell into deep sleeps (Gen. 15:12; Dan. 10), and yes, people fell under the power or presence of God (John 18:6; Rev. 1:17). But to call this being 'slain in the Spirit' is, in my opinion, irresponsible exegesis. Rather, we could affirm that being 'slain in the Spirit' is in harmony with Scripture by virtue of the instances where people fell because of the presence or power of God.[8]

Animal noises and behaviours

Of all the phenomena, animal noises, animal behaviours and roaring are the most controversial. Are they of God, the flesh, or the devil? How can they be of God when they are so unseemly and not supported in Scripture? There is no animal theology in the Bible! I know of only one verse where a godly person compares his experience to an animal behaviour. The prophet Micah, who, after receiving a terrifying word of judgment from the Lord concerning Samaria, shrank in appalling grief and stated, 'Because of this I will weep and wail; I will go about barefoot and naked. *I will howl like a jackal and moan like an owl*' (Mic. 1:8). Animal noises? Yes, probably. Should we develop a theology about them? No, probably not. Micah perhaps is only giving a poetic simile to illustrate his emotion.

In the current renewal, it is not impossible that some of the animal noises and behaviours could have God as their source. However, *animal noises and actions do not have a clear scriptural precedent. They have no biblical or theological framework per se.* In some cases there could be psychological or demonic causes as well, or a mixture. We must not encourage or showcase them. We should not defend them, draw attention to them or promote them.

The same goes for roaring. People cite Amos 3:8: 'The lion has roared – who will not fear? The Sovereign LORD has spoken, who can but prophesy?' This text connects hearing the voice of God with fearing him and prophesying, but the Lord does the roaring, not people. Some people equate this with a prophetic or intercessory experience, and it certainly is an emotional outburst of what God is doing inside the person. We are just not used to this type of outburst. Perhaps roaring is in the same emotional response category as crying, wailing, shouting and laughing.

When you interview people about their experiences of being slain in the Spirit or roaring, they almost always tell you that the experience was one of peace, joy, empowering, burdening, euphoria, healing, a vision of Jesus, and so on. Testimony is a powerful aid in merging Scripture and experience.

Answers to the objections to the phenomena

Everyone is entitled to explanations. Unfortunately, there are no absolute answers to every question, nor is there perfect understanding of all that occurs in renewal. Some things are mystery and wonder. If we think that we can and must give a response to every critic, we will become sidetracked and embroiled in controversy. Most hardened critics will not accept any evidence that is contrary to their position. We must apprehend the things of God through the eyes, ears and heart of faith, assisted by personal and corporate involvement in Scripture, tradition, reason and experience. The following are answers to the most common objections to the phenomena:

1. *'I don't understand them.'* Should our understanding of an event determine whether God would do it or not? Look at the cross. No one understood the cross. Even the disciples tried to stop it. Our understanding of an issue is an unreliable test to determine if something is of God or not. Throughout the Bible, God did things which people did not understand. Habakkuk did not understand why God let the evil deeds of Judah go unpunished, and then he did not understand how God could use the evil

Babylonians to judge his people (Hab. 1:2–4, 12–13). The Pharisees attributed the work of Jesus to Beelzebub (Matt. 12:24). After spending three years with Jesus, the disciples did not understand his mission and message (Luke 18:34). I don't understand how a black cow can eat green grass and produce white milk. Do men understand women? No! Does that mean they are not from God?! We don't understand most things in life. God's ways are not our ways.

2. *'Manifestations produce fear.'* Manifestations might frighten people precisely because they *are* of God. In the Bible, when God appears, he often causes fear. When God or the glorified Son appears, the immediate reaction is fear followed by an explanation and a word of comfort *not to fear*. Why? Because God, Jesus (or an angel) produced fear in the observer. Some might argue, 'But "perfect love casts out all fear." I'm afraid. Therefore, this must not be God.' This phrase is from 1 John 4:18: 'There is no fear in love. But perfect love drives out fear, because fear has to do with punishment. The one who fears is not made perfect in love.' This text deals with punishment and a cringing fear of God. God is not a capricious tyrant who produces fear.

People will and should fear God for his majestic power. The following people feared God: the Israelites at Mount Sinai (Exod. 20:18–20), Daniel (Dan. 10:7–9, 15–19), Zechariah (Luke 1:11–14), the disciples (Matt. 14:25–27) and John (Rev. 1:17). Other people fear because they do not understand what is happening. But again, to not understand and to fear does not mean it is not God. Fear is a natural response to the unknown.

3. *'God would not go against someone's will.'* A common view of God is that he is a gentleman who never imposes his will on people. But in the book of Isaiah God says: *'I say my purpose will stand and I will do all that I*

please' (Isa. 46:11). Are there any cases where God did override someone's will? Yes. God caused the company of soldiers and Saul to prophesy under the power of the Spirit (1 Sam. 10; 19); God overrode Balaam's will and caused him to prophesy a blessing over Israel (Num. 23); he also overrode Balaam's donkey by making it talk; the post-resurrection Jesus blinded Saul on the road to Damascus against his will (Acts 9). God sometimes does impose his will on people's wills.

As I was teaching a workshop at a conference I discussed this idea. A middle-aged pastor from Regina, Saskatchewan, said that he went to Toronto as a former Anglican priest who was resistant to the renewal but somewhat open. While close to getting a doctoral degree, he was studying the renewal and went to the Airport Vineyard to gather research in order to argue first-hand against it. While he was there, the Spirit of God hammered him. He shook, laughed, fell and was out on the carpet for several hours – all against his will. He did not ask for it or want it. Furthermore, his experience changed his theology and his church!

4. '*They look excessive and draw attention to the recipient.*' Yes, manifestations do look excessive. Perhaps that's why God causes them. For a visual aid, God commanded Jeremiah to bury his belt in the hole of a rock at the Euphrates River so that it would be marred and rendered useless. This was a symbol of Judah's pride, that God would mar and render useless (Jer. 13:1–11). God asked Ezekiel to erect a model siege of Jerusalem, and then to lie on his side for 390 days and then for 40 days, to parallel the number of years he would symbolically bear the sins of Israel and Judah (Ezek. 4:1–8). God commanded Hosea to marry a prostitute named Gomer as a prophetic sign of his

love for unfaithful Israel (Hos. 1:2–3; 3:1–3). God commanded Isaiah to go barefoot and naked for three years as a prophetic sign of his judgment accomplished through the Assyrians against Egypt and Cush (Isa. 20:1–6).

The preceding prophetic activities drew excessive attention! That is the purpose of signs and wonders. Signs point to something. Wonders draw attention and produce awe. God sometimes uses bizarre visual aids to get our attention.

5. *'God brings order, not disorder.'* The assumption is that our idea of order always conforms to God's. The Bible shows that God's order often *looks* messy. However, underneath, he controls it toward a positive goal. We confuse 'out of control' with disorder. We can still have controlled disorder that is healthy. For example, Saul and the prophets were disorderly (1 Sam. 10; 19); Acts 2 was disorderly; when Jesus cast demons out of the Gerasene demoniac into the herd of pigs, it was disorderly (Luke 8)! Dr J. I. Packer states: 'Churches tend to run in grooves of conventionality, and such grooves quickly turn into graves.'[9] Oh, what great 'order' there is in a graveyard!

People cite Paul's appeal, 'Let all things be done decently and in order' (1 Cor. 14:40). They apply this to the renewal, with its 'disorderly' meetings. For example, B. J. Oropeza spends a whole chapter in his book on this theme. He suggests that the cultural background of Paul's exhortation to the Corinthian church is rooted in allusions to the pagan worship of the god Dionysus, the son of Zeus. Dionysian pagan worshippers drank wine and secured divine power in spiritual ecstasy, resulting in miracles and supernatural phenomena.[10] Oropeza, commenting on 1 Corinthians 14:23, 40, suggests:

Paul may be warning the Corinthians that their charismatic activity in worship could reach a level whereby the outsider would think members of the church were 'possessed of a religious frenzy in the manner of the Dionysian and Cybele cults' ... Paul stressed propriety in worship knowing the maenadic background of some of the church members. Corinthian Christianity must not become another ecstatic mystery cult[11] ... *In many ways the maenads* [priestesses of Dionysus] *in Dionysian worship engaged in some of the phenomena we see in the current renewal* ... Dionysus offered freedom to cast off restraints and was 'the god of joy,' offering joyful cathartic experiences ... to outbreaks of dancing mania and similar manifestations of collective hysteria.[12]

This cultural background is helpful. Some of the Corinthians came out of Dionysian worship. Corinthians should have kept away from syncretism and pagan imitations or influences. Just as Israel was to be separate from the surrounding pagan cultures, so the church in Corinth and the church of today must do likewise. However, the problem with Oropeza's application to the current renewal is that most of the people who manifest in 'disorderly' ways are not coming out of pagan mystery cults, nor are they frenzied spiritual ecstatics involved in collective hysteria.

Furthermore, the context of 1 Corinthians 14 is that of 'ordering' tongues and especially prophecy. Paul writes, 'The spirits of prophets are subject to the control of prophets. For God is not a God of disorder but of peace' (1 Cor. 14:32–33). Gordon Fee remarks, 'The interesting opposite of "disorder," however, is not quietness or propriety, or even "order," but "peace." Minimally this refers to the sense of harmony that will obtain in a Christian assembly when everyone is truly in the Spirit and the aim of everything is the edification of the whole (v. 26).[13] Prophecy and tongues must be ordered in the context of love (1 Cor. 13). The church can still become sterile and lifeless – when old habits become entrenched order. Therefore, the change and transition are often messy and disorderly.

The American novelist Henry Miller remarked that 'Confusion is a word we have invented for an order which is not yet understood.' Even quantum physics research is discovering that there is random chaos at the sub-atomic level – underneath the apparent 'order' of the universe. Proverbs 14:4 notes that 'Where no oxen are, the trough is clean; but much increase comes by the strength of an ox' (NKJV). If we do not want a messy trough, then remove the oxen. But then we won't get much work done with them either. Even life itself is full of disorder – look at a nursery full of children! Let's still work to bring order in renewal.

6. *This renewal causes division.* The faulty assumption is, 'If this movement was from God there would be no division. God brings unity, not division.' But the Bible and history don't support that.

Jesus declared, 'Do not suppose that I have come to bring peace to the earth. I did not come to bring peace, but a sword. For I have come to turn a man against his father, a daughter against her mother, a daughter-in-law against her mother-in-law – a man's enemies will be the members of his own household' (Matt. 10:34–36). Wherever Jesus went, division resulted (notably among the Sadducees, the Pharisees, the teachers of the law, and even his own disciples). Wherever there is an intensified working by Jesus, there is a corresponding intensity of division.

Moses' leadership caused division between him and Korah (Num. 11). The inclusion of the Gentiles in God's church caused division (Acts 15). Paul and Barnabas divided over John Mark (Acts 15). Past and present renewals, reformations and revivals produced division. People opposed the Great Awakening in the early 1700s. The Pentecostal revival at Azusa Street in the early 1900s received the same unjust opposition. G. Campbell Morgan, a respected Bible preacher, called the Pentecostal Movement 'the last vomit of Satan'! His teaching produced division. But the ultimate thing which renewal and revival must produce is love. Without love all renewal and gifts of the Spirit will be as nothing (see 1 Cor. 13:1–3).

7. *'This is the flesh, emotionalism and manipulation.'* Because people cannot see *through* the emotion and phenomena, and are uncomfortable, and have no prior grid to interpret it through, they sometimes confuse it with fleshly behaviour. But God created emotions. The Bible is replete with emotional reactions to God's Spirit – such as fear, joy, wonder, weeping and even anger. 'When Saul heard their words, the Spirit of God came upon him in power, and he burned with anger' (1 Sam. 11:6). People's hostile, critical, divisive and smug reactions can become more fleshly than any of the emotions or manifestations. These people misunderstand what fleshly behaviour is according to New Testament theology.

In New Testament theology the 'flesh' denotes the seat of activity for the earthly human nature in its weakness and sinfulness. Fifteen works of the flesh, which are opposite to the kingdom of God and the fruit of the Spirit, are listed in Galatians 5:19. The flesh aggravates lusts and desires (Eph. 2:3), is contrary to the Spirit (Gal. 5:17) and cannot please God (Rom. 8:8). If one does not discern the heart and focus of people and look for spiritual fruit, it would be hasty to call the works of the Spirit the works of the flesh. Still, we need discernment. There might be some fleshly behaviour, but often it is no more than immaturity or over-zealousness. John Arnott retorts that 'I would rather contend with a little fleshly zeal than carnal resistance.'

Others declare that the phenomena are the results of manipulation and the power of suggestion. A theology professor at the University of Toronto, interviewed by a journalist on Canada's *Fifth Estate* television programme reporting on the 'Toronto Blessing', declared that people come to the meetings knowing how they are meant to act. My reply to that is, 'Do small children who come to the meetings and experience phenomena know in advance how they are meant to act?' Michael Green says, 'I challenge any clergy to get large numbers of a typical Anglican congregation to lie upon the ground of their church. I have not infrequently been praying for people myself and have been surprised when I looked round to find they had fallen to the ground. Far from manipulation, I did not even know it was happening.'[14]

Still others believe that manifestations result from the power of suggestion or mass psychological hysteria. But theologians assert this – not psychologists. One writer comments:

Dismissing the manifestations as 'mass hysteria' is quite meaningless, according to psychiatrist Richard Laugherne ... True hysteria is actually a very rare phenomenon, and those who bandy the word about in attempts to explain occurrences at Christian meetings are using the word in a loose colloquial sense, and not scientifically, to describe a verifiable clinical phenomenon.[15]

There might be some fleshly or over-zealous or immature aspects to the phenomena, and there might even be some manipulation, but that does not invalidate the genuine work of the Spirit. What we need is proper pastoring, administration and discernment.

8. *'This is a great deception invading the church.'* Because so many appear to be 'caught up' in the renewal, it might seem (and in some cases it may be true) that theology, sound reason and discernment have been abandoned. Careful analysts are wary of accentuating experience instead of the Bible. Because the Bible does not clearly endorse all the phenomena, some assert that a great deception has invaded the church (e.g. Matt. 24:4, 24). They assert that the rational must take precedence over the experiential. Clifford Hill, editor of *Prophecy Today*, feels that believers who are newly baptized in the Holy Spirit are susceptible to this deception. He warns:

> Those who are in the greatest danger are believers who have been newly baptized in the Holy Spirit and who lack maturity in the Word of God. They have opened their lives to the manifestations of the Spirit and they begin to judge everything on an experiential, rather than a rational, basis. If they lack a depth of sound teaching in the Word, they are an easy target for the enemy.[16]

On the surface, the assertion of deception appears accurate. However, it isn't. Most people in the renewal are not newly baptized believers. And the cumulative witness of thousands of mature pastors and people around the world testifies to Abraham Lincoln's dictum that 'You can fool some of the people some of the time but you cannot fool all of the people all of the time.' As well, the Bible affirms the subjective witness of the Spirit, who will guide us into all truth (John 16:13), who gives an anointing to know the truth (1 John 2:20, 27), and who testifies with our Spirit that we are God's children (Rom. 8:16). Furthermore, as John Arnott encourages, 'We can have more faith in God who will protect and lead us than in the Devil who will deceive us. The world has already experienced a great deception!'

In addition, if we ask for the Holy Spirit we must trust that God will not give us a snake or a scorpion (Luke 11:11–13). As well, it is not possible that false Christs and false prophets can deceive the elect (Matt. 24:24). By the Spirit and the Word in the community of faith, we will safely test the root and the fruit to discern if this is of God or of a deceiving spirit. Immersion in the Bible was not sufficient to keep the Pharisees from deception. Subjective assertions – such as the following from Clifford Hill – are even more dangerous: 'The reason I am writing this additional letter is to bring a solemn warning of the danger to which I believe God has alerted me of a deceiving spirit entering the churches.'[17] How does Clifford Hill – or any other person who feels that the renewal might be a great deception – know that he himself is not deceived into thinking this is a deception? How can anyone appoint himself as the watchman over the church?

Some appeal to Matthew 12:38–39 to prove that it is evil and a deception for Christians to seek and desire miracles:

Then some of the Pharisees and teachers of the law said to him, 'Teacher, we want to see a miraculous sign from you.' He answered, 'A wicked and adulterous generation asks for a miraculous sign! But none will be given it except the sign of the prophet Jonah.'

But we must observe the context. Jesus scorns the condescending, hard-hearted, rebellious, 'wicked and adulterous' Pharisees and teachers of the law, who constantly opposed him. They wanted him to prove himself. This Jesus would not do. He did, however, perform many miracles for those who asked in humility and worship.

What people must watch out for are false prophets and teachers who will introduce doctrines of demons which cause people to abandon the faith and love. But these false prophets will be known by their character and the false teachers will be known by their lying and dull consciences (see Matt. 7:15–20; 24:10–11; 1 Tim. 4:1–2). All demonic doctrines attack the authority of Scripture and the Person and work of Jesus Christ. The renewal is not a deception nor is it a habitation of demonic doctrines! The renewal *is* biblical.

Ultimately, God will allow or cause emotional and physical phenomena that do not contradict his character. The Bible allows for but does not command manifestations. Jonathan Edwards suggests that 'We ought not to limit God where he has not limited himself.'

THE HISTORICAL BASIS OF THE MANIFESTATIONS

Have manifestations happened before?

This is a secondary criterion. Even though some things have never happened before, this does not mean that they are not from God. Many things which God did, he did for the first time (the parting of the Red Sea and the pouring out of the Spirit on the Day of Pentecost). This has created great misunderstanding throughout church history. Every time something new happens or something is perceived as new, it is rejected and persecuted. Later people accept it as from God and then memorialize it (e.g. the prophets – they are killed and then honoured later).

It is the dilemma of wineskins. Jesus said, 'And no one pours new wine into old wineskins. If he does, the new wine will burst the skins, the wine will run out and the wineskins will be ruined. No, new wine must be poured into new wineskins. And no one after drinking old wine wants the new, for he says, "The old is better"' (Luke 5:37–39). The danger in religion is to stay with the old and familiar wine and wineskins – the content and container of what was. We can miss the new content and container of what God is pouring out now. When a new visitation occurs, it still may be God even without having a historical precedent.

Because we cannot find examples from Scripture for many manifestations that we see today, the next best help is to survey past movements of God to see if we can find similar or identical phenomena. There are mysteries that we cannot explain with Bible texts. With discernment, we can endorse many things that do not contradict the Bible. The following accounts, though extracted from their historical and literary contexts, provide striking similarities with today's events.[18] Today's manifestations and phenomena have historical precedents. However, historical precedents might only prove that the weirdness we see today has been seen before. What is important is their historical contexts and the reflections that people had on those experiences. People understood that they were encounters with the living God.[19] Many of the revival contexts bear ample documented testimony to the spiritual fruit of those encounters.

John Wesley, English Methodist revivalist (1703–91)

In 1759 John Wesley wrote about the extraordinary manifestations and behaviour of the people who were being impacted by the Spirit. He was troubled by both the presence and then the eventual absence of manifestations. Dr Patrick Dixon writes:

> Wesley continued to agonise over the place of manifestations in the church. On the one hand he felt uncomfortable about some of them – and afraid they would bring his work into disrepute, but on the other hand he was concerned when they all seemed to fade away, which they had done for well over ten years. After all, he had seen the fruit in people's lives and knew that the manifestations were often associated with lasting change. He also knew that manifestations were often a dramatic public sign of God's presence, power and authority, and were often used by God to draw many to meetings where they heard and responded to the gospel. He remarked,

'The danger was to regard extraordinary circumstances too much ... as if these were essential to the inward work, so that it could not go on without them. Perhaps the danger now is to regard them too little, to condemn them altogether, to imagine they had nothing of God in them, and were a hindrance to His work. Whereas the truth is, God suddenly and strongly convicted many; the natural consequences whereof were sudden.'

Richard Riss writes:

Of particular importance to Wesley was the outpouring of the Spirit in Everton during the summer of 1759. The vicar of Everton, John Berridge (1716–1793), had undergone a fresh understanding of justification by faith alone in 1757, and from that moment onward had resolved to preach Jesus Christ and salvation by faith. He had burned all of his old sermons, shedding tears of joy over their destruction. This attracted the attention of the entire neighborhood, and his church soon became crowded whenever he preached ... Within a year and a half, John Wesley was on the scene, and what he found made a profound impression on him, to the extent that he made occasional references to it in his Journal throughout the rest of his life. In one of his first references to it (July 29, 1759), he quotes a very long account of the work of God in Everton, probably by John Walsh, who wrote:[20]

'On Monday, July 9, I set out, and on Wednesday noon reached Potton, where I rejoiced at the account given by John Keeling of himself and others ... I discoursed also with Ann Thorn, who told me of much heaviness following the visions with which she had been favored; but said she was at intervals visited still with such overpowering love and joy, especially at the Lord's Supper, that she often lay in a trance for many hours. She is twenty-one years old. We were soon after called into the garden, where Patty Jenkins (one of the same age) was so overwhelmed with the love of God that she sunk down, and appeared as one in a pleasant sleep, only with her eyes open; yet she had often just strength to utter, with a low voice, ejaculations of joy and praise; but, no words coming up to what she felt, she frequently laughed while she saw His glory ...

'Sat. 14 – While Mr. B[erridge] preached in the church, I stood with many in the churchyard, to make room for those who came from far; therefore I saw little, but heard the agonizing of many, panting and gasping after eternal life. In the afternoon Mr. B[erridge] was constrained, by the multitude of people, to come out of the church and preach in his own close. Some of those who were here pricked to the heart were affected in an astonishing manner. The first man I saw wounded would have dropped, but others, catching him in their arms, did, indeed, prop him up, but were so far from keeping him still that he caused all of them to totter and tremble. His own shaking exceeded that of a cloth in the wind. It seemed as if the Lord came upon him like a giant, taking him by the neck and shaking all his bones in pieces ... Another roared and screamed in a more dreadful agony than ever I heard before ... Some continued long as if they were dead, but with a calm sweetness in their looks. I saw one who lay two or three hours in the open air, and, being then carried into the house, continued insensible another hour, as if actually dead. The first sign of life she showed was a rapture of praise intermixed with a small, joyous laughter.'

Jonathan Edwards, New England theologian and pastor (1703–58)

In 1740 Edwards wrote:

It was a very frequent thing to see a house full of outcries, faintings, convulsions, and such like, both with distress, and also with admiration and joy. It was not the manner here to hold meetings all night, as in some places, nor was it common to continue them till very late in the night; but it was pretty often so, that there were some that were so affected, and their bodies so overcome, that they could not go home, but were obliged to stay all night where they were ... and there were some instances of persons lying in a sort of trance, remaining perhaps for a whole twenty-four hours motionless, and with their senses locked up; but in the mean time under strong imaginations, as though they went to heaven and had there a vision of glorious and delightful objects.[21]

George Whitefield, English Methodist revivalist (1714–70)

Whitefield wrote in 1740:

> Thursday, May 15. Preached at Fagg's Manor ... The congregation was about as large as that at Nottingham [about 12,000]. As great, if not a greater commotion was in the hearts of the people. Most were drowned in tears, The Word was sharper than a two-edged sword. The bitter cries and groans were enough to pierce the hardest heart. Some of the people were as pale as death; others were wringing their hands; others lying on the ground; others sinking into the arms of friends; and most lifting up their eyes to Heaven and crying to God for mercy. I could think of nothing, when I looked upon them, so much as the Great Day. They seemed like persons awakened by the last trump, and coming out of their graves to judgment. One would imagine, none could have withstood the power, or avoided crying out, 'Surely God is in this place.'[22]

The Cane Ridge meeting, Kentucky (1801)

This account is by Moses Hodge, who witnessed the Cane Ridge meeting:

> The careless fall down, cry out, tremble, and not infrequently are affected with convulsive twitchings ... Nothing that imagination can paint, can make a stronger impression upon the mind, than one of those scenes. Sinners dropping down on every hand, shrieking, groaning, crying for mercy, convulsed; professors praying, agonizing, fainting, falling down in distress, for sinners or in raptures of joy![23]

The following account is by James B. Finley, who was also at the meeting:

> The noise was like a roar of Niagara. The vast sea of human beings seemed to be agitated as if by a storm ... some of the people were singing, others praying, some crying for mercy in the most piteous accents, while others were shouting most vociferously. While witnessing these scenes, a peculiarly-strange sensation such as I had never felt before came over me. My heart beat tumultuously, my knees trembled, my lips quivered and I felt as though I must fall to the ground. A strange supernatural power seemed to pervade the entire mass of mind there collected ... I stepped up on a log where I could have a better view of the surging sea of humanity. The scene that then presented itself to my mind was indescribable. At one time I saw at least five hundred swept down in a moment as if a battery of a thousand guns had been opened upon them and then immediately followed by shrieks and shouts that rent the very heavens.[24]

Peter Cartwright, Methodist Frontier circuit-rider (1785–1872)

The following is his account of 'the jerks' at an early Kentucky camp meeting:

> No matter whether they were saints or sinners, they would be taken under a warm song or sermon, and seized with a convulsive jerking all over, which they could not by any possibility avoid, and the more they resisted the more they jerked. If they would not strive against it and pray in good earnest, the jerking would

usually abate ... To see these proud young gentlemen and young ladies, dressed in their silks, jewellery, and prunella, from top to toe, take the jerks, would often excite my laughter. The first jerk or so, you would see their fine bonnets, caps, and combs fly; and so sudden would be the jerking of the head that their long loose hair would crack almost as loud as a waggoner's whip ... [25]

Charles Finney, revivalist preacher

This is Finney's account of the Revival at De Kalb in New York State in 1825:

I went to De Kalb; another village still farther north ... A revival commenced immediately, and went forward with a good deal of power for a place where the inhabitants were so much scattered. A few years before there had been a good deal of excitement; and many cases had occurred of what the Methodists call '*falling*' under the power of God. This the Presbyterians had resisted, and in consequence a bad state of feeling had existed between the Methodists and the Presbyterians ... I had not preached long, before one evening, just before the close of my sermon, I observed a man fall from his seat near the door, and that the people were gathered around him to take care of him. From what I saw I was satisfied that it was a case of 'falling under the power of God,' as the Methodists would express it, and supposed that it was a Methodist ... But on inquiry I learned that he was one of the principal members of the Presbyterian church that had fallen. And it was remarkable that during this revival there were several cases of this kind among the Presbyterians, and none among the Methodists. This led to such confessions and explanations among the members of the different churches as to secure a state of great cordiality and good feeling among them.[26]

Frank Bartleman, leader and journalist at Azusa Street (1907)

The following is an eyewitness account by this journalist at the 1906–1909 visitation at Azusa Street, Los Angeles. This was the revival which birthed the modern Pentecostal movement.

Someone might be speaking, Suddenly the Spirit would fall upon the congregation. God himself would give an altar call. Men would fall all over the house, like the slain in battle, or rush for the altar en masse, to seek God. The scene often resembled a forest of fallen trees. Such a scene cannot be imitated ... The whole place was steeped in prayer. God was in His holy temple. It was for man to keep silent. The Shekinah glory rested there.[27]

TESTING THE FRUIT WITH DISCERNMENT

Like at Azusa Street, after being 'slain in the Spirit' thousands of people have fallen to the floor. But as David Hope, Bishop of London, intones, 'I don't mind them falling down, what I want to know is if they are any good when they get up.' After people get up I like to ask them what happened. A few years ago I preached at a church on grace, and I felt the presence of God settle on these people like a gentle mist.

LET THE RIVER FLOW

After the message, I held a ministry time. One man, aged about 40, came to me with tears streaming down his cheeks. He stood with his arms uplifted, sobbing, and crying out: 'I'm so tired of striving, I'm so bound up, please help me!' I placed my hand gently on his forehead and prayed a simple prayer: 'Lord, may your grace come upon this man and heal him.' Within seconds, the Spirit of the Lord visibly rested on him as he fell to the floor. He heaved and wailed. After about ten minutes he started to laugh and cry simultaneously. Then, suddenly he blurted out, 'I am free, I am free!' That, for me, was a profound lesson in the school of renewal, where manifestations and God's power produced fruit. Later on, this man told me he became bound up by striving to please God and others through performance and perfectionism – this had led to legalism in his spiritual life. He went down bound up, but he came up a free man full of joy!

One evening there was 'a whole lotta shakin' goin' on' with a group of our youth. Many of them were laughing, falling, shaking, getting drunk in the Spirit, and so on. After several hours, you could tell that some of them were now imitating this behaviour to get attention and laughs. I walked up to the person at the centre of attention and asked privately if she could walk. She acted as if she could not walk for a while, but then she began to change her whole mood. She finished shaking, went and sat down, and that was the end of it. She knew that what she was doing was an imitation, and she stopped when she was gently confronted about it. During charismatic activity Paul's teachings and warnings in 1 Corinthians 14 are relevant: 'Let all things be done decently and in order' (1 Cor. 14:40).

108

However, there are two possible extremes that will bruise the fruit of a great move of the Spirit: *condemnation* and *fanaticism*.

Condemnation

Jonathan Edwards and George Whitefield are revivalist heroes to us now, but they were not so in their own day – at least under the opposing eye of the influential Boston pastor Charles Chauncy. Chauncy effectively opposed the First Great Awakening as he reacted to the 'enthusiasm' demonstrated by phenomena. He did not understand revival. Had he come to *discern* rather than to *condemn*, history may have looked different. Unfortunately, many Christians are more interested in being right than in being loving. Harshness and condemnation bring disunity to the church more than anything. The issue in most renewals and revivals is not doctrine but practice. Loving correction is needed but not punishment. But, there is another extreme that we can fall into: fanaticism.

Fanaticism

John MacArthur, in a narrow, negative and extreme way, wants to correct the laughter and the so-called 'mysticism' and 'reckless faith' in the current renewal. He asserts (but he does not prove or document) that to many evangelicals experience is more important than doctrine and '*thinking* is deemed less important than *feeling*'.[28] I contest that evangelicals are finally discovering that experience and feeling are as important as doctrine. They do not leave their brains at home when they enter the renewal. Some might go overboard sometimes, but many are finding that rationalist, anti-supernatural and anti-experiential cessationist theology is 'dead orthodoxy'. They want to *experience* the Holy Spirit.

However, MacArthur correctly warns that runaway passions, fanaticism and carnal enthusiasm can grieve the Holy Spirit and give advantage to Satan. He states that during the First Great Awakening 'many who were swept up in the emotion and excitement of the phenomena began to distrust any voice of caution.'[29] This is a sound warning for this renewal and the coming revival. In fact, Jonathan Edwards, in his biography of David Brainerd, suggests that fanaticism crept into and harmed the Great Awakening:

> An intemperate imprudent zeal, and a degree of enthusiasm soon crept in, and mingled itself with that revival of religion; ... neither people nor ministers had learned thoroughly to distinguish between solid religion and its delusive counterfeits; even many ministers of the Gospel, of long standing and the best reputation, were for a time overpowered with the glaring appearances of the latter.[30]

Guy Chevreau also warns against 'admixtures' when he cites Iain Murray:

> The course of a revival, together with its purity and abiding fruit, is directly related to the manner in which such excitement [about physical manifestations] is handled by its leaders. Once the idea gains acceptance that the degree of the Spirit's work is to be measured by the strength of emotion, or that physical effects of any kind are proofs of God's action, then what is rightly called fanaticism is bound to follow. For those who embrace such beliefs will suppose that any check on emotion or on physical phenomena is tantamount to opposing the Holy Spirit.[31]

Edwards, a great thinker and writer, emphasized what he called 'holy affections'. He felt that true religion was as much a matter of the head (i.e. the intellect) as it was a matter of the heart (i.e. affection). But to him, religious knowledge was an *experience* of God's grace leading to love and joy, with the will and the heart working together. Wouldn't you agree?

This is what we are seeing today. The renewal is biblical and is from God.

CHAPTER SIX

THE MINISTRIES
OF PROPHECY

It was a Sunday morning service in early 1988. Our church had hosted a weekend renewal conference with George Mallone (then Pastor of Burnaby Christian Fellowship near Vancouver) and Terry Lamb (a young man gifted in prophecy who was also on staff there). I was in my second year of teaching at a Bible college, fully convinced that God had called me to a long-term academic ministry. At the end of the service, Terry stood up and said that he had what he believed to be a 'word from the Lord' for me. He asked if I would stand. While anxiety raced through my body, I sheepishly stood. He said that while he was taking a shower early that Sunday morning he received something from the Lord for me. He looked straight at me and announced, 'You are going to become a pastor.' The atmosphere in the room grew quiet. He then asked, 'What do you think about that?' My reply was, 'I've thought about it.'

That was my introduction to real-life personal prophecy. The interesting thing is, earlier that year I had felt a small seed of desire being planted in my heart for pastoral ministry. There was no particular reason for me to have that desire. I was not moving in that direction, and so I did nothing about the word which Terry had spoken out except ponder it in my heart. This prophecy came true four years later, when I left the Bible college to join the pastoral staff of New Life Vineyard.

Prophecy has gained international notoriety – some good, some bad. John Paul Jackson reports, 'A pastor once said to me, "Of all the ministries in the church, the prophetic ministry scares me the most because it can simultaneously destroy and bring life with unparalleled spiritual velocity."' Prophecy is being poured out on men and women, children and youth, conservative and charismatic, often accompanied by manifestations. Peter's citation of Joel 2 in Acts 2 is a *normal* Christian experience, but intensified during times of renewal. The manifestation gifts of 1 Corinthians 12:8–11 are ways in which the Spirit 'shows' himself, especially in great outpourings. Over the last eight years, we have seen that prophecy is a major gift that bursts forth. Therefore, I felt that a separate chapter was needed on the ministries of prophecy.

WHAT IS NEW TESTAMENT PROPHECY?

I define New Testament prophecy as 'a Spirit-inspired ability to receive and communicate immediate divinely given revelation'. In other words, God speaks, someone hears and tells what God said. Prophecy is communicating with and for God. The Greek word *prophetes* in the New Testament means 'one who declares, proclaims, makes known, heralds; a spokesman'. It may include forthtelling or foretelling. According to David Aune, 'the term *prophetes* was freely applied to those who were regarded as inspired spokesmen of God.'[1] Prophecy and revelation are parallel words but with a nuance of difference (see 1 Cor. 14:29–31; Rev. 1:1, 3). Eugene Peterson writes: 'The emphasis in revelation is on seeing something, in prophecy on hearing something. God acts among us and we see what he does (revelation); God speaks to us and we hear what he says (prophecy).'[2]

Some believe that prophecy is preaching or teaching the Bible. J. I. Packer asserts, 'Prophecy has been and remains a reality whenever and wherever Bible truth is genuinely *preached* – that is, spelled out and applied, whether from a pulpit or more informally. Preaching is teaching God's revealed truth with application; such teaching with application is prophecy.'[3] However, the New Testament does not support this view. It shows that preaching (*kerusso*) always included announcing the gospel. It also shows that preaching, teaching and prophecy are separate activities. Preaching or teaching might contain a prophetic edge to it, or prophecy may be delivered through a preaching mode (e.g. Peter's and Stephen's sermons in Acts 2 and 7). But the gift of prophecy is fresh communication from the Holy Spirit, not merely the 'forth-telling' of already revealed truth that involves study and preparation. There is the gift of teaching (Rom. 12:6; 1 Cor. 12:28), the activity of preaching and teaching (Acts 15:35), and the gift of prophecy (1 Cor. 12:28; 14; Eph. 4:11). Also, prophets and teachers work together (Acts 13:1).

New Testament prophecy is where God addresses a situation rather than a universal announcement from heaven with absolute authority (1 Cor. 14:30–31). The gift of New Testament prophecy is not on a par with Scripture, nor does it carry the same authority. It will not contradict or contravene Scripture. It is neither an *alternative* for, nor an *addition* to Scripture.[4] Its purpose is to equip and edify the church (Eph. 4:11; 1 Cor. 14:3, 6). People must communicate prophecy with a measure of faith (Rom.

12:6). It takes risk and courage to deliver it in the church. The chance of being wrong and losing face is real.

OLD TESTAMENT PROPHECY

The Old Testament Hebrew word for prophet is *nabi*. There is scholarly controversy as to its root meaning. Suggestions are: (1) 'to announce', hence a spokesman; (2) 'to bubble up', hence to pour forth words; (3) 'to call', hence one who is called. According to Robert Culver, the most essential idea in the word is that of 'authorized spokesman' of a divine message. This is determined more by usage than by etymology.[5] The three major passages that show this are Exodus 7:1–2, Numbers 12:1–8 and Deuteronomy 18:9–22. A 'prophet' speaks on someone's behalf.

Old Testament prophets were 'covenant enforcement mediators'.[6] They enforced the covenant blessings and curses on Israel commanded by Moses. God enforced his Law through prophets. Prophets often addressed issues of social oppression, idolatry, immorality, religious corruption and making alliances with pagan nations. Also, some Old Testament prophets, such as Nathan, Gad, Asaph, Heman, Isaiah and Micaiah were consciences and consultants for the king. They were court advisers who represented the Lord in wisdom and guidance to Israel's kings. Still other prophets were preachers of righteousness to the nations – Isaiah, Jeremiah, Nahum, Jonah and Obadiah. The Word of the Lord was centralized in a few prophets. Prophecy was not universally available to all Israelites.

DIFFERENCES BETWEEN OLD TESTAMENT AND NEW TESTAMENT PROPHECY

We must not view New Testament prophecy through an Old Testament grid. The major differences between Old and New Testament prophecy have to do with function and fulfilment. We must view New Testament prophecy through New Covenant and Kingdom theological lenses. It is now freely given and available to all through the New Covenant, in fulfilment of Jeremiah 31:31–34 and Joel 2:28–32. Prophecy is a last-days phenomenon (Acts 2:17–19) and a manifestation of the Spirit's presence (1 Cor. 12:7–10). As the church lives between 'the already' and 'the not yet', prophecy has a different perspective. It is not like an Old Testament prophet, whom God raises up to declare or predict his Word to his people. Isaiah announced historical and last-days judgment and blessing, and portrayed the age to come. New Testament prophecy brings 'windows' of the age to come into this present age.

New Testament prophets were not covenant enforcement mediators, nor consultants or consciences to kings, nor social activists, nor preachers of righteousness to the nations. Some may do this today, but we do not see this in the New Testament. People like Chuck Colson and Leonard Ravenhill have had 'prophetic' ministries but are not prophets. In addition, Old Testament prophecy is fulfilled in Jesus Christ (Deut. 18:15–18; Matt. 5:17; Heb. 1:1–2). In the New Testament there are those who function in the gift of prophecy, while others function in the office of prophet. The difference is one of degree and calling. In the end, all genuine prophecy comes from or points to Jesus 'for the testimony of Jesus is the spirit of prophecy' (Rev. 19:10).

Many believe that New Testament prophecy is governed by Deuteronomy 18:18–22. Namely, a genuine prophet of God must have 100% accuracy. But is this what the text means? Here it is in full (italics added):[7]

> I will raise up for them a prophet like you from among their brothers; I will put my words in his mouth, and he will tell them everything I command him. If anyone does not listen to my words that the prophet speaks in my name, I myself will call him to account. But a prophet who *presumes* to speak in my name anything I have not commanded him to say, or a prophet who speaks in the name of other gods, must be put to death. You may say to yourselves, 'How can we know when a message has not been spoken by the LORD?' If what a prophet proclaims in the name of the LORD does not take place or come true, that is a message the LORD has not spoken. That prophet has spoken *presumptuously*. Do not be afraid of him.

The fuller context of Deuteronomy 18:9–22 shows that God was giving Israel a way to judge 'revelation' that a false prophet from a surrounding polytheistic nation who relied on magic, superstition and divination might give in the name of Israel's one true God. First, a false prophet would speak *presumptuously*. This Hebrew word literally means 'to boil up, to seethe', and carries the idea of acting proudly, rebelliously and insolently.[8] J. A. Thompson says these false prophets 'blurted out personal opinions for which there was no backing from Yahweh. Often the desire to please men lay behind such utterances' (Isa. 30:10; Jer. 14:14–15; 23:16, 21–27, 30–33; 27:9–10, 14–16; Mic. 2:11; 3:11, etc.).[9]

117

Secondly, a false prophet might also speak in the name of other gods and entice people into idolatry (Deut. 13:1–5; 18:20). The character and the content of the false prophet were the tell-tale signs. They were proud, they led people away from the true God, they were not consistent in their accuracy and they bore bad fruit in their character. This is also the test that Jesus gave (Matt. 7:15–20). Bad root, bad fruit.

However, God would reveal his will through a line of true prophets who would be from among the Israelites and not foreigners, who would have his words in their mouths, who would lead people to be loyal to the Lord and to his covenant, and who would be consistently accurate. Over time, the true prophet's character, content and consistency would emerge. To prophesy inaccurately would not make one a false prophet.

Scripture makes it clear that on occasions true prophets knowingly or unknowingly prophesied inaccurately, though they were not put to death or branded false prophets for such inaccuracies. (See, for example, 2 Sam. 7:3ff.; 1 Kings 22:15.) The difference between the two is *not* that the true prophets were 100% accurate, while false prophets made mistakes. False prophets bore bad fruit and seem to have been consistently inaccurate.[10]

There are, then, cases where the words of true prophets did not occur. Perhaps they were examples of conditional prophecies (e.g. Exod. 32:14; Jer. 18:7–10; 26:19; Joel 2:13ff.; Amos 5:15; 7:3; Jon. 3:8ff.).

Also, whereas Old Testament prophecy was for individuals and not available to all (Num. 11:29), New Testament prophecy is for the community and is available to all (Acts 2:17–18; 1 Cor. 14: 31, 39). It is not centralized in a few prophets but is distributed to many people. Because it comes through people's personalities and limitations, it can be counterfeited or given erroneously, and so it must be judged (1 Cor. 14; 1 Thess. 5:19–21). Prophecy comes mingled with the person's intellect, personality and language, under the inspiration of the Spirit.

There is the low-level revelation (inspiration) that a person speaks or summarizes in their own words. There is also the high-level revelation that conveys a greater clarity of God's heart (e.g., 1 Cor. 2:9–13; Rev. 19:9). I cannot find in the Bible any verse that states that people today will speak the very words *of* God, as the Old Testament prophets and the New Testament apostles did. They may communicate words *from* God, but they will not deliver the very words *of* God. Even Paul wrote some things that were not the very words of God but were *his* opinions (1 Cor. 7:10–12). He may never have known that he was writing the very words of God in his epistles.

Prophecy can come with lack of precision. The prophet Agabus predicted that the 'Jews at Jerusalem' would bind up Paul. However, it was the Romans, not the Jews, who bound him up (Acts 21:33). Agabus also predicted that the Jews would hand Paul over to the Gentiles. However, the Jews tried to kill Paul rather than hand him over (Acts 21:31). The overall gist of Agabus' prophecies was accurate, but his specific details lacked precision.

There are different levels of prophetic ministry. At the highest level is the office of prophet. At the middle and lower levels are ministry, gifting or simple prophecy. Mike Bickle has developed the four-fold grid illustrated below. However, where Bickle believes that it is possible for someone to reach a Level IV ability and consistently speak 100% accurate words of God, I would differ. Paul says that 'we know in part and we prophesy in part' (1 Cor. 13:9).

The New Testament does not give us a precedent that one can function at 100% accuracy. The apostles did, but we do not. We may have high degrees of accuracy, but it will be imperfect. Below is an adapted version and a brief discussion of Mike Bickle's scheme:[11]

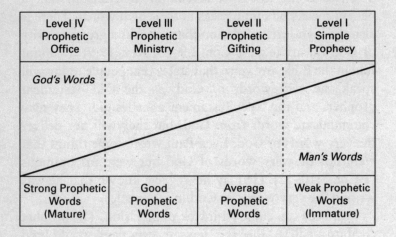

Level IV Prophetic Office	Level III Prophetic Ministry	Level II Prophetic Gifting	Level I Simple Prophecy
God's Words			
			Man's Words
Strong Prophetic Words (Mature)	Good Prophetic Words	Average Prophetic Words	Weak Prophetic Words (Immature)

Level I: Simple Prophecy

These are believers who speak something God has brought to mind (maybe even a 'word of knowledge'). This would be a 'gracelet' or inspiration of prophecy available to all Christians.

Level II: Prophetic Gifting

These are believers who regularly receive impressions, dreams, visions or other types of revelation. This would be the gift of prophecy resident and functional in those gifted this way.

Level III: Prophetic Ministry

These are believers whose gifting is recognized, mature, and who are commissioned for regular prophetic ministry in the local church. They have a full-fledged gift of prophecy.

Level IV: Prophetic Office

These are believers whose ministry is very much like the Old Testament prophets, who declare 'words *from* God' (not the Word *of* God) nationally and internationally, with predictions and revelation.

PROPHECY AND MISTAKES

If people prophesy and make mistakes, do they exercise the genuine gift? If they are not 100% accurate, are they false prophets (Deut. 18)? From the New Testament, I would say that *yes*, people can and will make mistakes and may still be genuine. They may give *erroneous* words, but this does not mean that they are *false* words. Sometimes people might 'prophesy' out of their thoughts or desires, or they may have a small piece of prophecy which they elaborate on. This is not false prophecy, but rather what John Blattner calls 'non-prophecy'[12] or what we could also call 'poor prophecy'. Concerning spiritual gifts, can we find anyone who exercises their gifts with 100% maturity? Are there any teachers, pastors, evangelists, healers or administrators who exercise their gifts perfectly? Of course not. Are they ever 'off'? Of course. The same applies for prophets.

A false prophet is one who prophesies from the spirit of the devil and leads people away from God to worship another god (Deut. 13:1–5). He will secretly introduce destructive heresies and might even perform signs and miracles to deceive (2 Pet. 2:1; Matt. 24:24). A false prophet is one who prophesies in the name of the Lord but whose origin is something other than God (Deut. 18:20–22). Because people prophesy in part (1 Cor. 13:9), their prophecy must be weighed and tested (1 Cor. 14:29–32; 1 Thess. 5:20–22).

TYPES OF PROPHETIC COMMUNICATION

Prophecy is hearing from God and communicating it. Prophetic ministries are the various ways in which God communicates to and through his people. The revelation can come in different forms. The Bible says, 'For God does speak – now one way, now another – though man may not perceive it. In a dream, in a vision of the night ... he may speak in their ears ...' (Job 33:14–16). I have seen different sorts of prophetic people receive and give prophecy in a variety of ways. Some people receive messages from God through several of the ways below, and communicate it through any number of ways as well. Others have more of a 'speciality' in how God reveals things to them and in how they deliver it. Still others will receive and communicate it in combinations. There are also levels of accuracy and significance to what someone gives.

Declaration and prediction

A person will deliver a declaration or prediction that is similar to an Old Testament prophet or to the New Testament Agabus. Sometimes a manifestation will occur with it. In Kelowna, over a five-year period, scores of people prophesied that God was going to give the Main Street

Public Market to us as our new church building. This was both a declaration and a prediction that came true. Personal and corporate prophecies can come in the forms of declaration or prediction (Acts 13:1–3; 21:10; Rev. 2:8–10). Not all prophecy carries prediction. God may announce words to people or address situations that only he could have knowledge about.

Written and spoken

Different people will submit hand-written notes or lengthy letters that communicate the heart of the Lord. Or they will merely speak it conversationally. This is where a person will deliver a prophecy that they received from God, usually while they were in prayer, worship or waiting on him. Sometimes it is a vision, a riddle, a parable or an analogy (Hos. 12:10; 2 Sam. 12:1–7). Rather than declaring it publicly, the person will probably ask someone else to read it out, or they may speak it out themselves informally (Jer. 30:2; Rev. 1:11).

Dreams, visions and visitations

There are instances where God speaks prophetically *to* people through dreams, visions and personal visitations. At other times he speaks prophetically *through* people by these means. The Bible is replete with instances of both (see Matt. 1:20–2:13; Acts 2:17; 8:26; 10:9–16; 16:9; 18:8–9; Rev. 22:16). Dreams and visions are normally symbolic. At other times God will speak to people through mental pictures which appear 'in the mind's eye'. They are clearer than dreams but not as clear as visions – similar to a camera snapshot. On rare occasions God will visit people through angels, theophanies or with an audible voice (Acts 22:6–10).

Music, songs and artistic expressions

God will also release prophetic music, songs, dance, drama and other artistic expressions. While a worship team is leading in worship, a team member might feel compelled to sing a spontaneous song that comes as prophecy. At other times the songs that people write or sing, or the symbolic actions in dance, drama or other art forms may carry a prophetic nuance that touches people's spirits or particular situations. How does an instrument or dance prophesy? The answer is that the spirit of the person playing the instrument or dancing can prophesy by playing or expressing what is inside. The outer speaks of the inner. As worship leader Kevin Prosch sings, 'God is speaking through the music' (see Exod. 15; Deut. 32:1–43).

Prayer ministry and Scripture

Sometimes prophecy will flow as people pray for others. People may not give advance thought to what they will pray. It unfolds *as they speak*. They pray according to the Spirit. They might pray something very personal and even directional without knowing it until after they talk to the person for whom they prayed. Also, there are times when the Spirit will inspire someone with a prophetic prayer (Luke 1:67–69) or tongues (1 Cor. 14:5–6). At other times, God will bring a verse or passage of Scripture to mind which speaks to a person or situation. God will even use a text that is previously unknown to the one who is praying.

Impressions and visual aids and actions

Sometimes people *feel* prophecy in their spirit or emotions. It will not necessarily have words. People have to put words to it, or at least they have to try to explain their prophetic feelings. The feeling or impression is the message, or the message comes through 'sanctified intuition' or spiritual perception. According to the King James translation, Jesus *perceived* in his spirit the reasoning of the Scribes (Mark 2:8). Peter *perceived* the bitterness of Simon the sorcerer (Acts 8:23). Paul, while sailing to Italy, *perceived* that the voyage was destined for disaster (Acts 27:10). The impression or perception might be a still inner voice, a thought, or a sense of knowing (1 Kings 19). At other times God will lead someone to do an action that serves as a prophetic visual aid. The action is the message (see Jer. 27:2–3; Ezek. 5:1–4; Acts 21:9–14).

Burden-bearing and intercession

This is similar to receiving impressions that are prophetic. The difference here is that God will lay burdens on people's hearts that often lead to intercession. He might place a strong compulsion in someone to pray for a certain person, community or nation. He might communicate his heart for the condition of a church or give calls for repentance, prayer, evangelism or revival. These can come as a felt burden that serves as the word of the Lord to incite intercession in and through people. The word 'burden' in the King James Version translated the Hebrew term for *prophetic oracle* (Heb. 1:1; Jer. 23:25–38; Rom. 8:26–27).

Discernment and direction

Finally, prophecy can come in a variety of unpredictable ways in which people might have an awareness in discernment and direction. They will have a certain sense that 'I know that I know.' It may be specific or unclear. For some, it might be a small 'check'. Others will function at the level of a *seer* or *visionary*. Through 'being in the Spirit', they will have spiritual eyes to see and discern the warning or guidance of God for a person, group or situation (see 1 Sam. 9:9; Mic. 1:1; Rev. 1:1–2; 22:8).

THE PURPOSE OF NEW TESTAMENT PROPHECY

For edification (1 Cor. 12:7)

As with all the gifts, prophecy functions to build up or edify the church for its good. The Holy Spirit who speaks through Scripture to teach, rebuke, correct and train also speaks supernaturally through prophecy, apart from Scripture, to edify.

For strengthening, encouragement and comfort (1 Cor. 14:3)

Prophecy is meant to empower, edify and encourage people. Its context is love (1 Cor. 13). The goal must not be to condemn, to be harsh, judgmental or embarrassing. From time to time God may give a corrective or judgmental prophecy, but its goal is always to strengthen, encourage and comfort (Acts 15:32). The spirit and goal in which it is given makes all the difference. Ideally, prophecy will not manipulate or hurt people.

A sign for believers and conviction for unbelievers (1 Cor. 14:24–25)

Supernatural revelation can convict the unsaved. When this occurs, prophecy functions as a sign of God's presence for believers.

To equip the saints for ministry (Eph. 4:11)

Along with apostles, evangelists, pastors and teachers, prophets are also called to help equip the saints for the work of ministry. Teachers and prophets can and should work together (Acts 13:1). In the gathered church *body-life* context, prophecy will instruct and encourage. Paul writes: 'For you can all prophesy in turn so that everyone may be instructed and encouraged' (1 Cor. 14:31). The church should both desire and honour prophecy (1 Cor. 14:1, 39; 1 Thess. 5:21).

HOW TO GROW IN PROPHECY[13]

The starting-gate is to eagerly desire prophecy (1 Cor. 14:1, 39). Prophecy flows from the inner person, in the recesses of the mind and the spirit. It is often subjective in origin but objective in results. Like the book of Revelation, it is a glimpse into the spirit-realm – often with symbols, imagery and associations. Prophecy is not a fixed entry point where one enters to 'get words' from God. It is more a place of viewing to see what God is revealing. If we desire to prophesy, we must hear clearly. James Ryle lists three prerequisites for hearing God clearly: (1) *a pure heart*; (2) *a hearing ear*; (3) *a responsive life*.[14] This is the fertile soil. Now let's look at the fruitful setting:

1. *Listen selectively and know it is partial* (1 Cor. 13:9). James Ryle comments:

> While *sensitive* listening increases what we are hearing all about us, *selective* listening draws out attention to the things we consider most important. For example, when a mother puts her newborn baby in its bed and goes to sleep herself, most noises throughout the night fail to wake her. But let that baby squeak even

once, and the mother is out of bed in an instant. The great value she places on her child determines her sensitivity to the baby's softest cry, while at the same time shuts out the nonessential racket of other things. Hearing the voice of God is much the same way. The value we place on hearing Him causes us to focus on His speaking, which in turn cultivates our sensitivity to hearing Him when He does speak.[15]

Hearing God's voice is like tuning in to the wavelength of a radio station. We are receivers and God is the broadcaster. To hear clearly requires getting alone with God in quietness and peace. Jim Goll says, 'Quietness is an incubator for revelation.'

2. *Speak it out in faith* (Rom. 12:6). You always have to take a risk whenever you prophesy. You do not absolutely know if what you are about to share will be accurate, received or rejected. It takes faith. When we see the Spirit begin to fall on people, and they begin to shake or look like they want to express what is going on inside, we will ask them to speak it out. Or we will ask them what is happening. Do they have something to share? Are they seeing or hearing or feeling anything? The more people speak it out, the more experienced they become, and they learn to recognize that 'Hey God, that was you after all!'

People prophesy when: (a) They feel a bubbling up inside which is accompanied by a word or phrase. These prophecies form in the mouth, not in the brain. (b) They see a vision or picture and feel they must describe it. After they describe it, they begin to interpret it. (c) They might receive a voice or thought in their mind, a biblical text, a sentence, or the whole prophecy. They store it up and then deliver it when they can.[16]

3. *Worship and pray.* An *ethos* of worship and prayer is the best place for prophecy to grow (Acts 13:2). Worship will help touch the spirit and release prophecy (2 Kings 3:15; 1 Sam. 19:18ff.; 1 Chron. 25:1). Prophetic people cannot thrive without this.

4. *Study prophecy, dreams and visions.* Study the major and minor prophets, symbols and prophetic people in the Bible and New Testament passages on prophecy, dreams and visions. Keep immersed in the Bible so that your hearing ear and your seeing eye will become more sensitive to the mind of Christ. In your study, look for good and bad principles. There are also good books on prophecy, dreams and visions (see the Bibliography).[17] Attend conferences and listen to tapes on prophecy. Get into a learning environment.

5. *Be in a learning environment with others.* Do not endorse solo, lone-ranger prophetic ministry. People should learn from and become accountable to others. You can use small prophetic prayer groups and training seminars and classes to help equip people. It is also good to help connect people with other prophetic people and to church leaders to have a context and channel through which to prophesy. More is 'caught than taught'.

6. *Bring your spirit under control and be patient.* Often, when prophecy is being released, people will sense a dire urgency or will be impatient to give their word. Paul calls prophets to control their spirits and to speak in turn (1 Cor. 14:32). God is not in a hurry. Learn to 'take the stairs instead of the elevator'. During meetings the Spirit may come *upon* people and they may become very ecstatic and frenzied. Prophecy can dominate the focus. But, as one commentary says,

Paul clearly did not define prophecy as some form of wild-eyed ecstatic phenomenon. The speaker had final control over how the prophetic word was proclaimed ... Those who prophesy are not out of control, driven into some ecstatic frenzy, nor are they so 'Spirit-possessed' that their personality is lost in the 'divine.' ... Prophecy was not to dominate, nor was it to have an independent authority.[18]

7. *Be responsive and obedient to the subtle ways in which revelation will come.* The Lord might bring a Scripture to mind; he may implant an impression in the mind or emotions; he may give a dream, vision, picture or insight that serves as an analogy between the natural and the supernatural. Be in community and in relationship with pastors, leaders and other prophetic people to 'compare notes', dialogue, submit and weigh what the Lord may be saying.

8. *Learn to wait with expectancy* (Ps. 130:5–6; 27:14; Mic. 7:7). Sometimes the Lord is not speaking, or he may be speaking slowly or withholding revelation. God constantly communicates, but only according to his purposes and timing. Therefore, it is important to wait on the Lord with an expectant faith.

9. *Learn to serve with pure motives out of love.* Ambition, pride, politics and the desire for position will bring prophetic people into disrepute. The goal should be to serve and bless people, *not* 'to give a word' (2 Kings 3:11). Prophecy is for encouragement, comfort and edification, not for fortune-telling or divination. For it to be effective, it must flow out of love and compassion. It can easily be used to manipulate or dazzle people. The end product will be a gift without fruit, and glory to the prophet rather than glory to God.

10. *Be accountable to pastoral leadership and to the church body*. God works through lines of authority. If prophetic people will not submit and not serve, they have no authority or blessing to prophesy. God despises rebellion (see Num. 16 and 1 Sam. 15:23). In humility they must build relationships with pastors and people. It is also dangerous to develop a 'lone ranger' ministry, where you avoid being accountable, or because you think 'The pastors aren't hearing from God and I am.'

11. *Avoid becoming religious or 'Gnostic'*. There are insecure people who make their talk sound 'spiritual'. They will appeal to the subjective 'God told me' to validate their behaviour or decisions. Or they might say, 'We don't need human leaders. We need the Spirit to lead us.' Or, 'We don't need structure, we need the Spirit to have complete freedom.' These people will lack lasting fruit as they act out their rebellion. They rely on 'inner knowledge' that is inaccessible to anyone else. They will use this to control and manipulate. I call this becoming religious or Gnostic. Feelings, 'revelation' and impressions become a steady diet for some. They avoid bringing their 'revelation' into accountability and submission to leadership. People who fall into this trap can become religious and harsh. The antidote is humility, grounding in the Bible, appreciating both the Spirit and structure, and servanthood.

12. *Overcome feelings of rejection, harshness or rebellion*. A common feeling for prophetic people is rejection, which can lead to self-isolation, harshness and rebellion. Because prophecy is easily misunderstood and prophetic people can be unnecessarily sensitive, this can lead to feelings of rejection bred by insecurity. Some prophetic people can get their gift so wrapped up in their personality that they seek to be known more by recognition than relationship.

131

Their gift is their identity. If leaders do not readily accept or follow their prophecies, or put them off for a season, this can be perceived as rejection rather than administration and waiting. The more a person feels rejected, the more isolated, harsh and rebellious they can also feel. The goal is love, with a desire to encourage and serve people.

PASTORING PROPHECY

In our church we have struggled with pastoring and administrating prophecy and prophetic people. We've worked on accountability structures to keep false prophets out, to keep immature prophetic people from hurting or manipulating others, and to release mature prophetic people to exercise their gift. We do not recommend that you allow a free-for-all environment where anyone can prophesy at will. Random, loose-cannon prophecy is out of order (1 Cor. 14). We also do not recommend that you let anyone give personal prophecy to people unless they are authorized. Leaders must have a vision to not despise prophecy but to properly pastor it in the church.

Believe in prophecy, desire it (1 Cor. 14:1), and do not be intimidated by prophetic people who 'hear from God'. I used to tell one person who was a very gifted prophet, 'I view you as a person, not a prophet.' Stir up the gift of prophecy in people by praying for them, teaching them about the gift, encouraging them, and providing a safe place for them to prophesy, where they can make mistakes or submit their revelation, which may seem 'weird'. Build relationships with prophetic people through informal meetings, small groups, and involving them in prayer and intercessory times. You might want to start small groups where prophetic people can gather to worship, pray, submit their revelation, and discuss interpretation with a pastor. You might start mentoring groups where seasoned prophetic people can help those who are immature or new in prophecy.

Incorporate prophecy into the life of the church, just as you would any other gift. You would call on people with gifts of teaching, worship leading, evangelism, administration, encouragement or helps to exercise their ministry. Also call on prophetic people to come and pray for people, to be at intercession meetings, to be ready to give something in a Sunday service, or to wait on the Lord at home to see if he is speaking about a particular area. Provide space at church services for prophetic ministry to be released in worship and prayer times, or in times of waiting on God. Prophetic people should be under the authority of the pastor and worship leader, and they should be given prior authorization to give words at the moment, if they are mature and have been recognized. Or during a meeting, you may have them first submit their prophecy to a pastor or leader, who can judge and authorize it to be given. If they are on the worship team, have the worship leader and team work out a system for giving space for prophetic song. During the week, have prophetic people write out their dreams, visions or revelation and submit them for interpretation, judging and application.

Work in a team context where those with gifts of pastor, teacher and administration work together with prophets to receive, communicate and implement what the Lord is saying (see Acts 13:1-4). Administration is the key to effectively acting upon and implementing prophecy. Help prophetic people to appreciate the need for structure and accountability. If a prophetic person cannot be accountable, led and corrected, leaders will not feel secure enough to authorize that person to prophesy. Develop written policies which explain the expectations for accountability, judging criteria, and guidelines. A good place for prophecy to develop is in small home-groups. Leaders of home-groups should be taught how to facilitate prayer and prophetic ministry in their meetings. Prophetic people should be accountable to their home-group leader and should allow their prophesying to be released in the right space and to be weighed.

Prophetic people often feel an urgency with their revelation and can tend to resist structure because they feel the Spirit will be quenched (1 Thess. 5:19–20). The opposite can also happen. If there is not enough structure, disorder can set in and the Spirit will likewise be quenched (1 Cor. 14). You must balance Spirit and structure and not be hasty in letting people give their prophecies, which seem so compelling to them. God is not governed by the tyranny of the urgent, and neither should we be.

Lastly, distinguish between public and personal prophecy. If a prophecy is for the congregation, everyone will hear and weigh it. Leaders will act on it. If a prophecy is given to an individual, it is wise to have a leader and another person present to hear and weigh it. The person should be encouraged to *not* act on it impulsively, but to wait for confirmation from other means and to ask God to implement it. Timing is always an issue with both public and private prophecy. It is also wise to tape-record public and private prophecies wherever possible for future recall, interpretation, weighing, application, and to protect the integrity of the prophetic person. Prophecy is one of the most difficult gifts to pastor, because you are dealing with supernatural revelation through natural people. Therefore, we must develop skill in pastoring prophecy. As Wesley

Campbell says, 'Pastors pastor and prophets prophesy.' It requires patience, risk and proper administration.

ADMINISTRATING PROPHECY

I owe the following structure for administrating prophecy to Mike Bickle, the Senior Pastor of Metro Vineyard Fellowship in Kansas City:

Revelation. This is the actual prophecy. It may come as a dream, riddle, story, declaration, Scripture, impression, vision, or any combination of ways discussed above. What is the content of the prophecy? Sometimes it is specific and straightforward; at other times it is unclear.

Interpretation. This is the stage where you seek to understand the prophecy. Revelation may come in several parts or in ways that are unclear. Usually a prophecy, like a parable, will have a 'bottom-line' meaning or theme. The Bible, prayer, spiritual knowledge and wisdom, and discussion are the elements which will help you to understand the prophecy.

Application. This is the stage where you administrate, pray through, and apply the prophecy. Who should hear it? In what form should it be shared and how much? How should someone respond to it? What action, if any, should they take? Is it a directional, predictive, exhortative, warning, correcting, or conditional prophecy?

CRITERIA FOR JUDGING PROPHECY

Over the years we have wrestled with prophecy in terms of its administration and release. It is a difficult gift to manage, but it is certainly worth the effort. Below are the criteria we developed in our church to judge prophecy.

1. Does the content line up with the Bible? Prophecy is not the word 'of' God but is a word 'from' God. All prophecies and prophetic people are under the authority of the Bible. (See 2 Tim. 3:16–17; 1 Cor. 14:37–38.)

2. Does it exalt Jesus Christ? Or does it exalt the prophetic person? (See John 16:14; 1 Cor. 12:3; 1 John 4:1–2; Rev. 19:10.)

3. Does it bear witness with the recipient or to the situation or does it seem way off? Is it spoken with love and in order, and does it edify, strengthen, and comfort? Is there confirmation from others, and is it consistent with what God is already doing or saying? (See Deut. 18:20–22; 1 Cor. 13–14.)

4. Is the character of the prophetic person and the fruit of his or her ministry Christ-like? Is there a willingness to have the prophecy judged and is the person in submission to authority? Does the prophecy condemn, manipulate, or stir fear and confusion? Or is it like the wisdom from God, which is 'first of all pure; then peace-loving, considerate, submissive, full of mercy and good fruit, impartial and sincere'? (See James 3:17–18; 2 Cor. 11:13–15; 2 Pet. 2:1–5; Matt. 7:15–20; Gal. 5:22–23; 1 Cor. 13:2; Deut. 13:1–5; Rom. 8:15; 2 Cor. 3:17.)

5. Does the leadership, as shepherds of the flock, receive and confirm it? (See Acts 20:28–30; Titus 1:9.)

RELEASING PROPHECY

Prophecy is desirable (1 Cor. 14:1). It should not be treated with contempt, but should be tested (1 Thess. 5:19–22). It edifies the church when it is exercised with order (1 Cor. 14). It would be released without respect of persons as a last-days outpouring of the Holy Spirit (Joel 2:28–29; Acts 2:17–18). Often prophecy is birthed or released in people with accompanying phenomena, like shaking, trembling, flailing and shouting. People will receive mental pictures and words, impressions, visions, Scriptures, burdens and revelation in their minds or emotions. When people are being impacted by God – shaking, 'looking agitated', and being overwhelmed with 'words', pictures and revelation – we should help them to release prophecy. When people shake, it is sometimes *unto* prophecy. People ask, 'What do I do?' Let me suggest at least the following:

1. When this gift is being imparted, stir it up with the laying on of hands and prayer by elders and/or other prophetically gifted people. The Holy Spirit will often bring an impartation and release by the principle of transference.

2. During ministry times, ask people to come forward for prayer to be released in prophecy. The Holy Spirit will sometimes indicate that there is an 'anointing' for prophecy. This may come as a word of knowledge, a prophecy, or a part of the 'ethos' of Spirit flow. Invite people to earnestly desire this gift (1 Cor. 14:1). Sometimes there will be prophetic 'epicentres' where the Spirit's anointing of prophecy is concentrated. People who are in the epicentre or are brought into it will often receive prophecy. At other times the Spirit will just come 'on' people and they will prophesy (e.g. Num. 11:25–26; 1 Sam. 10:6; Acts 2:18; 19:6).

3. If people begin to experience the things above (with or without manifestations), ask them to speak it out, to declare what they believe God has placed on their heart, and to report on the vision, picture or impression which they received. People need encouragement to express what is going on inside, so that there is an outlet. Tongues often result as well. Stay with the people, ask God to release and bless prophecy in and through them, and then get them to pray for people, with others who are mature alongside them to guide them and weigh their words.

Perhaps the prayer of Moses is fulfilled today, as God pours out his Joel 2 and Acts 2 Spirit:

> Then the LORD came down in the cloud and spoke with him, and he took of the Spirit that was on him and put the Spirit on the seventy elders. When the Spirit rested on them, they prophesied, but they did not do so again. However, two men, whose names were Eldad and Medad, had remained in the camp. They were listed among the elders, but did not go out to the Tent. Yet the Spirit also rested on them, and they prophesied in the camp. A young man ran and told Moses, 'Eldad and Medad are prophesying in the camp.' Joshua son of Nun, who had been Moses' aide since youth, spoke up and said, 'Moses, my lord, stop them!' But Moses replied, 'Are you jealous for my sake? *I wish that all the LORD's people were prophets and that the LORD would put his Spirit on them*!' (Num. 11:25–29)

PART THREE

DIRECTING AND RELEASING THE RIVER

CHAPTER SEVEN

OVERCOMING OBSTACLES

Every river has snags, rocks, twists and obstacles. If you want to traverse a river by canoe, kayak or raft, you have to overcome these. As long as it's pure, the goal is never to stop, divert or change the river but to cooperate with and overcome its obstacles. With the renewal, the goal is not to have it without difficulties or obstacles. Yet many do not accept or understand that all renewals and revivals have obstacles and difficulties. Some will want to control or change the river, or to stop it flowing. Others will 'wait and see'. Jonathan Edwards challenged this:

> It is probable that many of those who are thus wait-ing, know not for *what* they are waiting. If they wait to see a work of God *without* difficulties and stum-bling blocks, it will be like the fool's waiting at the river side to have the water all run by. A work of God without stumbling blocks is never to be expected.[1]

With the renewal, people have fear and discomfort which are often due more to emotional than theological reasons. Therefore, some will just want to wait things out to see. However, whenever the presence of God intensifies, the presence of Satan also intensifies as he provokes conflict, immature zeal, counterfeit and criticism. This is the nature of revival warfare.

141

Patrick Dickson suggests that 'the picture must be seen in perspective, and the evils must be weighed against the overall good.' He cites Dr William Patton, who declares that 'After drought, the copious rains often deluge the land and sweep away bridges, and otherwise do very much harm. But no one is so alarmed by the evils of rain, as to desire a continuation of the drought.'[2] Therefore, we must help each other to perceive the new thing that God is doing and to develop a new grid through which we may properly discern his work. If we can anticipate the obstacles before we get there, we will save ourselves from going under. Let not the prophecy of Isaiah ever be fulfilled in us: 'You will be ever hearing but never understanding; you will be ever seeing but never perceiving' (Matt. 13:14). We must see in but also beyond the physical phenomena.

ARE THE RENEWAL AND THE PHENOMENA FROM GOD?

The phenomena in the present renewal are sometimes bizarre. How do we know if they are from God or not? Could it be the devil or the flesh? There are four major possibilities for the root-causes of phenomena:

The flesh

We could say that the phenomena are psychologically induced by the power of suggestion or hypnotic states. Or we could say that people cause the phenomena themselves through imitation or psychosomatic disorder. If we cause it ourselves, or if it is caused in a way that it is not from God (and we think or teach that it is from God), this is *misperception*!

The devil

We could say that demons and the devil can counterfeit the phenomena and gifts. Many of the same things can occur in occult or demonized situations (as Hank Hanegraaff of the Christian Research Institute has alleged). If the devil or demons cause the phenomena and we think they are from God, this is *deception*!

The Lord

Because of faulty paradigms, people rule out the possibility that these phenomena can be from God. It is common for people at first to attribute them to everything except God. But if God does cause the phenomena and we say that we produced them ourselves, or someone else induced them, or that the devil or demons caused them, this is *blasphemy*! The Pharisees did this.

A mixture

If God causes the phenomena and the devil infiltrates them with the flesh or demons, we end up with a mixture. The task is to remove the chaff while retaining the kernel. This is *sanctification*! John Arnott has said, 'The question is not whether demons and the flesh are here, but whether the demons and the flesh are coming or going!'

The late Martyn Lloyd Jones, minister of Westminster Chapel in London for 25 years, addressed the issue of phenomena and the devil:

> It comes near to the rule that in revival phenomena begin to manifest themselves ... these phenomena are not essential to revival ... yet it is true to say that, on the whole, they do tend to be present where there is

revival. Here is a church in a period of dryness and drought, why should the Devil suddenly do something which calls attention to religion and Jesus Christ? The very results of revival, I would have thought, completely exclude the possibility of this being the action of the Devil ... There is nothing so ridiculous as this suggestion that this is the work of the Devil.[3]

Take a long view

We must observe the long-term effects in people's lives. Do they love God more? If they love God more, why would someone say this is from the devil or the flesh? People object that the phenomena are not biblical nor from God. If that person comes to a renewal meeting and observes that the worship and prayers of God-fearing people sometimes result in phenomena, they might still conclude that this is of the devil or the flesh. But how can these same God-fearing people assume that their worship and prayers are not also answered by the devil, just because they don't trust or haven't experienced phenomena? What is more important is that some people are so afraid of fleshly expressions in revivals that they themselves act in a fleshly, ungodly way by criticizing, condemning or anxiously worrying about what they see!

Does it produce spiritual fruit?

Jesus warned his disciples:

> Watch out for false prophets. They come to you in sheep's clothing, but inwardly they are ferocious wolves. By their fruit you will recognize them. Do people pick grapes from thornbushes, or figs from thistles? Likewise every good tree bears good fruit,

but a bad tree bears bad fruit. A good tree cannot bear bad fruit, and a bad tree cannot bear good fruit. Every tree that does not bear good fruit is cut down and thrown into the fire. Thus, by their fruit you will recognize them. Not everyone who says to me, 'Lord, Lord,' will enter the kingdom of heaven, but only he who does the will of my Father who is in heaven. Many will say to me on that day, 'Lord, Lord, did we not prophesy in your name, and in your name drive out demons and perform many miracles?' Then I will tell them plainly, 'I never knew you. Away from me, you evildoers!' (Matt 7:15–23)

The issue in the above passage is wicked people who masquerade as God's messengers. Outwardly they can do some of 'the stuff'. However, their fruit shows that they are unbelievers. They cannot bear genuine spiritual fruit. The issue is about false religion – external form without internal heart. Fruit is the measuring stick for salvation and sanctification. The question is not whether they are Christian false prophets, but rather whether these so-called prophets are Christians at all. When a person's work is biblical, is doctrinally sound, and is expressed through godly character, we must believe that this is the work of the Holy Spirit. It is not demonic.

CRITERIA FOR JUDGING THE PHENOMENA

We must judge the experience so that we can either welcome it, reject it or refine it. We must know if something is from God or not. We must not fall into deception or fanaticism. We are called to 'not put out the Spirit's fire; not treat prophecies with contempt; test everything; hold on to the good; avoid every kind of evil' (1 Thess. 5:19–22); and we are called to 'not believe every spirit, but test the spirits to see whether they are from God, because many false prophets have gone out into the world' (1 John 4:1). James Beverely, in his book *Holy Laughter & the Toronto Blessing,* tries to deal with the central issues that surface concerning the 'Toronto Blessing'. His book contains some helpful analyses, critiques and suggestions that leaders in the renewal should sort through. Because it is perhaps premature, the book appears to be adversarial and overly ambitious.

After citing 1 John 4:1, in chapter 2 Beverley offers 'ten tests for truth' to 'test the spirits' (of the renewal). They are: (1) the God test; (2) the Christological test; (3) the biblical test; (4) the moral love test; (5) the spirituality test; (6) the freedom test; (7) the church test; (8) the social/political test; (9) the prophetic test; and (10) the rational test. In the rest of the book he then critiques John Wimber, Rodney Howard-Browne, the Airport Vineyard, the manifestations, the Kansas City prophets, the Word-Faith Movement, and the Toronto Blessing. Below is part of what I wrote to Beverley on 19 August 1995 in response:

Your 'biblical test' of testing the spirits according to 1 John 4:1 fails to take into account the context of 1 John. The testing of spirits has to do with testing the false prophets who will inevitably demonstrate a deficient Christology [doctrine of Christ] and Soteriology [doctrine of salvation]. Your book contains little biblical material and your 'ten tests' are generally sound but subject to subjective application and interpretation. For example, what do biblical order, freedom, love, and prophecy look like? You fail to mention that

146

the main biblical tests are: a preached gospel of grace, love of one another, fruit of the Holy Spirit, the centrality of God's Word and the centrality of the incarnate Son of God.

He sent me a kind reply to some of my points. I now appeal to an expert in revival in order to judge the current renewal – Jonathan Edwards. I have adapted five criteria gleaned from his treatise, *The Distinguishing Marks of A Work of The Spirit of God.* On the basis of 1 John 4, he offered these principles to the opponents of the New England Awakening in 1741:

Does it esteem the Lord Jesus Christ?

'Every spirit that acknowledges that Jesus Christ has come in the flesh is from God, but every spirit that does not acknowledge Jesus is not from God' (verses 2–3). 'If anyone acknowledges that Jesus is the son of God, God lives in him and he in God' (verse 15). John Stott remarks that 'By this acknowledgment is meant not merely a recognition of his identity, but a profession of faith in him "openly and boldly" (Westcott) as the incarnate Lord.'[4] This is the first test: if the Holy Spirit is at work, a person will confess a living faith in the incarnate Jesus. A sure test that the Holy Spirit is at work in someone is when Jesus Christ is esteemed and glorified (cf. John 15:26; 16:13–15; 1 Cor. 12:3).

Does it operate against the interests of Satan's kingdom?

'You dear children, are from God and have overcome them, because the one who is in you is greater than the one who is in the world. They are from the world and therefore speak from the viewpoint of the world, and the world listens to them' (verses 4–5). The second test is whether the content of the teaching is of the 'world' or not. The world values 'the lust of the flesh, the lust of the eyes, and the pride of life' (1 John 2:16). Worldly teaching gains a hearing only from those in the world. Teaching from the Spirit gains a hearing only from those who have the Spirit (John 16:12–15; 1 John 2:20, 27). John declares that a true work of God overcomes the world and the spirit behind worldly teachers and false prophets because 'greater is he that is in you than he that is in the world' (verse 4).

Does it honour the Scriptures?

In verse 6 John asserts that he and the apostles carried the message of God, and those who know God will know that their message is true: 'We are from God, and whoever knows God listens to us; but whoever is not from God does not listen to us. This is how we recognize the Spirit of truth and the Spirit of falsehood.' The apostolic teaching and doctrine became Scripture inspired by the Holy Spirit. A work of the Spirit will always honour the apostolic message contained in Scripture. There are also close connections between God's Word and the hearers. God's people listen to it, and those who don't listen to it do not know God. Again, listen to Edwards:

The devil never would attempt to beget in persons a regard to that divine word which God has given to be the great and standing rule for the direction of his church in all religious matters, and all concerns of their souls, in all ages. A spirit of delusion will not incline persons to seek direction at the mouth of God.[5]

Does it operate as a spirit of truth?

John summarizes: 'This is how we recognize the Spirit of truth and the Spirit of falsehood' (verse 6). This means, as John Stott explains, that 'we can test the spirits, and "get to know" which is which (*ginoskomen* present tense), by examining both the messages they proclaim through their human instruments and the character of the audience who listens to them.'[6] Genuine renewals and revivals are empowered by truth and also empower truth. The Spirit of truth guides his followers into truth (John 16:13). Therefore, as Stott continues, 'if by observing the manner of operation of a spirit that is at work among a people, we see that it operates as a Spirit of truth, leading persons to truth, convincing them of those things that are true, we may safely determine that it is a right and true spirit.'[7]

Does it operate as a spirit of love for God and people?

From verse 7 till the end of the chapter, John dwells on the test of love. 'Everyone who loves God has been born of God and knows God. Whoever does not love does not know God, because God is love' (verse 7), and 'if we love each other, God lives in us and his love is made complete in us. We know that we live in him and he in us, because he has given us of his Spirit' (verses 12–13). If we can observe people loving each other and God more, we can be confident that this is a genuine work of God, who lives in Christians and has given them of his Spirit. Come Holy Spirit!

WHAT ABOUT THE EMPHASIS ON EXPERIENCE?

A central concern about the current renewal is the alleged emphasis on experience. For example, in his books *Charismatic Chaos* and *Reckless Faith*, John MacArthur charges that 'charismatics' rely more on mystical experience and emotion than on the 'objective' Word of God. The problem with this is that it doesn't consider the thousands of Anglicans, Baptists, Mennonites and Presbyterians who have been affected by the renewal and yet are not charismatics, and are generally well-trained, thinking and typically unemotional people. But we can over-react to the experiential excess that may at times be present. If there is experiential over-use, the answer is not disuse but proper use. We still, though, have to acknowledge the place of religious experience and its value.

Abraham Maslow wrote a book entitled *Religions, Values, and Peak Experiences*. In it he discusses the issues of people who have had private, transcendent, mystical 'peak-experiences' and those who haven't. He found that there are many 'non-peakers' who are afraid of peak-experiences, or who want to suppress, deny or forget them. These people usually value the rational, and organize their lives around denying and controlling the emotional and mystical. Non-peakers are generally ultra-scientific and extremely 'practical' people. However, he states,

> Organized religion can be thought of as an effort to communicate peak-experiences to non-peakers, to

teach them, to apply them, etc. Often, to make it more difficult, this job falls into the hands of non-peakers … The peak experiences and their experiential reality ordinarily are not transmitted to non-peakers, at least not by words alone, and certainly not by non-peakers.[8]

He says that non-peakers are generally more comfortable with the cognitive than the emotional. They have little security or familiarity with the mysterious, the unknown, the dangerous-to-know, and the ineffable.[9]

Part of renewal is where the Holy Spirit touches the emotions and the spirit of a person, which might result in physical non-rational manifestations, visions, miracles, laughter and so on. When a person has a peak-experience a non-peaker cannot describe or critique it with another non-peaker. Religious experiences are subjective in nature. But is not renewal effective because of deep peak-experiences? However, as Maslow suggests, the peak knowledge gained needs external and independent validation.[10] It needs objective critique.

We should not emphasize and encourage people to come back for more and more experience as the goal. Yet, thousands of overly rational and controlling people are having powerful peak-experiences that offend and frighten the non-peakers. But for once, many are enjoying an experience that is equal to their knowledge.

WHAT ABOUT DISAPPOINTMENTS WITH GOD?

To properly direct and release the waters of renewal, leaders must counsel people who do not experience phenomena and wish they did. Some go away feeling inferior, left out, or passed over by God. Some may say, 'Is my heart so hard that God can't touch me? Everyone prays for me and I don't fall down. I don't get these things, and I'm not prophetic.' People will experience 'disappointment with God'. The novice will look for what God is doing in others and may think that God doesn't love them. Some people who don't experience manifestations might want them so badly, that they will do anything. They will come to prayer lines five times in a row. They'll push and shove. They may imitate it. Then after a while, some begin to resent those who manifest. They might despise prophetically gifted people, and there will be division.

There must be wisdom to pastor the phenomena. God loves everyone, and works in a unique way with each person. Even though we may teach this, some won't believe it. 'That person was touched, why wasn't I?' They will need assurance. But some of these problems have to do with what we model: what messages do we speak, both with our words and with our actions? Do we give the impression that manifestations are more important than fruit? Do we focus on them? Yet even if we do not, some people will still feel that God is not fair.

Because the gifts of God are based on grace and not on merit, they appear to be unfair. God touches some people in certain ways and does not touch others in the same ways. Some are gifted and anointed in some ways while others are not. But, the Bible nowhere says that grace is either fair or equal. God's grace is free and unconditional: we cannot earn it, do not deserve it, and cannot pay it back – that's why it's grace! Grace is the landowner giving us a full day's wage for working in his vineyard when we came on the job at the last hour (Matt. 20:1–16). Grace is not fair – but then it has little to do with justice!

Therefore, people must be taught to not strive or unrealistically expect things to happen to them. Yes, they should seek the gifts and grace of God, they should be open to receive, but they should not set themselves up for disappointment or failure. They must be told not to compare themselves with others or walk away with remorse if they don't get what they want in the way that they want it. God works individually. He may move on some dramatically and on others in less dramatic ways. He may work quietly at home or in a public meeting. He may delay his work for the right time or accomplish something immediately.

Many people bring emotional issues to these things: they grow up thinking that unless they achieve and perform well they are not worthy or acceptable. They compare themselves with others and easily fall into envy, jealousy, competition or spite. But experiences in life and with God are not uniform. We must give gentle counsel and not fail to use models and testimonies of people who have renewal fruit but did *not* experience dramatic manifestations. The options in how God touches and how people are involved are:

- Some receive but did not ask.
- Some ask but have not yet received.
- Some ask and have received.
- Some did not ask and have not received.
- Some will receive in a different way than they expected.

First, some people may feel left out. We can validate the feeling, but we must correct the theology. No one is left out, all have gifts, callings and anointings of the Holy

Spirit. God cares for his children individually as he wills – there is no partiality. Second, anointings do not only come with manifestations – some do, some do not. The degree to which there are or not manifestations is not the degree to which there are gifts, callings and anointings. Third, the Bible declares that the church is a body. As parts of his church, we are attached to that body. We do not operate alone as mavericks with private agendas.

When we are part of a local body, we all share in prophecy, miracles, gifts, manifestations and anointings. They are all meant for the good of the whole body. As parts attached to the whole, we all benefit when another part is touched. Deep impartations, healing, and releases are often not dramatic. We welcome the variable grace of God, even when it appears unfair! It really isn't unfair, because God's gifts are not for the individual but for the whole body (1 Cor. 12:7).

WHAT ABOUT 'BOGUS BEHAVIOUR'?

Eventually, immaturity appears in any renewal and revival. Some people try to imitate manifestations or spiritual gifts, others will exercise them inappropriately, still others will get overly excited and do things that embarrass people. Others practice what I call 'charismatic Gnosticism'. 'Gnosticism' comes from the Greek word *gnosis* ('knowledge'). These people come across as having inner spiritual knowledge. They always talk about their 'revelation' and hearing God. But, because they are insecure, they will not submit their stuff for discussion and are not accountable. They express things in abstract and 'religious' language which sounds spiritual.

So, wherever there is renewal and revival there is also

'bogus behaviour'. Everyone will be at different stages of maturity. The task of leaders is to teach, correct, develop policies, engage in dialogue, and proactively oversee what is happening. We have called all our ministry team people aside several times for special teaching sessions on prayer protocol and manners. Within renewal settings we do not let immature, over-zealous or 'Gnostic' people get out of control. Leaders must take the initiative to not let people minister in ways that will embarrass or put others in an awkward spot. People will appreciate you for it.

WHAT ABOUT 'UNORTHODOX' LEADERS?

Some people object to the roots of the renewal by forming a logical case against its so-called unorthodox leaders. While I don't agree with the case, I will now explain how the argument is formed: the 'Toronto Blessing' has its roots in Benny Hinn and Rodney Howard-Browne, who both prayed for Claudio Freidzon, who prayed for John Arnott in Argentina. Howard-Browne prayed for Randy Clark at Kenneth Hagin's Rhema Bible Church in Oklahoma. Kenneth Hagin is the senior leader of the Word-Faith movement. Benny Hinn, also from the Word-Faith movement, is a friend of John Arnott. Rodney Howard-Browne had his roots as an associate pastor of a Word-Faith church in Johannesburg, South Africa, before coming to the USA in 1987. Furthermore, Howard-Browne's style of getting people to laugh and asking God to 'fill, fill, fill' while he prays, is suspect. Benny Hinn is already suspect because he blows on people and swings his coat while people fall down, and has preached a theologically deficient message. Some would say, then, that the renewal is suspect because of the unorthodox beliefs and practices of the key leaders.

Is this a valid logical case against the roots of the renewal? I think not, for the following reasons.[11]

No one in Christendom has perfect beliefs

Catholics believe in purgatory, Eastern Orthodox believe in using icons, Methodists are Arminians and believe in entire sanctification, Calvinists believe in limited atonement and unconditional election, Dispensationalists believe in cessationism, Anglicans believe in infant baptism, Baptists believe that immersion is the only mode for baptism, Vineyards believe in power evangelism and asking the 'Holy Spirit to come', Rhema churches believe in prosperity and Word-Faith, and the apostle Peter believed that Gentiles should follow Jewish laws, and so on ... My point? No one has perfect doctrine on which everyone will agree. We all contest one another – but usually on biblically unclear issues. How much orthodox theology must someone believe to receive salvation? (See Acts 2:21.) How much orthodox theology releases the blessings of renewal? How much orthodox theology must one believe for God to use and anoint someone? Precious little. Is he not beyond our historical and cultural theologies?

What we can agree on are the Apostles Creed and the basic tenets of biblical faith centred in the Person and work of Jesus Christ – fully God and fully man – in whom there is forgiveness of sin and justification by faith. Check out the beliefs of Arnott, Howard-Browne, Hinn, Hagin and Freidzon to see if they are in the 'faith once delivered unto the saints' (Jude 3). Sound theology is important, but who qualifies to sit as the theological council for all Christendom? Certainly not Hank Hanegraaff or John MacArthur, but rather the global church of Jesus Christ.

No one in Christendom has perfect practices

Russian Orthodox worshippers stand for the service, Anglicans sit on wooden pews, Pentecostals pray in tongues all at once, Presbyterians listen to their pastor pray, Charismatics use guitars and drums, Plymouth Brethren use nothing or only pianos, Catholics have priests, Protestants have pastors, and so on ... Also, renewals and revivals always produce 'unorthodox' practices. Luther used pub music set to Christian lyrics. Whitefield and Wesley preached in open fields. Charles Finney used his 'new measures'. Howard-Browne lines people up while he prays 'fill, fill, fill'. My point? No one has perfect practices that go uncontested. *The issue is usually more with style than substance.* God is bigger than our distinctive practices and uses them to fulfil his purposes.

The focus and the fruit must be biblical

Check the leaders and the churches in the renewal. Whom and what do they focus on? Are the worship of Jesus and submission to the Bible central? Is the fruit of their ministries in keeping with the Holy Spirit, passion for God, holiness, healing, evangelism, and love for others? Jonathan Edwards, Catherine Booth, Charles Finney, Billy Sunday, Kathryn Kulhman, William Branham, John Wimber, Benny Hinn and Rodney Howard-Browne have all been criticized and called unorthodox. Phenomena and practices themselves tell us nothing. Laughing, trances, prophecy, falling, tongues, shaking and healing can come from the occult, the cultic, the demonic, the flesh, or from God. The question is, what is the source, focus and fruit of their character and ministries? The answer is not difficult to discover. If one can show that the focus or the fruit contradicts Scripture, then correction is proper. Bad root, bad fruit. Good root, good fruit.

WHAT ABOUT FEAR AND SCEPTICISM?

Finally, people become either afraid or sceptical or both. Usually their emotions are saying 'no' even while their minds or hearts are saying 'yes'. Fear and scepticism are natural responses to things we do not or cannot fully understand. When you move into the supernatural it becomes difficult. The Bible is full of examples where godly men and women experienced fear or scepticism when God visited. In Luke 1:5–20 Zechariah the priest, John the Baptist's father, had an angelic visitation. The angel prophesied that his wife Elizabeth would bear a son and he would minister in the power of Elijah and prepare the way of the Lord. Notice Zechariah's reaction:

When Zechariah saw him, he was startled and was gripped with fear. But the angel said to him: '*Do not be afraid.*' Then Zechariah asked the angel, 'How can I be sure of this? I am an old man and my wife is well along in years.' The angel answered, 'I am Gabriel. I stand in the presence of God, and I have been sent to speak to you and to tell you this good news. *And now you will be silent and not able to speak until the day this happens, because you did not believe my words, which will come true at their proper time.*'

The godly Zechariah was both frightened and sceptical when an angel appeared to him. He could not believe that his wife Elizabeth would bear a son. God even disciplined him for his unbelief by closing his speech for nine months!

The angel gave him a prophetic word concerning his son, but Zechariah could not welcome it due to his fear and scepticism. This visitation was an answer to Zechariah's prayer for his barren wife to conceive. But he did not welcome or recognize it. This word came true. Zechariah became the father of John the Baptist, the prophetic forerunner to Jesus Christ.

The Bible says that 'perfect love casts out fear'. When bizarre things take place, the role of the church is to love, comfort, teach, encourage and help people to face their fears. As we love people we will help them overcome their fears and scepticism. Often, if people hear good teaching, see good modelling, and see good fruit, they will feel secure. But they must also be taught that fear is a natural response to encounters with God.

Even though God causes fear, he can be trusted, for he is good. C. S. Lewis teaches us a great lesson about fearing Jesus (depicted as Aslan the Lion):

Said Mr Beaver sternly, 'Don't you know who is the King of Beasts? Aslan is a lion – *the* Lion, the great Lion.'

'Ooh!' said Susan, 'I'd thought he was a man. Is he – quite safe? I shall be rather nervous about meeting a lion.'

'That you will, dearie, and no mistake,' said Mrs Beaver, 'if there's anyone who can appear before Aslan without their knees knocking, they're either braver than most or else just silly.'

'Then he isn't safe?' said Lucy.

'Safe?' said Mr Beaver. 'Don't you hear what Mrs Beaver tells you? Who said anything about safe? *'Course he isn't safe. But he's good*. He's the king I tell you.'[12]

CHAPTER EIGHT

RELEASING THE RIVER OF GOD

During times of renewal and revival people tend to fall into excess or depart from central priorities. Because people do not understand what is happening or do not know what to do, they sometimes do nothing or do the wrong thing. Rivers have banks and courses, boundaries and destinations. While raging rivers are powerful, they are still contained. As we release the river of God, we must not let it rage out of control by having no boundaries or destinations. Scripture should determine the boundaries. Maturity in Christ and the glory of God should mark the destinations. Several spiritual movements in the past fell into dishonour by failing 'to keep the plain things the main things'. A few principles are necessary if we want to let the river flow toward godly, long-lasting fruit.[1]

1. *We cannot become preoccupied with spreading phenomena*. If this is our goal, we will eventually de-rail the train. *Experience* cannot be the focal point, yet we do desire experience. Moreover, concerning experiences, Scripture clearly endorses some and allows for others. Some experiences we cannot explain, and we take away the mystery of God's sovereign ways if we try to. We must have a long-term view rather than a short-term view that is only concerned with immediate enthusiasm. Phenomena are often theatrical, but the renewal is not a theatre.

2. *We must always keep the central teaching of Scripture at the forefront.* John Wimber declares that 'the main things are the plain things'. For example, Acts 2:42–47 shows many main and plain things that will build an effective church: Bible teaching, prayer, fellowship, communion, sharing, Holy Spirit power, house-groups, worship and evangelism. Above all, the Person and works of Jesus Christ are central to the task of renewal and revival.

Though we cannot give a proof-text to *support* everything we see during renewal, neither can we give one to *counter* everything we see either. Many things have no clear explanation but are not prohibited by Scripture either. People criticize the renewal for not having strong exegetical and theological preaching. Perhaps, but how much exegetical and theological depth would we find in the preaching in most of our churches? Yes, let's all do good theological preaching.

3. *We should not draw attention to the manifestations and 'showcase' them like entertainment.* We should freely release manifestations of the Spirit which Scripture clearly endorses (e.g. the gifts in 1 Cor. 12–14) and those which Jesus models in the Gospels. If we bring people up front to demonstrate the phenomena, we focus our attention and priorities on the wrong place. We should welcome whatever God wants to do with manifestations, but we cannot take the focus away from Jesus Christ, Scripture, and the glory of God. As Margaret Poloma says, 'we cannot let the entertainment upstage the guest of honour.' Furthermore, we should not display everything that God is doing. Some people do not want to be a spectacle. Others desire to remain anonymous or to enjoy God's blessings in private. Furthermore, someone's experience might not edify the church. We must, like Paul, focus on building up others

(1 Cor. 12–14). A person who groans, wails or shakes violently may repel some people.

4. *Models control outcomes.* What you structure for, lead and model is what you get. The tendency is to develop a formula or programme that 'works'. People will watch a model and draw conclusions from it. If we always line people up front, pray for them, and most fall down or shake, people might unconsciously conclude that this is the method for receiving gifts, healing, manifestations, or whatever. If we always talk about the phenomena and focus our meetings on reproducing the phenomena, we communicate a subtle message to people. The result is that some will feel that without shaking, falling over, or prophesying the meeting is flat, or they are unspiritual or are having difficulty receiving. Pentecostals made tongues the central experience to seek. Today's renewal can make manifestations the central experience to seek. No model is perfect. Let us pick models that have the potential 'to keep the main things the plain things'.

5. *God is not always a God of 'order'.* He will use disorder to bring more divine order. Our definition of order and God's are often different. Most Westerners like control and order. But we need *biblical order and administration.* One of the supernatural gifts of the Spirit is *administration* (1 Cor. 12:28). We must administrate people, meetings and situations where the Holy Spirit is moving in renewal and revival. Many people do not have a theology of renewal and revival and have not experienced or observed many of these manifestations. Fear or doubt is often the result. We believe what we are taught, and we see what we are taught to see and expect.

However, we must be open to truth and experiences that we are uncomfortable with, as long as they do not contradict the Bible. We must explain what we can, teach what is plain, and pastor people through the process – particularly newcomers and visitors. We should bless the phenomena as we lead with order. The apostle Paul is against 'charismania' and free-for-all 'enthusiasm' (see 1 Cor. 14). This means we should not sit idly by and let everything happen in a random, 'uncontrolled' fashion. Things may look messy and out-of-order at times, but with proper administration and explanation we will guide things fruitfully.

6. *Some people unknowingly assume that sanctification and maturity accelerate during times of renewal and revival.* More prophecy and tongues, more being slain in the Spirit, more laughter and shaking, more visions and dreams do not hasten holiness. They do quicken the spirit and empower devotion, but they are no substitute for obedience, intimacy with God, and walking by the Spirit. These are biblical ways to develop godly character – and the process is slow but sure.

7. *At times there may be counterfeit manifestations or anointings* – but Satan and demons always want to take away from the genuine expressions of God. The New Testament acknowledges false anointings (1 John 2:27) but assures us of the inner teaching of the Holy Spirit to keep us from deception (1 John 2:20–21; John 16:13–15). Also, immature people who desire attention for themselves or who want to be part of what God is doing may try to imitate the manifestations. Though counterfeit or self-made manifestations might happen occasionally, this should not cause us to either fear or doubt the genuine. The wheat and tares grow together – we are called to test, discern, administrate, be proactive and lead.

8. A common question is: 'Why do I have to go to Toronto or attend a renewal meeting or conference in order to receive "the blessing"? Why can't it happen in my church or in the privacy of my home? Can't a sovereign God bless me here without my having to go elsewhere?' The answer to that question varies. God has given his Spirit to scores of churches and individuals who have not gone to Toronto. But he has also raised up Toronto as a 'watering hole' where his manifest presence is concentrated. There is something about God inhabiting the congregation, which is the corporate body of Christ. Biblically and historically, we can see that God sovereignly chooses certain locations and people to become centres and releasers of his impartation.

He chose Moses, the Tabernacle, the Temple and Jerusalem as centres and lightning rods of his presence in the Old Testament. He chose Jesus his Son as the centre and lightning rod of his presence until his ascension. As other centres and lightning rods of his presence, he chose the upper room and the 120 disciples in Jerusalem on the Day of Pentecost. He chose Northampton, Jonathan Edwards and George Whitefield in the First Great Awakening. He chose Cane Ridge and Barton Stone in the Frontier Camp Meeting Revival. And lately, to name just a few, he chose Rodney Howard-Browne conferences, John Arnott and the Toronto Airport Vineyard, Eleanor Mumford and Holy Trinity Brompton, London, in the current renewal.

Many who have not been blessed before are blessed when they go to Toronto or other places where renewal is breaking out. God works through people (incarnationally). If we want to hear preaching or prophecy we must go where a preacher or a prophet are (see Rom. 10:14–15). God builds bonfires of his manifest presence in concentrated areas, but he also lights campfires all over the landscape. He works through individual people, churches, centres and everything in between. The bottom line is: catch the fire wherever you can and however you can.

EXPERIENCE RAIN AND REFRESHING

We must release the Spirit – that is, we must give him freedom to move in our midst. As we do, we will experience 'spring rain' and 'times of refreshing'.

Joel 2:23–24 says: 'Be glad, O people of Zion, rejoice in the LORD your God, for he has given you the autumn rains in righteousness. He sends you abundant showers, both autumn and spring rains, as before. The threshing floors will be filled with grain; the vats will overflow with new wine and oil.' And Hebrews 6:7 says: 'Land that drinks in the rain often falling on it and that produces a crop useful to those for whom it is farmed receives the blessing of God.' The symbol of rain connotes refreshing, blessing, life and the Spirit. The rain of the Spirit is being poured out in tremendous measures today. In the summer of 1993, Wes Campbell preached near Toronto at a family camp on the subject of renewal. He began to compare the present renewal to rain. As he was speaking, it began to pour with rain outside, with lightning and thunder. It became a literal downpour in the natural of that which he was speaking about in the supernatural. I had a very similar experience also in Toronto at the same site during a youth retreat which I spoke at during that same summer. It is not by coincidence that these two events occurred at the same location during preaching on the subject of renewal and rain. It is also no coincidence that several prophetic words about rain have been given about this renewal.

'Repent, then, and turn to God, so that your sins may be wiped out, that times of refreshing may come from the Lord, and that he may send the Christ, who has been appointed for you – even Jesus' (Acts 3:19–20). Three successive blessings will occur. Forgiveness of sin, times of refreshing and the sending of Christ. The central messages of revival and renewal must be salvation and sanctification. Salvation is God's once-forever act of justification and forgiveness of sins which initiates spiritual rebirth by faith. Sanctification is our and the Spirit's progressive action of living the justified life and enjoying in the present the powers of the age to come. As we focus on repentance and turning to God, times of refreshing will come. Sin is the master culprit that renewal and revival must ultimately deal with.

Sin brings death, dryness, discouragement, pain and isolation to people. In the present renewal people are getting their sins wiped out and are experiencing times of refreshing which they have never experienced before. Read the following testimony of Dr Phil Taylor, former professor of pastoral ministries at Providence Theological Seminary in Winnipeg. He has a Doctor of Theology degree from Grace Theological Seminary. He is an elder in our church.

I have served the Lord over 27 years as a pastor, Bible college and seminary professor, chaplain and supervisor in clinical pastoral education. My renewal journey started five years ago. Trained as a 'cessationist' it took some time to make the paradigm shift to believe that 'sign gifts' are for today. *Because of renewal I have found more spiritual vibrancy and leading by the Spirit in these last months than in all my previous*

40 years as a Christian in my training, teaching, life and ministry.

CULTIVATING AN ETHOS OF SPIRIT FLOW

I have observed that there is a certain atmosphere or 'ethos' whereby the Holy Spirit is free to flow. The usual context is worship, waiting, prayer, expectant faith and listening. God honours these normative practices in his church. He will settle upon a gathering as the Word of God is preached and read, where contrite hearts are soft, and where a unity of faith lives. For biblical precedents see Nehemiah 8–9 and Acts 2.

I have also observed that God anoints some people or churches to function like a lightning rod for the Spirit's activities. When people come across the ministry of that person (such as Rodney Howard-Browne, Randy Clark or John Wimber) or into a specific location (such as the Toronto Airport Church or Holy Trinity, Brompton) the same results seem to regularly occur. For biblical precedents see 1 Samuel 10 and 19 and the ministries of Peter and Paul in Acts. Though not exhaustive, the following are some ways to release the Holy Spirit:

Worship, Word and warfare

Praise the LORD! Sing to the LORD a new song, and His praise in the assembly of saints. Let Israel rejoice in their Maker; let the children of Zion be joyful in their King. Let them praise His name with the dance; let them sing praises to Him with the timbrel and harp. For the LORD takes pleasure in His people; he will beautify the humble with salvation. Let the saints be joyful in glory; let them sing aloud on their beds.

Let the high praises of God be in their mouth, and a two-edged sword in their hand, to execute vengeance on the nations, and punishments on the peoples; To bind their kings with chains, and their nobles with fetters of iron; To execute on them the written judgment – this honour have all His saints. Praise the LORD! (Ps. 149:1–9, NKJV)

What was literal in the Old Testament is spiritual in the New Testament. In the New Testament, we are called to worship God in Spirit and truth (John 4:24), to wield the sword of the Spirit which is the Word of God (Eph. 6:17), and to wage war with a sword not against physical nations that oppose God's Kingdom as in the Old Testament, but against the demonic principalities and powers in high places (Eph. 6:1–18). A key to releasing the Spirit is to honour God with high praises in our mouths (worship), wielding two-edged swords in our hands (the Word), to execute vengeance on the nations (warfare).

I have seen people set free from demons, healed of physical or emotional sicknesses, have visions of Jesus or see angels, or start to manifest greatly under the power of the Spirit during intimate times of worship, Word and warfare. God honours Bible preaching, loud praise and worship, and intercession. This is aggressive warfare! For a biblical precedent, read the entire account of King Jehoshaphat in 2 Chronicles 20 and see the armour of God in Ephesians 6:1–18.

Wait and watch

At other times the ethos is that of waiting and watching. Sometimes the presence of the Lord can be so thick you can hardly move. People's responses range from settling into a holy hush, to silently weeping, to falling into a drunken spiritual state, to joyful laughter. The usual thing to do is wait and watch. We do not want to be in a hurry to get something going, or to get on with the programme. Often worship, Word, warfare, waiting and watching are connected.

In early November 1995 I was speaking at a renewal conference in Honolulu. On Friday evening a very powerful storm hit the islands with torrents of rain, wind, lightning and thunder. Before the worship leader could get us through the first song, the power and lights went out. There we were, hundreds of us sitting in a dark sanctuary with no power. One of the leaders asked me, 'What do you think we should do? Could this be a satanic attack?' I felt a peace and replied, 'Let's continue, let's wait on God and trust him with the outcome.' A local pastor invited all the people to come near the front to continue worshipping in the dark. Some of the sound people rigged up a small PA system and a spotlight with a battery.

I walked around the inside of the sanctuary and prayed for about 30 minutes. After I sat down, one of the leaders asked if I was ready to go up and speak. We were sitting in the dark, except for the small PA system and spotlight. I said I was ready. He introduced me. Just as I was about to get up and walk to the stage the power suddenly returned. The lights and PA system came back on! The timing was remarkable. I sat in my chair stunned. The presence and plans of God were evident. I realized that this was a prophetic moment for the islands. God was coming with a mighty wind, rain and fire to the Hawaiian Islands. He was calling people from darkness to light. Worship was the central priority. Waiting was the central practice. Acts 2, Psalm 27 and Isaiah 40 are good starting places for biblical encouragement for those who wait and watch.

Transference and laying on of hands

'Now Joshua son of Nun was filled with the spirit of wisdom because Moses had laid his hands on him. So the Israelites listened to him and did what the LORD had commanded Moses' (Deut. 34:9).

'Do not neglect your gift, which was given you through a prophetic message when the body of elders laid their hands on you' (1 Tim. 4:14).

'For this reason I remind you to fan into flame the gift of God, which is in you through the laying on of my hands' (2 Tim. 1:6).

A central proof that the renewal is spiritual and from God is that it is spreading around the world like an epidemic from person to person, church to church, conference to conference. The 'Toronto Blessing' is often transferred by prayer and the laying on of hands – much in the same way that blessings in the Bible were transferred (e.g. Gen. 48; Mark 10:13–16). The biblical precedent for transferring spiritual authority, blessings and gifts through the laying on of hands is well established. After prayer with the laying on of hands, I have seen hundreds of people shake and be released in new spiritual gifts such as prophecy, evangelism or healing. Sometimes a prophetic word will accompany the prayer for that person which 'calls forth' the blessing and impartation of God (e.g. Gen. 49).

The laying on of hands symbolized a person's authority or an appointment to a special task. This act conferred blessing (Gen. 48:18), induction to office (Deut. 34:9), and the setting apart of the Levites (Num. 8:10). Jesus laid his hands on children (Matt. 19:13, 15) and on the sick (Matt. 9:18). The early church laid hands on people for healing, for receiving the Holy Spirit (Acts 9:17), and for

171

setting people apart for particular offices and work in the church (Acts 6:6; 1 Tim. 4:14; 2 Tim. 1:6). Often accompanied by prayer (Acts 6:6), it was not a magical rite that gave people power.

At times, God will transfer the anointing from one person or group to another when they come into the ministry area of where those people are at, or when these people pray for them. Biblical examples are Saul and the prophets in 1 Samuel 10 and 19 and Moses and the elders in Numbers 11. Current examples can be found in the Introduction to this book. Though not through the laying on of hands but by a real mantle, this principle of transference is also illustrated when Elijah gave his mantle of prophetic anointing to Elisha (2 Kings 2).

There are some strange ways in which God chooses to transfer anointings and blessings. Elisha's anointing even went on after he was already dead and buried. Read the following bizarre account:

> Elisha died and was buried. Now Moabite raiders used to enter the country every spring. Once while some Israelites were burying a man, suddenly they saw a band of raiders; so they threw the man's body into Elisha's tomb. When the body touched Elisha's bones, the man came to life and stood up on his feet.
> (2 Kings 13:20–21)

While I don't understand it, I've read reports of people on the Internet whom God has touched in dramatic ways while talking with their computers to other Christians on an Internet Relay Channel (IRC) about the renewal. On 3 September 1995, one fellow wrote the following on the 'New-Wine' list:

172

After last night, I'm convinced there is a great renewal happening on IRC ... Last night, I got on the 'new-wine' channel and immediately I could sense that the Lord was there. I started praying for one of the people there. Then everyone joined in. That person really got soaked! Then everyone started praying for me. The Lord just ministered to me. Before I knew it, I was on the floor in my room. The Lord just showed me more of Him.

One of our missionaries in Japan was driving his car as he listened to a cassette recording of the dedication service for our facility in March 1994, where the Spirit revisited us. He began to shake right in his car as he was driving! I've had people tell me that in their small groups, while they have watched videos of meetings at the Toronto Airport Church, the Spirit of the Lord visited them in the same way as on the video. The principle of transference takes place when Christians open themselves to one another to allow the Spirit of God to flow through them to each other – even on the Internet, on cassette, and on video. Obviously, these are not substitutes for the laying on of hands, but they are examples of transference.

Bless what God is doing

Because God always blesses what he initiates, our role during this renewal (or at any time, for that matter) is to also bless what he is doing. This means that we acknowledge, affirm, cooperate with, and wish God's favour upon people and situations. When we wait and watch, we discover what God is doing. Jesus said, 'I tell you the truth, the Son can do nothing by himself; he can do only what he sees his Father doing, because whatever the Father does the Son

173

also does.' In a meeting, for instance, the ethos might be joy, repentance, healing or the release of spiritual gifts in corporate or private prayer. Our role is to stay in line with the 'flow' and not try to get things to our agenda. We may need to steer the direction, but we must know what God is doing so that we can jump on board and partner with him.

CHAPTER NINE

LEADING MEETINGS
AND PASTORING PEOPLE

HOW TO FACILITATE
LARGE-GROUP GATHERINGS

Much of what I am writing about occurs in large 'pools' and small-group 'tributaries' and 'back eddies'. Administration, goals and structure are high priorities when you gather a group of people: they need leadership, direction, boundaries and teaching. The following are principles and practices that we have found to be fruitful. You can use, modify or delete whatever best suits your context and style. I recommend that pastors and churches that have been significantly touched through this renewal should consider holding weekly, bi-weekly, or monthly renewal meetings if released by the Lord. I used to oversee our small-group ministry and help equip our lay-pastors. I have said, 'It's one thing to gather a group, but quite another thing to know what to do with them once they arrive.' You can gather a crowd in renewal, but once they arrive, what will you do with them? Below are some of the things we've learned in what to do.

Principles and practices for corporate meetings
1. Welcome and orient people. Begin with initial announcements and give a survey of what will take place for

the structure and content of the meeting. Greet visitors. You may want to give a summary with a brief explanation of what people can expect, but not in a way that you pre-program them into expecting phenomena. Be prepared to explain things as they happen 'on the spot'. Do not try to make something happen. Rather, seek for what the Father is doing and to bless and cooperate with that.

2. Enter into a time of worship and praise interspersed with some prayer and intercession (approximately 45 minutes). Worship and prayer are normative for renewal and revival.

3. After the worship you may want to summarize some of the things that have been occurring. Then it is helpful to bring to the front a few hand-picked people who have been touched in a significant way to give short *testimonies* (i.e. about three to five minutes each). 'Interview' people to help them talk and stay on track (about 15 minutes). Do not focus on phenomena as the testimony. It is OK to make reference to them, but the fruit and results are more important. Include less dramatic examples, which will help people hear what others are experiencing, validate the fruit and confirm that it is of God. Hearing from others also builds faith. Do not interview people to 'feature' their experience or to focus on it but to let them glorify the Lord in what he did for them. The model of Jesus with the woman at the well in John 4 is a good biblical precedent. Focus on Jesus Christ and the fruit not the phenomena (e.g. healing, closer intimacy with God, salvation, freedom from an addiction, more joy and peace, etc.).

4. Move to a brief time of Bible preaching or exhortation for the purpose of equipping and inspiration (approximately 40 minutes). I highly encourage that solid biblical and doctrinal preaching should always occur in the

meetings. God honours his Word, as it helps give under-standing, encouragement, teaching, exhortation and theo-logical anchoring to the experiences that people will have during times of worship and prayer ministry. The goal of the meetings is to release the outpourings of the Spirit unto Christian maturity and commitment for personal renewal and action in response. The goal of all *that* is for further outlets of service and witness for Christ. Preaching helps keep the momentum and manifestations on track. The Spirit will work through the Scripture to touch people's minds and hearts. Donald Gee said, 'All Scripture and no Spirit we dry up; all Spirit and no Scripture we blow up; all Scripture and all Spirit we grow up!'

5. Then, either call for a response to the preaching or have some more worship followed by prayer. This all de-pends on the 'flow'. Sometimes the Spirit will even begin to move on people during the preaching. This can look like an interruption, but it's OK. Wait, look and carry on if possible. Sometimes it is best to begin praying for people right on the spot where they are sitting or to have them come up to the front. You can even put the preaching closer to the beginning of the meeting after a shorter worship package, followed by a longer worship package and prayer ministry. Vary the structure of the meetings. But much will depend on the flow and 'ethos' of what is happening. In all, 'dial down' rather than 'dial up' the meetings.

6. Move to the prayer ministry time. I recommend that you orient people so that they know what to do or not to do. For example, you may want to exhort people to not seek to fall over, to not seek to manifest on their own, or to not always stand with their eyes closed. Often people will fall as they stand or even while they sit there. If people

stay aware of people in front of them, they can catch them if they fall. Encourage people to expect God to bless them and to wait on him. You can invite people to come to the front *as only one option*, or to remain where they are and have people pray for them (particularly prayer teams or those around them). Do not become stuck on only one model. Another good model for equipping the saints and encouraging body life is to have people pray for others and wait on God right where they are.

When ministry begins, look for those on whom the Spirit is beginning to rest. You may notice different people weeping, shaking, trembling, laughing, falling, swaying, eyelids fluttering, or ones that obviously have a look of a radiant engagement with God, and so on. You may feel an inner compulsion, being drawn to pray for someone. You must be patient and not be in a hurry to 'make something happen'. You may want to move several rows of chairs to allow for more room. Also, invite people to participate wherever they are. People will sit in the back or sides and become spectators. Encourage them to gather in clusters of friends and those around them to pray for one another or at least pray silently for what is happening in other parts of the meeting while they also wait on the Lord.

7. If you don't notice any emotional or physical manifestations outright, ask those who sense a strong anointing within them to come for prayer or to explain what is happening. Some people may have a prophetic word or word of knowledge for the group or individuals that may give some direction for prayer. Others may feel heat or burning, tingling, a euphoric lightness, a 'knowing', and so on. Encourage people to freely receive and assure them that it is OK if they do not experience a manifestation – that is not the goal. God will work individually as he sees fit. Also

encourage people to not fear or become overly critical of what they see or experience.

8. If there are some dramatic manifestations that occur – such as deep weeping and travailing, screaming, moaning, or laughing – it is wise to explain these things briefly on the spot over the microphone to minimize fear or scorn. These are 'teachable moments'. If a demon manifests by writhing, yelling, foaming and so on, 'dial it down' by invoking the peace, blessing and Kingdom of God over the person. Rebuke the demon in Jesus' name. 'Call the person back' and get them to exercise their will over the demon. Christians do not need to remain passive. Depending on the situation, either take the person to a private room where a team can perform deliverance or arrange for another time to deal with it. Do not let demons distract, confuse, or bring fear to the meeting. Above all, protect the privacy and dignity of the demonized person.

Pointers for prayer ministry

1. When you pray for people, watch for (with your eyes open) what the Spirit is doing. Do not be in a hurry to 'pray something'. Wait on the Lord as you gently speak words of agreement and blessing for what the Lord is releasing in that person. Sometimes you may want to ask the person for what they would like prayer. You may want to interview them to understand their need or to determine a prayer strategy. Other times you simply enter what the Lord is doing as they wait upon him. You can also ask people to describe what is happening or get them to pray out or declare what they see or are receiving through prophecy, word of knowledge, pictures and so on. If you have prophetic people who are delivering words to people, after they finish, ensure that several others gather around

them to 'pray in' blessing and agreement, if the words are 'on'.

2. If a person is about to fall in the Spirit (often called 'slain in the Spirit' or better, 'resting in the Spirit'), ensure that either someone comes up behind to catch them or have the person praying try to help them 'land softly'. To have a team of 'catchers' always available may or may not be a good model. But catchers are needed more to protect people from falling on others who have already fallen so they won't get hurt. If 'catchers' are used, they should not stand by passively but should actively participate in praying for those people. The message you might communicate is that 'falling' is expected and those who catch are not really involved in the prayer and ministry times. Sometimes you do not have the option, as it happens quickly with no warning! When they fall, continue to pray for them and seek to hear the Lord for any prophetic revelation or encouragement. Ask for more of the Spirit for them. Do not be in a hurry to leave them to move on to the next person. Minister to them and then perhaps leave them alone to 'soak in' and receive what the Spirit is releasing – often inner healing.

3. During the ministry time, if you have prophetic people, use them up front and to mingle in the congregation to deliver prophetic messages or words of knowledge. Always be 'in control' of the meeting, but do not try to 'control' the meeting. Let the Spirit move and watch the different waves and movements that will come to different locations in the room or upon certain groups of people. Usually things start slowly and build momentum as the meeting progresses. It is important to 'administrate' what is happening: feel free to direct traffic, teach and explain as things progress.

4. If you place your hands over or on someone during prayer, it is best to only very lightly touch their forehead or shoulder. It may even be better to not touch them at all unless someone else is present (particularly if praying for the opposite sex). I have even prayed for people while keeping my hands in my pockets, and have seen God move mightily on them! Be careful to not push people over, force ministry, or try to 'get words'. Also, if your hand or body shakes it is better to pray with your hands slightly away from the person.

5. It is fine to dialogue with people during prayer to find out what they want prayer for, what is happening, and whether things you are praying for are confirmed and 'on'. Do not suddenly walk away after praying for someone or when they fall. Bless and encourage them to keep 'soaking' in God's presence. Thank the Lord for what he is doing, ask him to increase and to do more, ask him to release his healing and filling, to set them free, to bless them (or whatever is taking place). You may want to pray scriptural prayers over them (e.g. Num. 6:24–27; Eph. 1:17–18; 3:16–19; Col. 1:9–11).

6. Try to tape-record public and private prophecies. If personal prophecies are given to people, have someone either tape them or write them down for future reference and give them to the person. You may even want to video-tape ministry times for future reference. However, the privacy and permission of the recipients must be respected and secured.

7. Be careful to not allow just anyone to speak over the microphone – you want 'quality control'. Only credible and tested people with anointing and authority should give leadership or prophetic messages over the microphone.

8. From the front, encourage people to 'get marinated' in the Holy Spirit. When people are being touched by the Spirit, do not be in a hurry to 'move on' to the next person unless there is a wave of the Spirit moving through. What you can do is invite them to 'soak' in the Spirit. If they fall down, encourage them to wait on the Lord and welcome his work. Often the Spirit will come in waves as he goes deeper.

HOW TO FACILITATE
SMALL-GROUP GATHERINGS

Principles and practices for small-group meetings

1. For small-group leaders, when something significant happens, don't freak out or fear – you are in charge and you have authority to lead. You must discern what is happening and determine what the context of flow is and where it might be going. People must be pastored through renewal and revival.

2. Sometimes during prayer or worship, people may start to manifest. If you are more used to this don't assume everyone in your group is! Ask the people manifesting what is happening or what they may be sensing God might be saying. Sometimes they do not know. You will have to discern what is going on, in that it may simply indicate the presence of the Spirit or an affirmation of what you as a group are praying or worshipping about, and so on. Use these as teachable moments and be proactive in deciding what you are going to do if something happens.

3. Sometimes a random or potentially 'offensive' manifestation may occur where a person may not always have the maturity or wisdom to know when things are inappropriate – such as immodesty, scary outbursts or physical

expressions, or something that doesn't seem to 'fit' and is out of context. In these cases do not ignore it. You may feel as if you don't know what to do – but as a leader, you must do something. Dial the person down, pray for them, and explain to the group what is happening. Do not let people give 'bogus' words or do random unexplained manifestations to, around or over people. Manifestations might happen as the Spirit moves – and these may appear to be random – but as you listen and see with the hearing ear and the eyes of faith you can usually discern what is happening through 'divine order'.

4. Release and bless what God may be doing. Get people to share what is happening. Perhaps they have a prophetic word, word of knowledge, or direction for prayer. Get people praying for others in the group; take charge and administrate; bring things into a productive focus. If you meet with a demonic manifestation, either dial it and the person down, pray for them later in private with a team, or use this as a teaching time in the context of the group. Above all, you must not embarrass the demonized person by doing deliverance right on the spot without their permission or by allowing it to turn into a spectacle. You must respect their dignity and privacy. You will have to decide if your group is mature enough and the timing and receptivity of the person is fitting to go for deliverance on the spot. In the Bible, it appears that most deliverance sessions Jesus and the early church engaged in were on the spot and very quick! If you are not a church leader and you run into problems, contact your pastor or small-group overseer/coach (if you have one).

Pointers for prayer ministry

1. Encourage the group to pray for each other. You can seat people on a chair in the middle of the room if they are comfortable – or off to the side – and have different ones pray for the person. Or, you can divide into smaller groups of two or three persons to pray for one another. You as a leader should set the tone and be a model by initiating and concluding the prayer.

2. Ask if there is anyone who feels they have something from the Lord to share for the group or for a person present. Get others to pray. Wait on the Lord in silence when praying as a group or for individuals. Again, do not be impatient with what may appear to be nothing happening. But do keep the momentum going forward and with a focus. Small-group meetings are an ideal context for the gifts and ministry of the Holy Spirit to take place.

HOW TO LEAD AND PASTOR
PEOPLE IN RENEWAL

1. Teach and preach on the biblical, historical and current experiences regarding renewal and revival. People need as much intellectual understanding as you can supply. Through the years we have taught on the subject of renewal and manifestations – much of what you are reading in this book we have taught our people. In 1994 we did an entire series especially for all the newcomers on the current renewal from a biblical, historical and contemporary perspective.

2. Help people to experience and learn first-hand and to overcome fear and wrong perceptions. You can ask people to share personal testimonies which demonstrate the fruit. You should also provide forums and meetings where

people can ask questions and where non-defensive dialogue can occur. Get people involved in worship, prayer, serving and intercession. Also, recommend good conferences, books, tapes, and videos that people can learn from and experience. Pastor the people, don't push the people. Remember to encourage a focus on God, not on renewal. We must be gentle and not argumentative or defensive. This is God's renewal, not ours.

3. Work with your key leaders and those being touched in key ways. It is difficult for two to walk together unless they be agreed. Therefore, it is important to consolidate your heart and vision regarding the renewal with your leaders. Leaders are influencers. If they buy in, most of the way will be paved. If they do not buy in you will have a very rocky road. I know many pastors who have lost their churches because of leadership conflicts over the renewal.

4. Seek after and emphasize the fruit. Help people to not judge the whole by the part. Most people work and perceive at the micro-level (the small picture, the details). Leaders must work and perceive at the macro-level (the large picture, the generalities). If we emphasize and look for fruit, and observe the whole rather than the parts, we will be able to lead with more skill and direction.

5. Establish boundaries and protocols for meetings and ministry times. Facilitate divine order but do not let things get 'out of control'. Things will look disorderly but that does not mean they are out of control. This is different from trying to control the renewal. Renewal is under God's control. Administration and facilitating order is under our control. People ask me what they should do with the shaking, the feelings of birthing, the groaning, the roaring and so on. I tell them to release it into positive directions – into prayer, intercession, prophecy, witness,

encouragement and worship. I also tell them to 'bring their spirit into subjection' according to 1 Corinthians 14:32 and yet not turn inward with their manifestations by bottling them up.

6. Continue to preach and practice the whole counsel of God with Christ at the centre. The tendency is to keep the Spirit at the centre, but his ministry is to glorify Christ (John 16). Keep all home-base ministries functioning. While it is easy to jettison the more 'mundane' things of church life, do not fall prey to this temptation. Some pastors would like to commit themselves primarily to renewal meetings. John Wimber warns, 'When you made that choice, you gave up your church. You'll not end up with a church. You'll end up with a "revival" centre full of strangers that have had a common experience. In seeking something that is good, be careful not to sacrifice the best.'[1] We must work for obedience to God, not just fascination with God. Many people will seek the renewal with the phenomena, the supernatural and the miraculous. But do not let people become enamoured with the supernatural. Eugene Peterson sounds a warning: 'It is easier to pursue a fascination with the supernatural than to enter into the service of God. And because it is easier, it happens more often. We have recurrent epidemics of infatuation with religion. People love being entertained by miracles.'[2]

Having said this, *incorporate* renewal and the supernatural into the goals and ministries of your church and organization. Release prayer, prophecy, intercession, worship and the gifts of the Holy Spirit into your cell-groups, Sunday school, youth ministry, Sunday evening services and so on. However, as you do, always seek to keep the 'plain things of Scripture the main things' of practice. Continue to 'equip the saints' for ministry (Eph. 4:11–12).

7. Pastor the flock of God in and beyond renewal. God's people still live in a very real world of frustration, pain and stress. They still have families, jobs, ministry and personal problems. Renewal will not replace the need for pastoral counselling, small groups, children's and youth ministries, good Sunday morning services and so on. Keep the plain and the main going. Renewal will certainly improve things, but it cannot be a substitute. Pastors will say, 'Well, we have held renewal meetings for the past six months now and things seem to be dying out. We can only preach to and pray for ourselves for so long. Is something wrong? What shall we do?' My reply is this: there comes a point when the people are renewed! If you hold renewal meetings and don't keep adding new wood to the fire by way of new people coming in, the old wood is burned up and the fire begins to subside. This is natural and not bad, as you cannot sustain an indefinite renewal. What is needed is new green growth. Just as new green growth sprouts after a forest fire, so the green growth of released ministry should sprout after renewal and revival fires.

After people become renewed and filled by the Spirit as on the Day of Pentecost (Acts 1:8), they must let the waters of renewal be released into their spheres of influence by being witnesses with power in mission, mercy ministry, evangelism, the multiplication of cell groups, church planting, community service and so on. If the waters of renewal are contained and controlled, people and churches will become like the Dead Sea, which has the fresh waters of the Jordan River flowing into it, but without an outlet. Thus the Dead Sea becomes a dead reservoir of water. Christians must become channels for the river to flow through and not become containers of God's blessing. I deal with this at length in chapters 10–12.

8. Continue to provide outlets for ministry and encourage an outward versus an inward focus. We must always work at multiplying cell groups, sending missionaries, serving in the community, and releasing evangelism and church planting. It is easy to become a reservoir that collects the blessings of God's river rather than become a conduit that channels the blessings to others. God gives vision for ministry ideas to many people in our churches. Part of pastoring is to equip for and facilitate the vision and ministry of others (Eph. 4:11–12). We must unleash the church to do the ministry as we promote the digging of irrigation ditches in which the waters of renewal can flow.[3]

9. Be prepared for resistance, criticism, opposition and 'the cost'. Every renewal and revival provoked resistance, criticism and opposition. Whenever the manifest presence of God comes, there is fall-out. Even Jesus himself caused much resistance and opposition to his ministry. Edwards said: 'There never yet was any great manifestation that God made of Himself to the world, without many difficulties attending to it.' The cost may be rejection, loss, alienation or misunderstanding. Are we prepared to pay the cost of renewal and revival? I've met dozens of pastors who have been forced to resign from their churches or denominations because of the renewal. Many have gone on to other churches or church planting to bear fruit a hundred-fold.

10. Train your prayer people and prophetic people. Establish proper guidelines and structures. It is unwise to turn loose just anyone who wants to pray for or prophesy over people. We have a two-level system of authorized prayer and prophetic people and apprentices who must work with the experienced ones and get further training. Well-meaning people caught up in the frenzy of renewal activity can bring harm and cause conflict if they pray or prophesy without maturity and wisdom. See chapters 6 and 10 for a fuller treatment. Also, many people are beginning to experience burdens for intercession, prophecy, evangelism and spiritual warfare. People will often begin to heave inside, feel as if they are 'in labour', roar, or will do 'vertical sit-ups'. The emotional and spiritual reactions they feel must be released. They need outlets. Get them to pray out or prophesy their feelings, to impart to others, to worship God, and in a sense to 'bring their spirits under control' (1 Cor. 14:32). Otherwise, they will get 'jammed' inside and will not know what to do with what they feel.

11. Do not model or promote an *anti-intellectual* spirit. Do not model or promote hasty giving of prophecy and 'words'. Prophecy must follow the New Testament guidelines with wisdom and patience. Do not let people become prophecy, dreams, visions, manifestations and experience 'junkies'. People must not throw out their minds and common-sense wisdom. Granted, many evangelicals have more Bible in their heads than Spirit in their experience. But because they are finally getting the experience the tendency is to get sloppy in their Bible and theology. However, don't let them swing so far that they reach the ozone layer. Do not announce 'healings' before the facts are thoroughly verified. Do not model or promote unrestrained 'enthusiasm' and so-called 'abandonment'. There is a vast difference between promoting freedom in the power of the Spirit, biblically governed, and careless emotion-driven euphoria.

12. Above all, lead by example. Be proactive and preventive. Pastor the church as elders and shepherds of God's flock. Keep current in what is happening, where, and who is endorsing and writing about this renewal. Read the Bible and good books on renewal and revival as you immerse yourself in relevant literature so that you – like the men of Issachar – will be able to understand the times and know what to do (1 Chron. 12:32).

As I realize that the subject of pastoring people and churches in renewal is larger than what I can tackle in this book, I am writing another book that will deal with this subject in more detail. I want to call it *Leadership in Renewal and Beyond.*

PART FOUR

LETTING THE RIVER FLOW

CHAPTER TEN

GETTING YOUR SAILS UP FOR THE WIND OF THE SPIRIT

> There's a wind a-blowin'
> All across the land
> A fragrant breeze of Heaven
> Blowin' once again
> Don't know where it comes from
> Don't know where it goes
> But let it blow over me
> Oh, sweet wind
> Come and blow over me.
>
> (VMG, David Ruis, *Winds of Worship #3*,
> © 1994, Mercy/Vineyard Publishing,
> used by permission.)

People are using three main metaphors for the renewal: fire, rain, and *wind*. In Acts 2:2 Luke says, 'Suddenly a sound like the blowing of a violent *wind* came from heaven and filled the whole house where they were sitting.' The day of Pentecost was windy! People want to welcome the wind of the Spirit. They want to personally appropriate the renewal. Winds bring change. Renewal and revival brings change. The Bible connects wind and Spirit, freedom and faith, the visible and the invisible.

The wind blows wherever it pleases. You hear its sound, but you cannot tell where it comes from or where it is going. So it is with everyone born of the Spirit. (John 3:5–8)

I would like to learn just one thing from you: Did you receive the Spirit by observing the law, or by believing what you heard? Are you so foolish? After beginning with the Spirit, are you now trying to attain your goal by human effort? Have you suffered so much for nothing – if it really was for nothing? Does God give you his Spirit and work miracles among you because you observe the law, or because you believe what you heard? (Gal. 3:2–5)

THE WIND OF THE SPIRIT

When the natural speaks of the supernatural

We cannot see the wind, but we can see its effects. We can hear and feel it. We can see trees bend and sway, leaves fall and dirt swirl. There are different kinds of winds, with different velocities and temperatures – breezes, gales, hurricanes, warm winds and cold winds. The natural principle is: *'The wind blows wherever it pleases. You hear its sound, but you cannot tell where it comes from or where it is going.'* The supernatural principle is: *'so it is with everyone born of the Spirit'* (John 3:8). The Spirit is like the wind. The disciples waited in the upper room for the promised Holy Spirit. When he came at Pentecost, he came as a *violent wind* (Acts 2:2).

The Greek word for 'Spirit' is *pneuma*. The English word 'pneumonia' comes from this Greek root. *Pneuma* means 'wind' or 'breath'. The Spirit is a wind that might blow like a mighty gale or a gentle breeze over a crowd or over a single person. We can observe his effects by the physical, emotional and spiritual reactions. That is what happens during renewal and revival.

God's people should understand the things of the Spirit. We should not respond to him with scorn, scepticism or unbelief. He should be familiar to us. But the 'religious' community is not always familiar with the Spirit. The Pharisees and the teachers of the Law misunderstood Jesus and the Spirit. Jesus was 'unorthodox' and offensive. He did miracles on holidays, he associated with 'sinners', and he taught strange things with authority. He challenged legalism. Paul flatly opposed attempts to appropriate the Spirit through legalism. He asked: 'Does God give you his Spirit and work miracles among you because you observe the law, or because you believe what you heard?' (Gal. 5:5). This does not mean that someone who has difficulty with the effects of the Spirit is a Pharisee. But despite any discomfort that we may feel, we must still let the Spirit blow into our sails.

Of sailing and the Spirit

When the men had hoisted it aboard, they passed ropes under the ship itself to hold it together. Fearing that they would run aground on the sandbars of Syrtis, they lowered the sea anchor and let the ship *be driven along*. (Acts 27:17)

For prophecy never had its origin in the will of man, but men spoke from God as they were *carried along* by the Holy Spirit. (2 Pet. 1:21)

The Greek for 'carried along' and 'driven along' in the two passages above is *phero*. It means 'to be moved' or 'to be driven' (literally by the wind and the weather, and figuratively by the Spirit of God). As the wind drives a sail-boat, so the Holy Spirit drives (or carries) people. The Spirit who inspired Scripture and prophecy moved or carried along the authors and prophets to write or speak the Word of God. Picture yourself as a clipper ship cutting through the water on the open sea, with bulging sails full of the blowing wind. You have hoisted your sails; you are steering the ship by its rudder; you are in for a breathtaking ride!

HOW TO GET YOUR SAILS UP
TO CATCH THE WIND OF THE SPIRIT

Be in community and be accountable

We should all commit ourselves to work in community and accountability. An effective church community will value correction, teaching and evaluation. We should not fall into 'charismatic gnosticism', in which experience cannot be tested. Be in a place where the Spirit has freedom to blow, but where it is safe to dialogue and test.

Be in the Scriptures and in prayer

Read the Bible and pray frequently. Ground your experience in the Bible, but empower your experience with prayer. We must not put the Bible on the shelf so that we can jump into experience.

Be at rest and be receptive to God working in new ways

Relax. Meditate on Mark 6:31–32. Don't strive to attain his Spirit (Gal. 3:1–5). Be open. Don't be a negative critic or a sour antagonist, like a member of the Sandhedrin. We need to defend the renewal, but we must not fall into Pharisaic attitudes that work to straighten and constrict the move of God. Be flexible and receptive to a God who will change your models of reality.

Be full of grace and discernment

Renewal and revival are never entirely pure. Human and demonic 'admixtures' will always be there. Let's be gracious. We do not have to get angry. We can encourage each other towards love and good deeds. We must discern and test people's teachings, practice and character in order to know whether they are of God, but we must also be gracious when people make mistakes.

Evaluate with your heart and your mind

Participate. Be involved at whatever level you can. My eleven-year-old daughter Melissa handed out paper tissues during one of our renewal meetings. Others might pray for people, teach, 'catch', serve on the worship team, set up chairs or clean up. Develop outreaches to the community in mercy ministry, food distribution and servant evangelism. Ask questions, study, read books, listen to tapes, observe and evaluate with your mind *and* your heart. You can reach the mind with scholarship, but you must reach the heart with the Spirit. As Paul Cain says, 'God will offend the mind in order to reveal the heart.'

HOW TO POSITION YOURSELF TO
CATCH THE WAVE OF THE SPIRIT

Of surfing and the Spirit

Surfing is a good illustration of how to appropriate the Spirit. I surfed in Southern California in my high-school days. Surfers paddle out, get in to position, and then ride the waves. Waves come in sets of six to eight for about ten minutes, and then there is a calm for about ten minutes in between sets. As you wait for the next set, you rest and watch. You sense the currents swirling underneath. On the horizon you will see the swell moving toward you and then the process resumes. You cannot fight the waves; you must cooperate with them. You calculate where you need to position yourself to catch the wave. So it is with the Spirit.

The natural speaks of the supernatural. The Spirit moves in sets. You can observe his coming at a distance. You position yourself by faith to ride the Spirit waves of renewal. You cannot fight the Spirit; you must cooperate with him. Between times of renewal and revival the Spirit seems to be less active. But when 'the surf's up', you ride! This is a time of exhilaration and intense action. Between sets you wait, watch and rest. You will even see this pattern during meetings.

Some people expect endless surfing. When the set is over, they may think the Spirit is not moving. They enjoy the excitement. They may conclude that unless they are always riding the crest of the wave, the time in between sets is not valid. But surfers know that time in between sets is needed to get a rest, to get a little sun, and then to paddle back out to get repositioned.

In between renewals and revivals there are 'down times' when there are lulls in the action. The intensity of the

Spirit changes. It is like the ebb and flow of the tides. There are low tides and high tides. The height and speed of the tides' ebbing and flowing varies from lesser to greater, and then after the cycle they go from greater to lesser. So it is with the Spirit. The eyes of faith will know how the Spirit is moving and that he moves in different ways. When he moves quickly, you ride the crest. When he moves slowly, you 'cruise'. When he slows down to a standstill you wait, watch and discern the swirling currents beneath you. He will be working in the depths.

The way to get the best of both winds and waves is to go windsurfing! It takes more skill and endurance, but oh, what a ride! Maximum renewal and revival are like windsurfing. You need to get your sails up to catch the winds and position yourself to ride the waves. The following are some of the keys to catching the winds and waves of the Spirit.

Develop a passion for God

Love the Lord your God with all your heart and with all your soul and with all your mind. This is the first and greatest commandment. And the second is like it: Love your neighbour as yourself. (Matt. 22:37–39)

Most people who have been touched by the Spirit develop a greater passion for God and love for others. We have seen partners in business who have had very strained relationships with each other, cry and pray together after breaking down their walls of hostility. We have seen marriages saved, young people turned on for Jesus, and prodigals come back to church after a significant touch by the Spirit. Gerald Hiebert is a man in our church who was a nominal Christian for 20 years. During our renewal meetings he encountered God in a very personal way. He declares that the last four years have been the most exciting years of his life. He has since left a well-paid job to join our staff as our church administrator. He is so excited about God that one Sunday morning he placed a cheque like this in the offering basket:

Gerald Hiebert
Kelowna, BC

585

8 NOV. 1994

Pay to __JESUS CHRIST__

the order of __EVERYTHING__

$ ALL

Royal Bank of Canada
Orchard Park Branch

Memo FOR THE REST OF MY LIFE

Gerald Hiebert

Walter Hilton, a 14th-century English Augustinian monk, wrote a devotional book for laypeople entitled *Toward a Perfect Love*. Using the analogy of the hound running after the hare, Hilton illustrates passion for God. A hound that runs after the hare only because he sees the other hounds running will eventually get weary and give up. But if he runs because he can see the hare first-hand, he will run until he catches up with it. So it is with Christians. If they are only attracted to the activity of renewal, they will eventually get weary and will give up the race. It is only those Christians who see and experience God at first hand who will stay in the race. Hilton wrote, 'Do not fear to desire from God as much as you are able for ... Whoever can most intensely desire God shall most intensely experience him.'[1]

In October 1995, while I was leading a renewal conference in Regina, Saskatchewan, about a thousand hungry and hurting people showed up ready for the 'winds of change'. I was particularly drawn to a man named Albert who was confined to a wheelchair. He came to the ministry team training session on the night before the conference and served on the team during the conference. He was 48 years old and had been born with cerebral palsy. He could barely talk and couldn't walk or use his right arm. But he did use his passion for God. As he wheeled around the conference he prayed for people. I saw him hug and pray for a little girl. During the conference I prayed for him. As I did, he called out, 'Oh Jesus, Jesus! I love you, Jesus! Thank you, Holy Spirit! Fill me, fill me!' Later he looked at me with his compassionate eyes and told me that he felt God had called him to preach and pray for the sick. He is not waiting till he is healed, for his passion for God compels him to do it now. He said, 'All I want to do is serve Jesus.' This desire to serve the Lord is a major sail to catch the wind of the Spirit.

Don't strive to attain the Spirit

In late June 1995 I was in England, doing a renewal conference. During a prayer time, the host pastor (an Anglican rector) was resting in the Spirit and was down for about 30 minutes. The next day he reported that he had had an experience in which he felt as if he were a large boat which was being propelled by a set of large oars in troubled waters. People were swimming in the troubled waters, trying to enter the boat. He felt himself working harder with the oars. Then he felt the Lord say that he needed to drop the oars, hoist his sails and become a sailing ship. He needed to open his sails to receive the wind of the Spirit. As he did so in his vision, he felt freedom. He also got the oars out of the way to allow the people in the troubled waters to enter the boat.

He felt that this experience was a picture of his ministry, which was characterized by him working harder and striving with little effect. It even hindered people from entering his church. The next morning I shared this story. Suddenly, a lady told how the week before she had painted two pictures – one of a Viking ship with oars and the other of a sailing ship! What neither of them knew was that at the last session of this conference I had planned to speak on getting our sails up to catch the wind of the Spirit.

Two mornings later I led a clinic on prophecy. As we waited on the Lord, one lady remarked, 'I feel the Lord is saying that we need to get our sails up to catch the wind of the Spirit. We need to not strive under our own power, but to allow him to give us freedom as he sends the wind of his Spirit.' Faith filled the room! I asked, 'Were you at any of the other meetings this week?' She said 'No.' I spoke that night with the two paintings as visual aids.

Many people use faith for salvation but use works to attain the Spirit for Christian living after they become Christians. I meet hundreds of tired Christians who strive for the Spirit, work for God's blessings, and are tangled up in legalism and religion to attain freedom. But instead they get law, bondage and fatigue. They are foreigners to grace. As Eugene Peterson says, 'Excessive activism is typical of those who do not live by grace.'[2] Don't strive to *attain* the Spirit and renewal. Hoist up your spiritual and emotional sails and allow the wind of the Spirit to propel you.

Continue to ask for the Holy Spirit

So I say to you: Ask and it will be given to you; seek and you will find; knock and the door will be opened to you. For everyone who asks receives; he who seeks finds; and to him who knocks, the door will be opened. Which of you fathers, if your son asks for a fish, will give him a snake instead? Or if he asks for an egg, will give him a scorpion? If you then, though you are evil, know how to give good gifts to your children, how much more will your Father in heaven give the Holy Spirit to those who ask him! (Luke 11:9–13)

The verbs for 'ask', 'seek' and 'knock' are all in the present tense. They suggest continuous, regular, persistent actions. It is God's will to give his good gifts to those who continue to ask by faith. The Holy Spirit is the best gift that he could give.

Believe that God's kingdom works in small ways with big results

He told them another parable: 'The kingdom of heaven is like a mustard seed, which a man took and planted in his field. Though it is the smallest of all your seeds, yet when it grows, it is the largest of garden plants and becomes a tree, so that the birds of the air come and perch in its branches.' He told them still another parable: 'The kingdom of heaven is like yeast that a woman took and mixed into a large amount of flour until it worked all through the dough.'
(Matt. 13:31–33)

It's difficult for people to be patient with God. We often desire quick and spectacular results. However, God's kingdom works in small and subtle but effective ways. Jesus was born in a stable in a small village. He grew up as a poor carpenter and died a common criminal's death. The disciples were a band of uneducated, awkward, Galilean fishermen. Yet, because of Jesus and the disciples, the world has never been the same. With a small beginning, Christianity became the official religion of the Roman Empire in AD 380–81.

The Azusa Street revival began in a ramshackle mission hall. Its leader was William J. Seymour, a black holiness preacher who was blind in one eye. The Toronto renewal meetings began with Randy Clark, a little-known pastor of a small St Louis church, together with John Arnott, the pastor of an average-sized church located at the end of a runway in a very humble warehouse facility. God will plant the seeds and yeast of his kingdom. When he finds receptive hearts, those seeds and the yeast of that kingdom grow into something substantial. One sermon, one prayer, one prophecy, one healing, one encounter with God or one idea planted in someone's heart can often have a substantial impact. People feel as if they are small and insignificant and therefore not effective. Well, Betty Reese says, 'If you think you are too small to be effective, you have never been in bed with a mosquito.'

Earnestly desire spiritual gifts

Be zealous for spiritual gifts and prophecy (1 Cor. 12:31; 14:1). Be open to receive, get your emotional and spiritual jug under the tap of the Spirit and fill it up (Eph. 5:18). Be like Elisha, who asked Elijah to grant him a double portion of his spirit (2 Kings 2:9). Be like Jacob, who wrestled with the angel until he received the blessing (Gen. 32:26). Be like the widow, who had nothing, was in debt, and only had a little oil. She responded to Elisha's command to go around and collect empty jars and begin to pour oil into them. For as many jars as she collected, she poured enough oil into them to pay her debts (2 Kings 4). Ask God for 'more'. By faith, expand the capacity of your heart, your vision and your will to receive.

Be zealous in service and faithful in prayer

Be devoted to one another in brotherly love. Honour one another above yourselves. Never be lacking in zeal, but keep your spiritual fervour, serving the Lord. Be joyful in hope, patient in affliction, faithful in prayer. (Rom. 12:10–12)

Finally, to get your sails up for the wind of the Spirit, love others and give away what God has given to you. Bless others. Do not hold it all in for yourself. Do not keep asking for 'more' unless you are prepared to be a channel of blessing who gives it away in service. If you don't give away the blessing, you will become stale. Give out your waters of renewal to refresh others. Build up others in love, using your spiritual gifts. Keep your zeal alive with spiritual fervour as you serve the Lord.

CHAPTER ELEVEN

DIGGING IRRIGATION DITCHES

WHAT COMES DOWN MUST GO IN AND OUT

Asked by a reporter, 'Where is this going?' John Arnott replied, 'This has the potential to rescue the planet!' Many believe the goal is *renewal* unto *revival*. Christians and churches experience renewal *so that* they will be empowered to take the gospel of the Kingdom to the world *unto* revival.[1]

The renewal comes down from God to go *in to* the church for refreshing. Then it is going *out of* the church for revival. I believe that 'What comes down must go in and out.' Let us catch the fire but also spread the fire. Let us receive the River but also release the River. Let us be conduits, not just containers. Let us pray a 'down and out' prayer: 'Your Kingdom come' (down); 'your will be done on earth as it is in heaven' (out). Evangelism is becoming a prominent 'outing'. The renewal has now sparked British prisons with 'cell-group' evangelism. This is what *National and International Religion Report* had to say:

Inmates at Lewes Prison call chaplain David Powe "Sky Pilot" because he directs them to heaven ... An Anglican vicar, Powe became chaplain of the 500 inmates at the East Sussex, England, prison 15 months ago. Since that time, 315 have become Christians ...

Lewes is similar to a county jail and prisoners do not stay long before being released or transferred to long-term prisons. One reason God is using Lewes is because transferred inmates 'take their new faith with them' to other prisons.

Outsiders are also coming in. The Brownsville Assembly of God Church in Pensacola, Florida started renewal services on Father's Day, 18 June 1995 and has continued them five nights a week. Texas evangelist Stephen Hill, who planned to preach only once, extended his stay when spontaneous revival broke out. By May 1996, half a million people had visited the very conservative, traditional church located in the worst neighbourhood of town. By then, some 18 thousand people had come to Christ. In any given meeting, as many as one hundred will re-dedicate their lives to or come to Christ. Many came directly from local bars to attend the services, which usually lasted until 2 a.m. The church is near pawn shops and used-car lots. Several nightclub actors, performers and musicians reportedly have come to Christ and testify that they have quit performing at the bars. Prostitutes and drunkards stand next to men in three-piece suits at the services. One woman said, 'It's the very poor next to the very well off, all looking for prayer together.' Their motto is 'stay hungry, humble, and holy, and trust God for the rest.' [2]

As the current renewal progresses, it appears to be moving out in three phases:

1) *Renewal.* This is the phase of *wind*. The Holy Spirit is blowing across the land. When storms come, the wind is usually the first expression. This is a season of

refreshment. People are getting 'blown' away by the wind of the Spirit.

2) *Repentance*. This is the phase of *fire*. As storms progress, fire (lightning) begins to burn. God is purging sin in the church. Many who have been in the wind for a time are beginning to experience a 'holy gripping' beyond renewal into confession, intercession and the fear of God. When we ask for the fire, let's remember that we are not only asking for power but also for purity.

3) *Revival*. This is the phase of *rain*. As the storm arrives, the rain comes while the wind and fire also continue. A church renewed and repentant becomes a strong force in the hands of God. Many prophetic people and church leaders around the world are predicting revival. Already, it is occurring in many parts of the world. Even business consultant John Naisbitt predicts a religious revival in America as we near the year 2000.[3] On 19 February 1996, Christian researcher George Barna predicted that America is headed for anarchy or revival in five to ten years.[4] I believe that both will happen!

TOWARDS A THEOLOGY OF REVIVAL

The current renewal is not man-made, nor emotionalism, nor mass hysteria, nor fanaticism, nor is it a 'laughing re-vival'. It is not a 'new' thing in terms of God giving new revelation about an end-times prophecy movement and super-church. It is not the Latter-Rain Movement or Pentecostalism resurrected, and it is not a great deception. It is a visitation of God. Its process is renewal. Its goal is revival. J. I. Packer describes revival as:

God comes down:

'He makes known his inescapable presence as the Holy One, mighty and majestic, confronting his own people both to humble and exalt, and to reaching out into a wider world in mercy and in judgment.'

God's Word comes home:

'The Bible, its message, and its Christ reestablish the formative and corrective control over faith and life ... The divine authority and power of the Bible are felt afresh ... '

God's purity comes through:

'As God uses his Word to quicken consciences, the perverseness, ugliness, uncleanness, and guilt of sin are seen and felt with new clarity, and the depth of one's own sinfulness is realized as never before.'

God's people come alive:

'Repentance and restitution, faith, hope, and love, joy and peace, praise and prayer, conscious communion with Christ, confident certainty of salvation, uninhibited boldness of testimony, a readiness to share, and a spontaneous reaching out to all in need become their characteristic marks.'

Outsiders come in:

'drawn by the moral and spiritual magnetism of what goes on in the church'.[5]

How does revival happen? Is Charles Finney right when he says that 'a revival of true Christianity is not a miracle but the right exercise of the power of nature ... the right use of God-given means'?[6] Or is it as Jonathan Edwards understands, a miracle, an 'extraordinary' or 'surprising' work of God where he by sovereign choice initiates a revival of religion?[7] It depends on your perspective – human or divine? I asked Mike Bickle what he believed about how revivals occur. I agree with him. He stated that after reading much material on revival – including Finney and Edwards[8] – he concluded the following:

God initiates. By the Holy Spirit, God stirs up conviction, penetrates people's hard hearts, incites an awareness of holiness, and promotes joy, devotion and prayer. God initiates revival.

People respond. God initiates conviction, repentance, prayer, and gifts of the Holy Spirit, which lead to renewal and revival. People then respond to his initiative.

God responds to people's response. As God initiates, he seeks a response. People respond by praying, preaching and prophesying revival. God then responds to their response by pouring out his Spirit with renewal and then revival.

DIGGING IRRIGATION DITCHES

We must also dig irrigation ditches in which the waters of renewal can flow. As he was arriving for a Canadian national pastors' conference in August 1994, John Wimber received the following open vision:

God showed me a mountain lake. [A gentle rain was falling into the lake.] The water spilled over a dam and cascaded into a river that came down into a large plain where there were thousands of acres of vineyards. I saw men working in the fields, *digging irrigation ditches*. I said, 'Lord, what does it mean?' In my mind, he gave me 'The lake is the blessing I'm pouring out ... The cascading stream is the church. I'm pouring it first into the church.' I recognized these irrigation ditches as 'Ministry to the poor, ministry to the weak, sick, broken, and lost.' There were different kinds of vineyards with different kinds of fruit growing on the vines. Then he said 'This blessing can either stay in the church, with great meetings that eventually end or we can pull the gates up and let the water begin flowing. If you want, you can direct the water, the blessing, into the fields.' I got the clear impression of co-labouring. God was pouring out his blessing. But *if we don't dig the channels*, if we don't go out into the highways and byways, if we don't put evangelism forward, revival won't spread.[9]

As the water comes down from God and in the church for renewal, where should the church direct it? Which vineyards need irrigation ditches for this water? Let me mention ten of them.

1. *Ministry to the needy and oppressed*

Every major revival and revivalist of the past helped the needy and oppressed. John Wesley and George Whitefield preached to the poor, prisoners, coal miners and children. George Fox and the Quakers, and William Wilberforce and the Clapham Sect, opposed the slave trade. George Müller 'fathered' thousands of orphans in Bristol. Revival brings freedom to the needy and oppressed. But today's church is often busy with internal strife, materialism, and legalism. The modern church can be important and big in the religious business while never reaching God's clientele – those that are poor and sick.

Jesus is our model. He announced: 'The Spirit of the Lord is on me, because he has anointed me to preach good news to the poor. He has sent me to proclaim freedom for the prisoners and recovery of sight for the blind, to release the oppressed, to proclaim the year of the Lord's favour' (Luke 4:18–19). Today many oppressed people are not only those who have no money but also those who have no husbands or fathers – the widows, orphans and single mothers. Our schools are full of children who come from single-parent families. What will the church do? A passage which captures the Lord's heart in this area is Isaiah 58:6–11:

Is not this the kind of fasting I have chosen: to loose the chains of injustice and untie the cords of the yoke, to set the oppressed free and break every yoke? Is it not to share your food with the hungry and to provide the poor wanderer with shelter – when you see the naked, to clothe him, and not to turn away from your own flesh and blood? Then your light will break forth like the dawn, and your healing will quickly appear; then your righteousness will go before you, and the glory of the LORD will be your rear guard. Then you will call, and the LORD will answer; you will cry for help, and he will say: Here am I. If you do away with the yoke of oppression, with the pointing finger and malicious talk, and if you spend yourselves in behalf of the hungry and satisfy the needs of the oppressed, then your light will rise in the darkness, and your night will become like the noonday. The LORD will guide you always; he will satisfy your needs in a sun-scorched land and will strengthen your frame. You will be like a well-watered garden, like a spring whose waters never fail.

We must dig irrigation ditches to help the River flow in ministry to the needy and oppressed.

2. *Ministry to children and youth*

God is touching children and youth. Children and youth who have never prophesied before are now doing so. John Paul Jackson tells of an occasion when he was speaking that during the ministry time a four-year-old Downs Syndrome boy came up to the platform. John Paul felt led to pick him up. The boy began to point out people on whom the Holy Spirit was moving. Those people began to fall, cry, and shake as he called for 'more power, more power'.

The renewal mixed with repentance has begun to affect the students at dozens of major campuses in the USA. On 22 January 1995, two students from Howard Payne University stood up and confessed their sins at Coggin Avenue Baptist Church in Brownwood, Texas. Others began to do likewise. Four days later, a similar event occurred on the campus of Howard Payne. Students received invitations from other campuses and students from those campuses invited others, and so on. At Wheaton College, during a meeting in March, five large garbage bags filled with bottles of alcohol, tobacco, drugs, pornography and secular music were collected. Young people were coming forward to receive Christ and many young people from area churches also attended. By April 1995 thousands of students and some faculty participated in confession, restitution and reconciliation in colleges such as Asbury

College in Wilmore, Kentucky, Northwestern College in Minneapolis, Minnesota, and Taylor University in Upland, Indiana.

God is going on-campus. Children and youth are getting more than an education! At the Atlanta '96 Youth Conference in February 1996, 7,000 youth workers from 100 denominations gathered around the theme of awakening, renewal and cooperation. Their common goal is to reach every kid, every campus, every community. They have set up a database of 56,000 schools with students in the sixth grade and higher.[10] Young people who are told to 'get a life' are getting God! This generation are the next generation of leaders in the church and society. Let's challenge them to be world-changers who will, as William Carey said, 'Expect great things from God [and] attempt great things for God.'

We must dig irrigation ditches to help the River flow in ministry to children and youth.

3. Ministry to men

Across North America a revival of manhood thunders ahead like an avalanche. Recent men's ministries such as *Promise Keepers* are front-runners. Founded in 1991 by Bill McCartney, former football coach of the University of Colorado Buffaloes, it is taking the USA by storm. The first conference attracted 4,200 men. By 1995, 720,000 men packed thirteen stadiums at *Promise Keepers* national conferences. In 1997, another conference is planned for Washington DC with the goal of gathering a million men. In February 1996, nearly 40,000 pastors gathered in Atlanta under the theme of 'breaking down the walls'. God is calling men back to be leaders in their homes, churches and communities.

A new magazine called *New Man*, published by Strang Communications, premiered on 20 January 1994 (the same day the Toronto Airport Vineyard began its meetings with Randy Clark). With a circulation of over 200,000, it outsells the popular *Charisma* magazine, also published by Strang Communications. *New Man* gives current understanding of what is happening in ministry to men.[11] Our churches must empower men through retreats, training and prayer. Our church sponsors two men's retreats per year, where they come to hear talks by each other and build bonds with other men. We average 50 men per retreat. Many start E-teams (encouragement teams), where they meet regularly with four to six other men for relationship and accountability. Many say that these retreats are some of the most significant times in their lives.

We must dig irrigation ditches to help the River flow in ministry to men.

4. *Evangelism*

Even though a flood of evangelism is filling the earth, most churches are not doing *proactive* evangelism. For example, at an evangelism convention of 250 Fellowship Baptist pastors in British Columbia in November 1995, handouts highlighted a study by Reginald Bibby, a Christian sociologist in Canada. His study 'shows that 80 percent of churches claim to be involved in evangelism but only 10 percent of church growth can be attributed to this activity. Bibby concludes that "most people aren't looking for churches to attend, and most churches aren't looking for people."'[12]

However, a lot is happening. The popular *Alpha Course*, developed by Nicky Gumbel at Holy Trinity Brompton, is spreading like wildfire. Thousands of churches are using it as part of an evangelistic strategy that includes a dinner and home-group study for the unchurched. God is also using evangelistic drama such as *Heaven's Gates and Hell's Flames*. For example, in early 1995 the Calvary Temple Worship Center in Modesto, California hosted the drama, which ran for six weeks and performed 28 times in their 3,000-seat church. Get this: 33,000 people made first-time decisions for Christ! Then, in late 1995, First Assembly of God in Bakersfield, California hosted the play, where over 10,000 people made decisions for Christ – including a TV cameraman who was covering the play. Also, there are over 2,000 global plans to evangelize the world by the year 2000. As of 1990, two-thirds of these plans were making active progress.[13] Something *big* is about to happen.

Every major revival of the past produced new converts and new churches. The New England Great Awakening (1734–43) added between 25,000 and 50,000 (in a popu-lation of about 340,000) to the churches, and 150 new Congregational churches were formed.[14]

We must dig irrigation ditches to help the River flow in evangelism.

5. Missions

Every major revival of the past either directly influenced or produced the most prominent missions expansions ever. Dating from the early 1700s, some of the first Protestant missionaries were the Moravians – a group of Lutheran Pietists led by Count Nicholas von Zinzendorf. Their offi-cial birth occurred in a communion service on 13 August 1727.[15] The Moravians were bathed in prayer. Earle E. Cairns writes: 'All day prayer began on 12 August, 1729, with twenty-four men and twenty-four women praying each hour of the day. This prayer ministry, coupled with

Zinzendorf's zeal to spread the gospel, led to missionary work in which the Moravians are credited with one missionary for every sixty members.'[16] That prayer structure lasted for a century! Their missions outreach extended all around the world. Their influence was a factor in the Evangelical Revival in Britain in the 1700s (in which Whitefield and Wesley were outstanding) and in the conversion of John Wesley.

Between the middle 1700s and 1914, many missionaries and missionary societies flourished, such as David Brainerd, William Carey, Adoniram Judson, David Livingstone, J. Hudson Taylor, Robert Morrison, Samuel J. Mills, the Scottish Society for the Propagation of the Gospel, the Baptist Missionary Society, the ReligiousTract Society, the Wesleyan Methodist Missionary Society, and the American Board of Commissioners for Foreign Missions.

The Lausanne Covenant declares that 'The church is at the very centre of God's cosmic purpose and is his appointed means of spreading the Gospel.' David Livingstone said: 'God had an only Son and He was a missionary and a physician.' The renewed church must gear up for short- and long-term missions around the world – particularly where the fields are ripe.

We must dig irrigation ditches to help the River flow in missions.

6. Social impact

Charles Finney believed that the gospel was meant to do more than save people. It was also meant to salvage society. He aligned himself with Arthur Tappan, a wealthy silk merchant, who believed that well-to-do Christians were obligated to give to the Kingdom of God. Tappan built teams to form a 'Benevolent Empire' of organizations to address the ills of society. By 1834 the annual income of this 'Empire' was today's equivalent of 130 million US dollars – which easily matched the major expenditures of the US federal government. They addressed problems of slavery, temperance, vice, women's rights, prison reform, and education.[17]

Past revivals produced reform leaders and agencies such as William Wilberforce and the Clapham Sect with anti-slave trade laws in England; Hannah Ball with the Sunday School; William and Catherine Booth with the Salvation Army; George Williams with the YMCA; Arthur Broome with the SPCA; Lord Shaftesbury with women and children labour laws and reforms for insane asylums; John Howard with prison reform; and Jerry McAuley with rescue mission work.

We took a survey of our congregation and learned that over 80 of our people serve as volunteers on boards or in community service. In our city a number of Christian leaders have formed a social impact society called the Christian Coalition of British Columbia. Its mission is to inform and mobilize people of faith politically around traditional family values. There is a link between revival and social impact. Richard Lovelace asserts: 'It is a clear lesson of history that there can be no effective social witness without a revived church.'[18]

We must dig irrigation ditches to help the River flow in social impact.

7. Interdenominational unity and prayer

David Ruis wrote the song 'Break Dividing Walls'. In November 1994 he flew to Fort Collins, Colorado to sing that one song at a meeting where 400 city and state leaders were gathered. That was all the Christian hosts wanted! Why? Because unity is a major need in the political and spiritual arenas. John 17, Ephesians 4:1–6 and Phillipians 2:2 clearly show that unity is important. We either hang together or we hang apart. Christians are called to 'make every effort to *keep* the unity of the Spirit through the bond of peace' (Eph. 4:3). Rather than try to *make* unity let us *keep* the unity we have in all the essential areas. As Charles Colson says, 'Unity is a matter of obedience.'[19] Unity has a twin sister: prayer.

According to David Barrett, today there are 160 million Christians worldwide who are daily praying for revival and world evangelization. He also states that there are 1,300 global prayer networks and 10 million prayer groups that have revival on their agenda.[20] Concerts of Prayer International reported that as of January 1995, 180 prayer summits were either confirmed or being considered.[21] The 'prayer summits' are where pastors and laypeople gather for worship, repentance and prayer for their churches, communities and nation.

Jonathan Edwards wrote the tract *An Humble Attempt to Promote Explicit Agreement and Visible Union of God's People in Extraordinary Prayer of the Revival of Religion and the Advancement of God's Kingdom on Earth*. His bottom line was unity and prayer concerts. As David Ruis sings, 'Those walls are comin' down.'

We must dig irrigation ditches to help the River flow in interdenominational unity and prayer.

8. Worship and the creative arts

God is restoring worship and the creative arts back to their rightful places in the church. He is releasing new styles of music, dance, drama, art and worship in the hearts of artists. Worship is also going to the streets in various evangelistic forms. In August 1990 James Ryle, Senior Pastor of Vineyard Christian Fellowship in Boulder, Colorado, had three dreams from the Lord. They spoke of a new kind of song that the Lord was about to release in the streets. According to these dreams, a new and distinctive anointing and sound will be restored to music that will attract people to Jesus Christ. This will happen

> when the church gets beyond the limits that she set for herself, into His grace, and takes the praise that is in the sanctuary and makes it music in the streets ... The time will come when the Lord God will release into the streets an army of worshipping warriors known as 'the Sons of Thunder.' They will bring forth praise into the streets that will birth evangelism and praise and give many children to God.[22]

He goes on to state that there are three groups that will make up the Sons of Thunder: (1) the musicians; (2) the evangelists who are not musicians; and (3) the musicians who are evangelists. The Sons of Thunder are both the musicians and evangelists who work together.[23]

If this is an accurate prophecy from the Lord, it is not unlike the past, where music and worship were at the centre of revival. Charles Wesley was the musical counterpart to John Wesley, the preacher in the English Revival. The 'Singing Sisters' worked with Evan Roberts in the Welsh Revival. Ira Sankey worked with D. L. Moody. Worship is at the heart of renewal conferences today all around the world. Perhaps the movie *Sister Act* portrays a timely message for the church to be culturally relevant in its worship.

We must dig irrigation ditches to help the River flow in worship and the creative arts.

9. Healing and miracles

Jesus commissioned the church to heal people and cast out demons as they preached the gospel of the Kingdom (Luke 9:1–2). Lois Gott of Sunderland Christian Centre in England 'had a wonderful prophetic word about how we are now in an introductory and preparatory phase of the Blessing,' writes John Arnott. 'There is much greater power and anointing yet to come. Her prophecy indicated that we are currently in a time similar to the ministry of John the Baptist, which is preparing the way for a soon-coming time resembling the ministry of Jesus where powerful signs, wonders and miracles will take place.'[24] Paul Cain has prophesied that there is coming a time when TV stations will have little to report except good news. They will show stadiums filled with people worshipping Jesus, where miracles and healings will occur. Instead of sports events there will be healing events.

We must dig irrigation ditches to help the River flow in healing and miracles.

10. The restructuring of Christianity and global revival

Mike Bickle has shared the following message for years. In mid-September 1982, while in a little hotel room in Cairo, he began to pray around 8:30 p.m. God spoke to him with what he calls an 'internal audible voice'. Mike reports that the Lord said, 'I will change the understanding and expression of Christianity in the earth in one generation.' The 'understanding of Christianity' meant the way that unbelievers would view the church. The church would

221

again become relevant and the world would see God's wonderful yet terrifying power in the church. The 'expression of Christianity' meant the way the church expresses its life together. It will be a healthy church with God's love and power present, rather than being meeting- and programme-based.[25] A visiting Chinese pastor once said about the American church, 'I am so surprised at how much the American church can accomplish without God.' But that's changing. Mike believes that 'the understanding and expression of Christianity is going to be changed by a great outpouring of the Spirit that will cross all kinds of national, social, ethnic, and cultural barriers.'[26]

As God restructures the church, the result will be global revival. In his book *The Coming Revival*, Dr Bill Bright of Campus Crusade for Christ tells of a powerful message he received repeatedly from the Holy Spirit during a 40-day fast which began on 5 July 1994. Over a period of time, Bill felt God called him to this fast to pray for a great spiritual awakening in America and the fulfilment of the Great Commission. During this fast he was assured by the Holy Spirit that this would occur. He made the following prediction:

America and much of the world will, before the end of the year 2000, experience a great spiritual awakening. This divine visit of the Holy Spirit from heaven will kindle the greatest spiritual harvest in the history of the Church ... The Holy Spirit gave me this assurance during a forty-day fast. I have spent fifty years studying God's Word and listening to His voice, and His message could not have been more clear.[27]

Billy Graham, the eminent evangelist, also senses something in the works. On 1 July 1994 at the North American Conference for Itinerant Evangelists he declared that 'America is at the centre of a great revival. Seldom has the soil of the human heart and mind been better prepared than today. I've never seen so many come to salvation in such a short time.' He also said, 'I am praying for a new touch of the Holy Spirit.'[28]

We must dig irrigation ditches to help the River flow in new structures of Christianity and global revival. Where is this River going? It is going down from heaven *into* the church for renewal and *out* to the world for revival.

WALKING IN THE AUTHORITY OF BLESSING

> The LORD had said to Abram ... 'I will make you
> into a great nation and I will bless you; I will make
> your name great, and you will be a blessing ... and all
> peoples on earth will be blessed through you.'
> (Gen. 12:1–3)

On the afternoon of 3 April 1995, a major trauma occurred at our home. My wife was babysitting the three
young sons of Tom and Judy Tearoe, who are friends of
ours in our church. I was at home that afternoon gathering
my thoughts for a talk that I was to give that evening. My
wife was preparing an early supper so I could get going.
Judy works several days each month as a nurse at the hospital. As usual for the past few years, the boys are dropped
off for the day by Tom while on his way to work. We loved
and treated their three boys as our own (we also have two
boys). Our youngest son Micah was six and the Tearoes'
oldest son Andrew was to be six that month. They were
best buddies. They would play hard after Micah would
come home from school until Tom would arrive to pick up
Andrew and his two younger brothers on his way home
from work.

We have a four-foot rock retaining wall in our front
yard that overlooks a grass area alongside the street. After

our two boys and Andrew had played several hours they decided to have a contest to see who could jump the farthest off the wall. Our oldest son Joel jumped first and landed on his feet. Andrew then jumped but landed prostrate. Then Micah jumped. Andrew did not get up. Because he lay motionless and started to breathe in an odd way, Joel ran into the house to tell my wife and me. My wife carried a very limp Andrew into the house. He was unconscious and not breathing. Later he appeared to have no pulse. Panic set in. We phoned for an ambulance, while I performed mouth-to-mouth resuscitation on him. We thought that he was just winded and would eventually come through. He did not respond. His face began to turn blue. We knew this was serious. We prayed.

The fire department and paramedics arrived and tried to revive him without success. They rushed him to emergency. The emergency team got Andrew's heart beating, but on his way to the operating room he died. Only 90 minutes earlier he was playing at our home. Now his life was gone. We were stunned and grief-stricken. He had a freak accident. Later we learned that he immediately went unconscious and died of a neck and spinal injury. God could have prevented the accident or could have spared his life. Why didn't he? It didn't seem fair. The loss is almost unbearable. Over 800 people came to the funeral five days later. And now life must go on. But it will never be the same. Not for Andrew's family and not for ours.

I tell you this story because it is a bleak contrast to the excitement of renewal. The irony is that pain, grief and death are still a fact of life, even during an unprecedented outpouring of the Spirit. How can these parents who lost their first-born son be excited about renewal? It goes broader. How can the people who lived through the atrocities of Rwanda or Bosnia get excited about 'holy laughter'? How can people in the Middle East or Northern Ireland who live in a time-bomb of fragile peace put the current renewal into their context? What about the families who lost their loved ones in the Oklahoma City bombing? Or in any given church, there are scores of people who suffer from depression, loneliness, anxiety, fear, insecurity, dysfunction and bondage. Going to another renewal meeting for some of these people is just not where they are at. How can there be devastating circumstances for some people while others revel in the euphoria? The reality is that the blessings of God co-exist with the curses of a fallen world. In life 'under the sun' there is a time appointed for each purpose. The book of Ecclesiastes makes the point:

> There is a time for everything, and a season for every activity under heaven: a time to be born and a time to die, a time to plant and a time to uproot, a time to kill and a time to heal, a time to tear down and a time to build, a time to weep and a time to laugh, a time to mourn and a time to dance. (Eccl. 3:1–4)

I also tell you this story because I learned a profound lesson in the school of God's grace working through people. After I left the chapel with Andrew's father and two friends who had arrived at the hospital, several of our pastoral staff and elders greeted us in the hallway. They said very little. There was nothing they could say. But a very special strength entered my spirit at the very sight of these people. They really didn't do anything. They gave hugs and wept but the most important thing is that *they were there*. Under the weight of trauma, we felt propped up.

This initial strength only lasted a short while though. The reality of the loss began to affect our sleep, our concentration, our ability to cope with work and family and basic living. We felt isolated. Momentary care helps, but ongoing care made a difference. In the weeks to follow, people gave meals, cards, phone calls and prayers.

THE MINISTRY OF BEING THERE

I call this the ministry of 'being there'. I write this near the end because I want to encourage my readers to never forget that as we release the waters of renewal there are still the tragedies and pain that people will have in the midst of this. In our joy, let us never overlook those in pain. Most people in pain need short and regular shots of care, not long sessions of counselling. We are to love one another and bear one another's burdens. A key way is to simply 'be there'. People don't know what to say to a family who have just lost their son. We don't need to say much. To say nothing is worse. To ask 'How are you doing?' when we come across their path is unavoidable. The difference is when *we* are proactive – when *we* initiate.[1]

Does this mean that we pull away from renewal or somehow scorn it because it is difficult to relate to for those who hurt? Do we direct the renewal away from the joy and excitement, to minister to these people so that they don't feel on the outside? I would say definitely not. The renewal is bigger than pain, it is bigger than the individual lives that it touches. Yet renewal ought to motivate us to care even more, especially for those who hurt. We must bless and endorse the overall purposes of God – even when it may for a season be seemingly out of sync with our personal experience. God works at many levels at once. He

227

ministers his comfort and care as a high priest to those in weakness, while at the same time he overwhelms people with his presence. God works the macro and micro pictures all at once. We are called to simultaneously 'know Christ and the power of his resurrection and the fellowship of sharing in his sufferings' (Phil. 3:10). Resurrection and suffering have fellowship. Revival and pain are compatible.

WALK IN THE AUTHORITY OF BLESSING

Our mandate is to walk in the authority of blessing. I believe that in the renewal 'what comes down must go in and out'. This is about receiving and giving away the blessing of God in our daily lives. Just as Abraham was blessed and called to be a blessing, so we, as sons of Abraham, have been blessed and are also called to be a blessing (Gal. 3–4). God releases blessing through those whom he blesses. He has blessed us with every spiritual blessing in Christ (Eph. 1) and 'from the fullness of his grace we have all received one blessing after another' (John 1:16). A blessing is anything that confers well-being to another. In Christ, God gave us spiritual authority, which is the right to exercise his power. We should walk in that authority by blessing others, and that includes simple acts of help and kindness.

Once I was teaching on 'walking in the authority of blessing'. I ministered to a Dutch couple in the front row. As I prayed for them I felt that they had a ministry of encouragement through care and hospitality. They began to weep as many heads nodded with affirmation. I was later told that they use a truck with a kitchen inside. They feed and clothe needy people from that truck. After the meeting, I saw the truck parked outside. Painted on the side were the words, 'House of Blessing'. They were a living illustration. In renewal, our response should not be to just ask for 'more'. Our response should also include looking for ways to be channels of blessing to others as witnesses sent out into the world.

Luke reports that

> on one occasion, while he was eating with them, [Jesus] gave them this command: 'Do not leave Jerusalem, but wait for the gift my Father promised, which you have heard me speak about. For John baptized with water, but in a few days you will be baptized with the Holy Spirit. But you will receive power when the Holy Spirit comes on you; and you will be my witnesses in Jerusalem, and in all Judea and Samaria, and to the ends of the earth.' (Acts 1:4–5, 8)

In Acts 1 and 2, Jesus went up, the Holy Spirit came down, and the church went out:

The Ascension	Pentecost	Mission-witness
Jesus goes up	The Holy Spirit comes down	The church goes out

The purpose of the Spirit who was sent on Pentecost was not for tongues or the founding of the church or revival. His purpose was to *empower* the church to be a *witness* (see Luke 24:45–53; Acts 1:8; 4:29–33). Notice in Acts 1:8 that after the church came *upon* them – not *in* them – the disciples would *be* witnesses. They were not called to 'go witnessing'. This is a state. They were called to *be* a church that testifies for Jesus, not called to *go* to church for Jesus. We are not called to go to church so as to be out of the world. We are called to be the church in the world. As Chuck Colson writes, 'What we do, therefore, flows from who we are.'[2]

As I stated earlier, the Dead Sea is dead even though fresh Jordan waters flow into it. It has no outlets. It has become a reservoir of fresh water gone stale. The same applies to the church. If we become only reservoirs of God's River and don't channel it outward, we will become stale and dead. Let us be channels rather than containers of God's blessing. Abraham is God's pattern for us. God said to him, 'I will bless you and you will be a blessing' (Gen. 12:2).

SOCIAL JUSTICE

Walking in the authority of blessing includes social justice and mercy and missions. What does social justice and the Kingdom of God mean to you? Justice in the courtroom? The battle over abortion or homosexual rights? Militant protests, lobbying or the Moral Majority? Or is social justice and the Kingdom of God simply helping the poor and praying for the sick?

Some Christians think the church should not get involved in political, moral and social issues, that its mission is only spiritual. Yet, what is the spiritual dimension of giving 'a cup of water in my name because you belong to Christ … '? (Mark 9:41). Kingdom ministry releases the rule and righteousness of God on earth in all areas of life as it is in heaven (Matt. 6:10, 33). Kingdom justice is political, moral, social and spiritual. For example: 'Endow the king with your justice, O God, the royal son with your righteousness' (Ps. 72:1); 'Defend the cause of the weak and fatherless; maintain the rights of the poor and oppressed. Rescue the weak and needy; deliver them from the hand of the wicked' (Ps. 82:3–4); 'He has shown you, O man, what is good. And what does the LORD require of you? To act justly and to love mercy and to walk humbly with your God' (Mic. 6:8).

Rights for the individual are central to justice. Love – with a desire for the well-being of people – is the issue, while justice is the instrument. Stephen Mott states that 'One needs justice in addition to love to carry on what love starts but cannot finish alone. Love is the greater factor, but justice is a necessary instrument of love.'[3] Love for God and neighbour fulfils the Law and the Prophets (Matt. 22:37–40). Love is the flame that ignites the tinder of social justice. We must address poverty, oppression and racism. Our communities include many people living on welfare and on the streets. Our prisons are packed with young rebels from abusive homes. Our schools are full of children from single-parent families. Our communities have racial tension between whites, blacks, Asians, Hispanics and Native Indians. What will the renewed church do?

The early church impacted their world with social justice.[4] By AD 313 the church had so infiltrated the Roman Empire that Constantine granted toleration for Christianity. In AD 380–81 Theodosius I issued edicts that made Christianity the official State religion. The vision for this is *what comes down must go in and out by walking in the authority of blessing* – to take what God blessed us with to bless others. The church is a 'counter-community' which is in the world but not of the world. It must influence and impact culture, not separate from it. We are the light of the world to shine with good deeds (Matt. 5:14–16).

Light is a penetrating force which overcomes darkness and establishes justice (Isa. 9:2–7; 42:1–7). Good deeds serve as light. Luke says 'In Joppa there was a disciple named Tabitha ... who was always *doing good and helping the poor*' (Acts 9:36). Jesus was anointed 'with the Holy Spirit and power, and how he went *around doing good and healing all who were under the power of the devil* ... ' (Acts 10:38). After we 'take another drink' of the Holy Spirit, let us do good, help the poor, pray for the sick, and help our neighbours in need – whatever that need might be.

MERCY, MINISTRY AND MISSIONS

On the west bank of the River of God is the renewal of our churches – power, passion and praise. On the east bank of the River of God is the revival of our communities – salvation, signs and wonders, and social change. The bridge from renewal to revival is God's heart for mercy, ministry and missions. What is the effect of renewal in people's lives? Let the following accounts from people in our church help tell the story of how to build the bridge.

Frank and Kathy Pullen

The first example is one of our deacon couples, who, as a result of renewal, came into an empowered awareness that simple acts of kindness, service and prayer are significant in God's kingdom.

Frank and Kathy's pilgrimage began in a fundamental-ist denomination which taught cessationism. They moved from another city and began to attend what was then called New Life Fellowship Baptist Church (now New Life Vineyard Fellowship) in Kelowna. During those formative years, they grew because of solid Bible teaching and an em-phasis on acts of service – that is, until renewal came to New Life Vineyard. They then saw things which didn't fit into their worldview. Their old teaching was shaken after they saw credible people whom they knew move in super-natural gifts. Some of these people also manifested. God used that to guide their hearts in a search for the truth. They began to see that he was bigger than their teaching and experience.

Frank is a task-oriented engineer who is comfortable with 'order' and logic, and he had little faith when it came to praying for people and getting excited about renewal. God confirmed in Frank's heart that the renewal was from him, but Frank still had no desire to be any more than a spectator. Nevertheless, the box in which he had put God was getting bigger, as he saw God speak directly into peo-ple's lives through prophecy. One night, at a prayer meet-ing, someone gave Frank a long prophetic word in a tongue, followed by an interpretation. Two mornings later, as he lay in bed praying, his arm began to shake. During the next month, every time he prayed, he also shook. God was reminding him how important his prayers were, and this encouraged him to pray for people more often. At Frank's request, leaders in the church prayed that God would give him gifts of prophecy and healing. He began to learn to hear God's voice. He was getting excited about his faith!

Frank is now on the prayer team, often praying for people after the church service. He has also led a small group for many years in his home, where he and Kathy have pastored many needy people. Also, Frank has been faithful in sharing his money and resources to help others. Because of renewal, Frank has also dedicated his work to God, and as a result he has gained the favour of his fellow employees. He now goes to work praying for his supervisor, and he also seizes opportunities to naturally share his faith. He also loves his children more and has a desire to spend time with them.

Kathy is a high achiever who is always busy helping people. She began to see how spiritual gifts edified the church. However, the key which freed her to embrace renewal as being of God was an experience of 'the fear of the Lord' during our repentance weekend in early 1988. Following that weekend, God took her 'black-and-white faith' and gave her 'colour vision' instead. He added a new depth of intimacy and clarity to her relationship with him. There were still many hurdles for her to cross before she could fully embrace renewal, but now she gained confidence that God would instruct her. In prayer she received a new understanding of Jesus' parable of the wineskins in Matthew 9:16–17. God revealed to her that she could not pour the 'new wine' of renewal into the 'old wineskin' of conservatism. Kathy prayed for the Holy Spirit to give her a new wineskin in her heart which would be open to his teaching.

Renewal also provoked in Kathy a desire for personal holiness and a strong urgency to train up her children in God's ways. She also became compelled to reach out to those around her in simple acts of kindness and service. She organized 'Mothers Who Care', a group of mothers who meet regularly to pray for the local public school and to do 'good works' for the teachers. Renewal has refreshed her prayer life with a boldness in God's sovereignty to enter into areas which she would not have entered before.

Kathy started a weekly ladies' Bible study in her home, where mothers and their children could come for lunch. The children play while the mothers have their study and pray for each other. Because of her renewed spirit, it was a joy for her to serve others, not a burden. The parable of the talents in Matthew 25:14–30 challenged Kathy's attitude. God convicted her by the example of the servant who had received one talent and buried it because of fear. Although she has seen a lot, Kathy has never experienced the outward manifestations associated with renewal. However, she has experienced an inner transformation which has changed her life for ever.

Because of renewal, Frank and Kathy have gone to great lengths to help 'the poor in spirit', to practise hospitality as a lifestyle, to give generously to those in need, to pray for and pastor the dozens of people in their circle of influence, and to serve whenever needed. They and their four children also came with me and a team from our church to Russia on a ministry trip. In their home or in the world, they are an example of bridge-building from renewal to revival through simple acts of mercy, ministry and missions.

John and Sandra DeVries

The next example is a middle-aged couple with a Christian Reformed and Presbyterian church background, who, as a result of being challenged by renewal, made radical lifestyle changes and dedicated their home and business life to mercy, ministry and missions.

John and Sandra worked for 14 years with young adults, and were involved in evangelism and eldership.

They realized that their service for God was for their own self-gratification and out of duty. They resigned and moved to another city to start a business. The business prospered but their marriage began to deteriorate. In some Pentecostal employees, they saw a vibrancy for the Lord that they wanted. They moved to Kelowna in 1984 to get a new start. They yearned for renewal. In 1987–88 they came to New Life. Their hearts were stirred for the first time as they experienced praising God.

This was during the first visitation of God to our church. Sandra attended the intercessory meetings, where the Spirit fell upon her. She started to shake at the church and at home. This upset John. For answers he quizzed Wes Campbell and listened to John Wimber tapes. After the entire family had attended a Bill Gothard Seminar, John's outlook on his business, his Christian faith and his family life was changed. He terminated his unequal partnerships and dedicated his business and finances to God. The Lord also placed in him and Sandra a vision to help the needy. Later, John and Sandra went to a Spiritual Warfare Conference in Anaheim. It was here that John experienced a surge of God's power that lasted two weeks. He resolved to do whatever God wanted him to do.

During the height of Operation Rescue (a pro-life movement), John founded the Kelowna Right to Life organization, along with others. God also opened John and Sandra's hearts to take in single mothers and those from broken marriages. Later, their children began to invite their hurting friends in to live with them as well. This spawned a vision. Using his own money – and government money later – John founded the Society of Hope, a non-profit organization which builds and acquires housing for single parents. But this was not enough. Because God prospered him in his business and challenged him to share – not own or keep – everything he had, he committed himself to give at least 30% of his income to the Lord's work. Not only that, but John, with others, founded Hope for the Nations – a non-profit organization with a vision to establish orphanages, to disciple underprivileged children through education and support, and to develop local businesses that will support the orphanages. So far, they have targetted Nepal, Indonesia, Bhutan, Mexico and Russia.

Renewal changed John and Sandra's lifestyle dramatically. They take in all sorts of people and disciple them, they have led care-groups, they open their home to host numerous gatherings and meetings, and they help in financial and administrative areas of the church. John even hires people to pray that his businesses will prosper, so that he can give more to the Lord's work. Another example of bridge-building in mercy, ministry and missions.

This final example is a Canadian First Nations (i.e. Native Indian) couple who were saved during the renewal and came to realize that they were significant in the body of Christ. They also received a burden to reach their native peoples through their home and in missions outreaches.

Clyde and Marilyn Jack

Clyde and Marilyn have a deep burden for their people and have always taken in the homeless and foster children. In 1989, during a home-group meeting in Saanich, BC, the Holy Spirit fell on the Christians gathered there during a time of worship and prayer. Shaking, prophecy, tongues and singing in the Spirit sovereignly came upon the group. That was the beginning of renewal for the Jacks. However, a pastor from Victoria, BC came in and shut everything down because he declared it demonic. The Jacks became disillusioned.

After they moved to Kelowna and joined our church five years ago they experienced re-renewal. They came into a deeper understanding of how they fit into the body of Christ and our local church. They used to feel inferior and out of place as Native Indians in a predominantly white (though multinational) church. During our church's 21 days of prayer, fasting and nightly renewal meetings in June 1994, the Spirit revisited the Jacks. Shaking, prophecy and intercession seized Marilyn. Clyde did not experience physical phenomena but did experience a heart change.

As they sang David Ruis' song 'Break Dividing Walls', they began to work towards this in their relationships with people. Soon God placed a vision in their hearts to work with our Manna Room (a ministry to street people and those needing food, etc.), and they began to distribute food and to minister to families in their native housing complex. They started a home cell-group and developed a ministry with a vision to be 'bridge builders who will bring non-native and native people together'. They have taken teams to various reserves and are planning other out-reaches with their home cell-group.

On 20 July 1995, Clyde and Marilyn were on their way with a team to minister to their native people in their home area of Saanich Peninsula on Vancouver Island, BC. While driving on the highway they pulled into an area that over-looked Saanich. They prayed, and then the team waited in the van for Marilyn. While she continued to pray with her eyes closed, she heard the audible voice of God. She said it sounded like 'the voice of many waters and a rushing wind', but more, as your mind and body can't contain it.

238

God was calling his native people. This is what the Lord said:

> I revealed myself to those who did not ask for me; I was found by those who did not seek me. To a nation that did not call on my name, I said, 'Here am I, here am I.' All day long I have held out my hands to an obstinate people, who walk in ways not good, pursuing their own imaginations [a direct citation of Isa. 65:1–2]. Come, Rise up Oh Saanich nation for I have a place for you. You have a place at my throne that I have called you to. You are my people. I have a place for you in the battle. And you will bow. And now is the time you must rise up and come. Even though you do not seek me you will come. I created you as warriors.

As I sat in the Jack's living-room tape-recording this interview, Marilyn recounted the above story, and then under the power of God, she re-gave this prophecy. What he audibly gave to her in July she prophetically gave to me in October, and also to our church at a Sunday service. Clyde and Marilyn are committed to reaching the native peoples of Canada and to inviting people from different nations into their home. Clyde and Marilyn embody mercy, ministry and missions as they walk in the authority of blessing. They call their home 'The House of Nations'.

CONCLUDING THOUGHTS

I've led you through a broad field of biblical, theological, historical and practical detail. It may be used as a reference work again and again. My purpose has been to write a ministry manual that will help readers to perceive, welcome and release the River of God in their churches in fruitful ways. This is difficult for many. People have unresolved and legitimate questions about Scripture and experience, cessationism, the manifestations, prophecy, and practical issues related to fun, fanaticism and fruit. We must be experiencing *and* thinking Christians. Jonathan Edwards asks, 'For who will deny that true religion consists, in great measure, in vigorous and lively actings of the inclination and will of the soul, or the fervent exercises of the heart?'

As renewal empowers our minds and hearts to engage in true religious affections, we must look beyond the River with a vision for directing the water to the irrigation ditches of a thirsty world. As the church catches the wind and waves of the Spirit, it must then walk in the authority of blessing by releasing the waters of renewal in practical acts of kindness and service through social justice, mercy, ministry and missions.

Mercy, ministry and missions are ways to build bridges from renewal to revival. Walking in the authority of blessing puts it all into perspective. I think John Wesley knew what this meant when he exhorted, 'do all the good you can, and in all the ways you can, and in all the places you can, and at all the times you can, to all the people you can, as long as you ever can.'

The River is here. Let it flow!

NOTES

INTRODUCTION: THE RIVER IS HERE

1. John B. Taylor, *Ezekiel: An Introduction & Commentary*, Tyndale Old Testament Commentaries, Vol. 20, IVP, 1969, p. 252, citing E. W. Hengstenberg, *Commentary on Ezekiel*, English trans., 1869.
2. Ibid., p. 253.
3. I don't believe, as Mark Stibbe does (see his *Times of Refreshing*, Marshall Pickering, 1995), that today's renewal is a precursor to the fourth wave of the Spirit in this century, as illuminated by Ezekiel 47:1–12. He writes that the ankle-deep water of verse 3 was wave one, Pentecostalism; the knee-deep water of verse 4a was wave two, the Charismatic Movement; the waist-deep water of verse 4b was wave three, the Protestant Evangelical Renewal; and the river that no one could cross in verse 5 will be wave four, the Global Revival. A principle of biblical interpretation is to ask, 'Could the author *intend* this meaning?' I deal with biblical interpretation in the next chapter. While Dr Stibbe's view is interesting, I believe that it can only serve as an illustration of the renewals of this century, not as an interpretation of them.
4. Eugene H. Peterson, *Reversed Thunder*, HarperCollins, 1988, p. 172.
5. As reported in the brochure, *Welcome to Our 3rd Year of Renewal* and in verbal announcements during the second anniversary meetings at the Toronto Airport Church.
6. Reported in Revival Christian Church, *Hong Kong and China Ministry Report*, Aug. 1995, pp. 4–5.
7. Internet address: http://www.grmi.org/missions/fsu.

1: FORGETTING THE FORMER THINGS

1. *Meditations of a Parish Priest* as cited in John Bramblett, *When Good-Bye is Forever*, Ballantine Books, 1991, p. 140.
2. Guy Chevreau helped to shape my thinking on this subject at a pastors' teaching session at the Toronto Airport Church in January 1996.
3. John Kilpatrick, *Feast of Fire*, self-published, 1995, p. vii.
4. Recounted by Larry Randolph while giving a message entitled 'Why God is Moving Powerfully in the 90s' at New Life Vineyard Fellowship, Kelowna, BC, Canada, Jun. 1994. I also confirmed this in a telephone conversation with Larry.
5. Adapted from Guy Chevreau, *Catch the Fire*, HarperCollins, 1994, pp. 28–33, and Marc Dupont, *Mantle of Praise Ministries*, photocopy.
6. James A. Beverley, *Holy Laughter and the Toronto Blessing*, Zondervan, 1995, chap. 9.

2: SCRIPTURE AND EXPERIENCE

1. See 'Church Growth' and 'Statistics, Global' in Stanley M. Burgess and Gary B. McGee (eds), *Dictionary of Pentecostal and Charismatic Movements*, Zondervan, 1988, pp. 186–7, 812–13.
2. He writes about this in his book *Spiritual Power and Church Growth*, Creation House, 1986.
3. For a more detailed treatment see Charles Kraft, *Christianity with Power*, Servant, 1989; Paul Hiebert, 'The Flaw of the Excluded Middle', *Missiology*, Vol. 10, 1982, pp. 35–47; Colin Brown, 'Enlightenment', in Walter Elwell (ed.), *The Evangelical Dictionary of Theology*, Baker Book House, 1984, pp. 355–6; John Wimber, *Power Evangelism*, HarperCollins, 1992, chaps 18–22.
4. Ray Anderson, *Ministry on the Fireline: A Practical Theology for an Empowered Church*, IVP, 1993, p. 27.
5. Ibid., p. 29.
6. We shall deal with the issue of experience a bit more in chapter 7.
7. Anderson, op. cit., p. 101.

8. For a fuller discussion see Guy Chevreau, *Catch The Fire*, HarperCollins, 1994, pp. 62–9. Italics his.

9. Ibid., pp. 67–8.

10. As pointed out by Guy Chevreau in *Pray With Fire*, HarperCollins, 1995, p. 78, in citing Gordon Fee, *God's Empowering Presence: The Holy Spirit in the Letters of Paul*, Hendrickson Publishers, 1994, p. xxi, and N. T. Wright, *The Interpretation of the New Testament 1861–1986*, Oxford University Press, 1988, p. 203.

11. *Paraclete*, Winter 1992.

12. Ibid., p. 17.

13. Gordon Fee offers understanding and good ideas for these issues in *Gospel and Spirit*, Hendrickson Publishers, 1991, and *How to Read the Bible for All Its Worth*, 2nd edn, Zondervan, 1981, 1993.

14. See Gordon Fee, *Gospel and Spirit*, Hendrickson Publishers, 1991, pp. 89–94. I have adapted his major points in the following discussion.

15. See Eugene Peterson, *Working the Angles*, William B. Eerdmans, 1987, pp. 107–45.

3: SURPRISED BY THE GIFTS OF THE SPIRIT

1. Jack Deere, *Surprised by the Power of the Spirit*, Zondervan, 1993, pp. 54–5.

2. Ibid., p. 99.

3. Victor Furnish, *II Corinthians*, The Anchor Bible, Doubleday & Co., 1984, p. 553.

4. Deere, op. cit., p. 112.

5. Gordon Fee, *The First Epistle to the Corinthians*, The New International Commentary on the New Testament, Eerdmans, 1987, p. 645–7.

6. Ibid., p. 643–4, n. 17.

7. For a historical survey of cessationist opposition, see William DeArteaga, *Quenching the Spirit: Examining Centuries of Opposition to the Moving of the Holy Spirit*, Creation House, 1992.

8. See C. Peter Wagner, 'Church Growth', in Stanley M. Burgess

and Gary B. McGee (eds), *Dictionary of Pentecostal and Charismatic Movements*, Zondervan, 1988, p. 184.

9. *City of God*, 22.8.

10. John MacArthur, *Charismatic Chaos*, Zondervan, 1992.

11. For a more detailed refutation of his book, see Rich Nathan, *A Response to Charismatic Chaos*, Apr. 1993, Association of Vineyard Churches, PO Box 17580, Anaheim, Ca. 92817–7580, or Roger Helland, *A Review of Charismatic Chaos*, self-published, 2041 Harvey Avenue, Kelowna, BC, Canada, V1Y 6G7.

12. Consult John Wimber, *Power Evangelism*, HarperCollins, revised edn, 1985, 1992, Appendices A and B, pp. 215–44.

13. Deere, op. cit., pp. 55–6.

4: THE MANIFESTATIONS AND PHENOMENA

1. This story is from the Airport Vineyard's *Spread the Fire*, Aug. 1995, Vol. 1, Issue 4, p. 16.

2. The following list is a compilation of what Wes Campbell and I put together in an early draft of *Welcoming a Visitation of God*, an unpublished manual.

3. *The 'Toronto' Blessing*, Kingsway Publications, 1994, p. 138.

4. For a full treatment of medical perspectives on manifestations and the idea of altered states of consciousness, see Dr Patrick Dixson, *Signs of Revival*, Kingsway Publications, 1994, chap. 5.

5. In his *Holy Laughter & the Toronto Blessing*, Zondervan, 1995, pp. 95–6.

6. John White, *When the Spirit Comes With Power*, IVP, 1988, pp. 116–19.

7. Ibid., pp. 82–3.

8. As reported by Daina Doucet, 'David Mainse: A Channel for God', in *Spread the Fire*, May/Jun. 1995, Vol. 1, Issue 3, p. 6.

9. Margaret Poloma, *By Their Fruits: A Sociological Assessment of the 'Toronto Blessing'*, distributed at the Toronto Airport Christian Fellowship, 19 Jan. 1996.

10. Gordon Fee, *God's Empowering Presence*, Hendrickson

Publishers, 1994, p. 448, n. 280.

11. William F. Fry, 'Using Humor to Save lives', abstracted from an address given at the Convention of the American Orthopsychiatric Association, Washington DC, Apr. 1979. Also for a fuller treatment on medical perspectives on laughter see 'Medical Perspectives on Humor: An Interview with Dr. William Fry' in *Humor and Health Letter*, Jan./Feb. 1993, and Dr Patrick Dixson, *Signs of Revival*, Kingsway, 1994, pp. 233–41.

12. George Lavington, *The Enthusiasm of Methodists and Papists Compared*, 2nd edn, London, printed for J. and P. Knapton in Ludgate Street, 1749, Vol. 2, pp. 71–3, as cited by Richard M. Riss on the Internet, 'New Wine News', #2 from *Catch the Fire*, 5 May 1995, p. 2, RRISS@drew.edu.

13. As cited by Joe Maxwell, 'Is Laughing for the Lord Holy?' in *Christianity Today*, 24 Oct. 1994, p. 79.

5: IS THE RENEWAL BIBLICAL?

1. Derek Morphew, *Breakthrough: Discovering the Kingdom*, Struik Christian Books, 1991, pp. 56–8.

2. Beverley, *Holy Laughter & the Toronto Blessing*, Zondervan, 1995, p. 157 (italics his).

3. Ibid., p. 158.

4. D. Spiceland, 'Miracles' in Walter A. Elwell (ed.), *Evangelical Dictionary of Theology*, Baker Book House, 1984, pp. 723–4.

5. *Could You Not Tarry One Hour?*, Creation House, 1987, p. 94.

6. From the rough-draft manuscript of chap. 7 of Wesley Campbell's *Welcoming a Visitation of the Holy Spirit*, Creation House, 1996.

7. *The Acts of the Apostles*, Tyndale New Testament Commentaries, IVP, 1980, p. 107.

8. A good discussion of this phenomenon is Francis MacNutt's *Overcome By The Spirit*, Chosen Books, 1990.

9. *Keep in Step With the Spirit*, Fleming H. Revell, 1984, p. 253.

10. J. Oropeza, *A Time to Laugh*, Hendrickson Publishers, 1995, pp. 131–44.

11. Ibid., p. 139.

12. Ibid., pp. 139–40 (italics mine).
13. Gordon Fee, *The First Epistle to the Corinthians*, The New International Commentary on the New Testament, Eerdmans, 1987, p. 697.
14. 'The Blessing? It's all in the Bible!' in *The Church of England Newspaper*, 23 Jun. 1995, p. 9.
15. Ibid.
16. '"Toronto Blessing" – True or False?' in *Prophecy Today*, Sep./Oct. 1994, p. 12.
17. 'A Word of Warning', a letter to *PWM Team Ministries*, 28 Nov. 1994.
18. I originally compiled the following accounts in a longer form for *Welcoming a Visitation of God* by Wes Campbell and myself.
19. I am indebted to Guy Chevreau for these insights which I gleaned from his teaching tapes, *Catching the Fire (1995)* and from a telephone conversation with him in Feb. 1996.
20. These paragraphs by Richard Riss explaining the context for Wesley's accounts and the quotes to follow are cited from a post which he made to 'New-Wine News' via the Internet (15 Sep. 1995).
21. *Jonathan Edwards on Revival*, Banner of Truth Trust, 1965, pp. 151–4.
22. *George Whitefield's Journals*, Banner of Truth Trust, 1960, p. 425.
23. 'Spiritual Awakenings in North America', *Christian History*, Vol. VIII, No. 3, Issue 23, p. 26.
24. Winkie Pratney, *Revival*, Whitaker House, 1984, p. 125–6.
25. From Peter Cartwright's *Autobiography*, quoted by Keith J. Hardman, *The Spiritual Awakeners*, Moody Press, 1983, p. 145–6.
26. Garth Rosell and Richard A. G. Dupuis (eds), *The Memoirs of Charles G. Finney*, Zondervan, 1989, pp. 133–4.
27. Frank Bartleman, *Azusa Street*, Logos, 1980, pp. 59–60.
28. John F. MacArthur, *Reckless Faith*, Crossway Books, 1994, p. 166.
29. Ibid.
30. As cited by MacArthur, op. cit, p. 167, from *The Life of David Brainerd*, New Haven, Yale University Press, 1985, p. 154.

31. Guy Chevreau, *Pray With Fire*, HarperCollins, 1995, p. 253, citing Iain Murray, *Revival and Revivalism: The Making and Marring of American Evangelicalism*, Banner of Truth Trust, 1994. p.163.

6: THE MINISTRIES OF PROPHECY

1. *Prophecy in Early Christianity and the Ancient Mediterranean World*, William B. Eerdmans, 1983, p. 195.
2. Eugene Peterson, *Reversed Thunder*, HarperCollins, 1988, p. 20.
3. J. I. Packer, op. cit., p. 217 (italics his). Against this view see David Pytches, *Prophecy in the Local Church*; George Mallone, *Those Controversial Gifts*; Wayne Grudem, *The Gift of Prophecy in the New Testament and Today*; and Michael Green, *I Believe in the Holy Spirit*.
4. Charles Hummel, *Fire in the Fireplace*, IVP, 1993, p. 110.
5. Harris, Archer and Waltke, 'Nabi' in *Theological Wordbook of The Old Testament*, Vol. II, Moody Press, p. 544.
6. *How to Read the Bible for All its Worth*, Zondervan, 1981, 1993, pp. 167ff.
7. I owe some of the following observations and ideas to Cindy Jacobs, *The Voice of God*, Regal Books, 1995, pp. 95–8.
8. Brown, Driver and Briggs, *Hebrew and English Lexicon of the Old Testament*, Clarendon Press, 1907, p. 267.
9. J. A. Thompson, *Deuteronomy: An Introduction & Commentary*, Tyndale Old Testament Commentaries (D. J. Wiseman, General Editor), IVP, 1974, p. 214.
10. Jacobs, op. cit., pp. 95–6.
11. Mike Bickle, *Growing in the Prophetic*, Kingsway, 1995, pp. 133–40.
12. *Pastoral Renewal*, Mar. 1988.
13. Three excellent books to consult are: Mike Bickle, *Growing in the Prophetic*, Kingsway, 1995; Cindy Jacobs, *The Voice of God*, Regal Books, 1995; and Graham Cooke, *Developing Your Prophetic Gifting*, Sovereign World, 1994.
14. *Hippo in the Garden*, Creation House, 1993, p. 52–66.
15. Ibid., p. 52.

16. Adapted from John Wimber's notes in the 'Facing the 90s' conference notebook.
17. Regarding dreams and visions, I recommend: James Ryle, *A Dream Come True*, Creation House, 1995; Kevin J. Conner, *Interpreting the Symbols and Types*, revised edn, Bible Temple Publishing, 1992; David Pytches, *Spiritual Gifts in the Local Church*, Bethany House, 1985, chap. 16; George Mallone, *Those Controversial Gifts*, IVP, 1983, chap. 6.
18. 'Prophecy, Gift of', in Stanley M. Burgess and Gary B. McGee (eds), *Dictionary of Pentecostal and Charismatic Movements*, Zondervan, 1988, pp. 732–3.

7: OVERCOMING OBSTACLES

1. *The Works of Jonathan Edwards*, Vol. II, Banner of Truth Trust, 1992, 273a.
2. *Signs of Revival*, Kingsway, 1994, p. 210.
3. *Joy Unspeakable*, Kingsway, 1980, as cited by Patrick Dixson, *Signs of Revival*, Kingsway, 1994, pp. 211–12.
4. John R. W. Stott, *The Letters of John*, Tyndale New Testament Commentaries, revised edn, IVP, 1988, p. 157.
5. Ibid., pp. 113–14.
6. Stott, op. cit., p. 162.
7. Ibid., p. 115.
8. Abraham Maslow, *Religions, Values, and Peak Experiences*, Penguin Books, 1976, p. 24.
9. Ibid., pp. 24–6, 41.
10. Ibid., p. 70.
11. For fuller treatments of this topic see Derek Morphew, *Renewal Apologetics*, VCF Cape Town, and Don Williams, *Revival: The Real Thing: A Response to Hank Hanegraaff's 'Counter Revival'*, Coast Vineyard in La Jolla, California.
12. C. S. Lewis, *The Lion, The Witch, and the Wardrobe*, Collier Books, 1970, pp. 73–6.

8: RELEASING THE RIVER OF GOD

1. I give credit to John Wimber, who helped to shape my thinking in a few of these areas.

9: LEADING MEETINGS AND PASTORING PEOPLE

1. John Wimber, 'The Biblical Context for Revival', *Equipping the Saints*, First Quarter, 1995, p. 19.
2. *Reversed Thunder*, HarperCollins, 1988, p. 186.
3. See Chapter 12 for a fuller treatment. Also see my article, 'From Vision to Vehicle: Putting Wheels on Your Ideas for Ministry' in *Equipping the Saints*, First Quarter, 1995, pp. 9–12, and Frank Tillapaugh, *Unleashing the Church*, Regal, 1982 and *Unleashing Your Potential*, Regal 1988.

10: GETTING YOUR SAILS UP FOR THE WIND OF THE SPIRIT

1. Walter Hilton, *Toward a Perfect Love*, trans. by David L. Jeffrey, Multnomah Press, 1985, pp. 61–2.
2. Eugene H. Peterson, *Reversed Thunder*, HarperCollins, 1988, p. 129.

11: DIGGING IRRIGATION DITCHES

1. Some of the material in this and the next chapter appeared in an article I wrote entitled 'Becoming Entrepreneurs in Kingdom Justice' in *Equipping the Saints*, 4th Qtr 1995, 1st Qtr 1996.
2. *National and International Religion Report*, 4 Sep. 1995, 2 Oct. 1995, 18 March 1995; *Charisma & Christian Life Magazine*, June 1996.
3. See his *Megatrends 2000*, Avon Books, 1990, chap. 9.
4. *National and International Religion Report*, 18 March 1996.
5. Packer, op. cit., pp. 244–5.
6. *Lectures on Revival*, Bethany House, 1988, p. 13.
7. See J. I. Packer, *A Quest for Godliness*, Crossway Books, 1990,

chap. 19, and *Jonathan Edwards on Revival*, Banner of Truth Trust, 1965.

8. Iain Murray in *Revival & Revivalism*, Banner of Truth Trust, 1994, deals a devastating blow to Finney and those who were influenced by his Arminian theology and practice of 'revivalism', which is not the same as 'revival'.

9. Adapted from John Wimber in *Vineyard Reflections*, Jul./Aug. 1994, pp. 6–7 (italics mine). Used by permission. He also mentioned publicly at the 'Let the River Flow' conference at my church in May 1995 that there was a gentle rain falling into the lake.

10. *National and International Religion Report*, 19 Feb. 1996.

11. See my article, 'Father Power' in *HomeLife*, Jun. 1996.

12. Reported in *Christian Info News*, Dec. 1995, p. 25.

13. Statistics from the Lausanne Statistics Task Force cited by Bill and Amy Stearns, *Catch the Vision 2000*, Bethany House, 1991, pp. 88–9.

14. Earle E. Cairns, *An Endless Line of Splendor*, Tyndale, 1986, pp. 242–3.

15. Ibid., p. 38.

16. Ibid.

17. 'Spiritual Awakenings in North America', *Christian History*, Vol. VIII, No. 3, Issue 23, p. 31, and Keith J. Hardman, *Charles Grandison Finney: Revivalist and Reformer*, Baker Book House, 1990, pp. 244–56, 297–9

18. Lovelace, op. cit., p. 381.

19. Charles Colson, *The Body*, Word Publishing, 1992, p. 102.

20. Andres Tapia, 'Is Global Awakening Just Around the Corner?', *Christianity Today*, 14 Nov. 1994.

21. Tom Phillips, *Revival Signs*, Vision House, 1995, pp. 96–7. For examples, read Joe Aldrich, *Prayer Summits: Seeking God's Agenda for Your Community*, Multnomah, 1992.

22. James Ryle, 'The Sons of Thunder', *The Morningstar Journal*, Vol. 1, No. 4, 1991, pp. 23–9.

23. Ibid., p. 29.

24. 'Moving Into Increasing Anointing', *Spread the Fire*, May/Jun. 1995, Vol. 1, Issue 3, p. 2.

25. Mike Bickle, *Growing in the Prophetic*, Kingsway, 1995, pp. 30–32.

26. Ibid., pp. 31–2.
27. Bill Bright, *The Coming Revival*, NewLife Publications, 1995, p. 29.
28. *National and International Religion Report*, Vol. 8, No. 15, 11 Jul. 1994.

12: WALKING IN THE AUTHORITY OF BLESSING

1. My wife and I recommend the following three books to those who need strength or must give strength in times of pain and grief: Marilyn Willett Heavilin, *Roses in December: Finding Strength Within Grief*, Thomas Nelson Publishers, 1993; H. Norman Wright, *Recovering From the Losses of Life*, Fleming H. Revell, 1991; and C. S. Lewis, *The Problem of Pain*, Collins, 1940.
2. Charles Colson, *The Body*, Word Publishing, 1992, p. 281.
3. Stephen Charles Mott, *Biblical Ethics and Social Change*, Oxford University Press, 1982, p. 53. I highly recommend this book, along with Charles Colson's *The Body*, op. cit.
4. For a good discussion, read Ramsay MacMullen, *Christianizing the Roman Empire*, Yale University Press, 1984.

SELECTED
BIBLIOGRAPHY

Anderson, Ray S. *Ministry on the Fireline: A Practical Theology for an Empowered Church*, IVP, 1993.

Arnott, John. *The Father's Blessing*, Creation House, 1995.

Beverley, James A. *Holy Laughter & the Toronto Blessing*, Zondervan, 1995.

Bickle, Mike. *Growing in the Prophetic*, Kingsway, 1995.

Cairns, Earle E. *An Endless Line of Splendor*, Tyndale House Publishers, 1986.

Campbell, Wesley. *Welcoming a Visitation of the Holy Spirit*, Creation House, 1996.

Campbell, Wesley and Helland, Roger. *Welcoming A Visitation of God*, unpublished manuscript, 1994.

Chevreau, Guy. *Catch The Fire*, Harper Perennial, 1994. *Pray With Fire*, Harper Perennial, 1995.

Deere, Jack. *Surprised by the Power of the Spirit*, Zondervan, 1993.

Dixson, Dr Patrick. *Signs of Revival*, Kingsway Publications, 1994.

Edwards, Jonathan. *Jonathan Edwards on Revival*, Banner of Truth Trust, 1965; *Treatise on Religious Affections*, Baker, 1982; *The Works of Jonathan Edwards*, 2 Vols, Banner of Truth Trust, 1992.

Fearon, Mike. *A Breath of Fresh Air*, Eagle, 1994.

Fee, Gordon and Stuart, Douglas. *How to Read the Bible for All Its Worth*, 2nd edn, Zondervan Publishing House, 1981, 1993.

Greig, Gary S. and Springer, Kevin N. (eds). *The Kingdom and the Power*, Regal Books, 1993.

Grudem, Wayne. *The Gift of Prophecy in the New Testament and Today*, Crossway Books, 1988.

Hardman, Keith J. *The Spiritual Awakeners*, Moody Press, 1983.

Jacobs, Cindy. *The Voice of God*, Regal Books, 1995.

Kraft, Charles H. *Christianity With Power*, Vine Books, 1989.

Mallone, George. *Those Controversial Gifts*, IVP, 1983.

Morphew, Derek. *Breakthrough: Discovering the Kingdom*, Struik Christian Books, 1991; Renewal Apologetics, self-published, May 1995.

Mott, Stephen Charles. *Biblical Ethics and Social Change*, Oxford University Press, 1982.

Murray, Iain. *Revival & Revivalism*, Banner of Truth Trust, 1994.

Oropeza, B. J. *A Time to Laugh*, Hendrickson Publishers, 1995.

Packer, J. I. *Keep in Step With the Spirit*, Fleming H. Revell, 1984.

Poloma, Margaret, *By Their Fruits: A Sociological Assessment of the 'Toronto Blessing'*, 1996.

Pratney, Winkie. *Revival*, Whitaker House, 1983, 1984.

Pytches, David. *Spiritual Gifts in the Local Church*, Bethany House, 1985; *Prophecy in the Local Church*, Hodder & Stoughton, 1993.

Riss, Richard. *A Survey of 20th Century Revival Movements in North America*, Hendrikson Publishers, 1988.

Roberts, Dave. *The 'Toronto' Blessing*, Kingsway Publications, 1994.

Ryle, James. *Hippo in the Garden*, Creation House, 1993.

Trueblood, D. Elton. *The Trustworthiness of Religious Experience*, Friends United Press of Richmond, Indiana, 1979.

Wagner, C. Peter. *Your Spiritual Gifts Can Help Your Church Grow*, revised edn, Regal Books, 1979, 1994.

White, John. *When the Spirit Comes With Power*, IVP, 1988.

Williams, Don. *Revival: The Real Thing*, Coast Vineyard (La Jolla, California), 1995.

Wimber, John. *Power Evangelism*, HarperCollins, 1985, 1992; 'Season of New Beginnings', *Vineyard Reflections*, May/Jun. 1994; 'Refreshing, Renewal and Revival', *Vineyard Reflections*, Jul./Aug. 1994; Board Report, Oct. 1994.

Roger Helland, B.A., Th.M., serves as the Associate Senior Pastor and is a member of the founding team of New Life Vineyard Fellowship in Kelowna, British Columbia, Canada. He is a graduate of Dallas Theological Seminary with a Master of Theology degree in Old Testament. He loves to teach on church renewal, leadership, the gifts and manifestations of the Holy Spirit and hermeneutics. As a Bible teacher he has ministered in a variety of interdenominational settings in various parts of the world, with his vision to see people equipped, empowered and released to fulfil their vision serve Jesus Christ. Roger lives in Kelowna with his wife Gail and their three children, Melissa, Joel, and Micah. His favourite pastimes are relaxing on the beach, reading and eating ice cream!

For conference ministry and teaching tapes contact:

Roger Helland
New Life Vineyard Fellowship
2041 Harvey Avenue
Kelowna, British Columbia
CANADA
V1Y 6G7

Fax: (604) 765 1323 or (604) 861 3844

For a catalogue of teaching tapes, books, materials, worship CDs and conference ministry from others on our pastoral team, as well as our training schools and internship programme, contact *The Grapevine* at the above address or fax: (604) 861 3844 or phone: (604) 762 4255

CATCH THE FIRE

The Toronto Blessing
An experience of renewal and revival

Guy Chevreau
Preface by John Arnott

'Lord, I have heard of your fame and I stand in awe of your deeds, O Lord. Renew them in our day, in our time, make them known'

Habakkuk 3:2

Catch The Fire, the globally acclaimed best seller, explores the remarkable work of God known as 'The Toronto Blessing'. From the moment news of the revival spread, newspapers, television and radio reports were buzzing with stories of whole congregations laughing, weeping and falling under the power of the Holy Spirit. Since then, its effects have been rippling throughout the world, transforming individuals and local churches everywhere.

Guy Chevreau, the internationally renowned speaker and member of the Toronto Airport Vineyard, was there from the beginning. In this inspirational book, he discovers a biblical foundation and historical precedents for such dramatic signs. Recounting many experiences of lives and ministries completely changed, he issues a crucial challenge to all Christians and church leaders who yearn to see the power of God released into their lives, the Church and the world.

PRAY WITH FIRE

Interceding in the Spirit

Guy Chevreau
Preface by John Arnott

'If I have the gift of prophecy, and the knowledge of
every hidden truth ... but have no love, I am nothing'
1 Corinthians 13:2

The outpouring of God's spirit that has become popularly
known as the Toronto Blessing has left many Christians
deeply changed. In this move, God is calling his people to
engage in prophetic, intercessory prayer – the kind of
prayer that can make individuals more like Christ and
bring renewal to the Church and revival to our communities.

Where God calls, he also equips for effective service. In
this fascinating sequel to *Catch The Fire*, Guy Chevreau
traces the power of intercessory prayer and prophetic ministry in the scriptures and in the history of the Church and
recounts telling testimonies of the Holy Spirit's impact in
our own day.

KEEP THE FIRE

The Toronto Blessing
Allowing the Spirit to transform your life
John Arnott

'You will receive power when the Holy Spirit has come upon you; and you will be my witnesses ... to the ends of the earth'

Acts 1:8

'Since we live by the Spirit, let us keep in step with the Spirit'

Galatians 5:25

The Holy Spirit has swept through your being, filling you with an overwhelming sense of God's love, and nothing will ever be the same again. Or perhaps you are praying to receive such an outpouring, but nothing has happened.

Keep The Fire is for you. This warm, personal and practical book explores what receiving the Toronto Blessing means for you, your church, your friends and those who have not yet heard the good news of Jesus Christ.

No encounter with the Holy Spirit is ever an end in itself, rather it is a gift to be shared. John Arnott offers down-to-earth biblical guidelines on the privileges of receiving such a treasured gift and on the personal and pastoral responsibilities that result.

LIVING THE MESSAGE

366 Daily Reflections based on *The Message*
Eugene H. Peterson

Living The Message is a spiritual companion with daily readings from *The Message*, Eugene H. Peterson's best-selling translation of the New Testament, Psalms and Proverbs, which has already sold over a million and a half copies. For each day of the year, there is a verse or passage from *The Message*, with a commentary by the author, for reflection and meditation. Eugene H. Peterson's vivid contemporary translation of God's Word is combined with his compelling insights into the Christian life, to produce a daily devotional which speaks powerfully to the needs and concerns of today's world.

Eugene H. Peterson is Professor of Spiritual Theology at Regent college, Vancouver. He has been a favourite author in America for over 35 years. He is the author of numerous books including *The Quest*, *The Journey*, *The Gift* and *Answering God*.